Barcelona

INSIGHT *City* GUIDES

Edited by Andrew Eames
Commissioning Editor in Spain: Don Murray
Editorial Director: Brian Bell

APA
PUBLICATIONS

Barcelona

First Edition

ABOUT THIS BOOK

Cityguide: Barcelona is the sixth book on Spain by the Insight team, following hard on the heels of Insight titles *Spain* (which won the Vega Inclan award), *Mallorca and the Balearics, Tenerife and the Western Canaries, Gran Canaria and the Eastern Canaries,* and *Southern Spain.* The experience that went into the production of this volume is tried and tested, but *Cityguide: Barcelona* is unique in the series in that most of the editorial was written originally in Spanish by journalists living in Barcelona.

Barcelona's overall editor is **Andrew Eames**, who has also edited four of the previous Spain books, as well as Apa's *Cityguide: London.* Eames is managing editor responsible for the Spanish group of titles, shortly to be increased to eight with the addition of new books on Catalonia and Madrid.

Eames first became interested in Insight Guides while working in South-east Asia as a young aspiring journalist. Since then he has published his travel autobiography, *Crossing the Shadow Line*, and has recently been working on a book about his experiences in Scotland.

The Writing Team

For local editing and commissioning in Spain, Eames enlisted the support of **Don Murray**, a Canadian photojournalist who worked on *Insight Guide: Mallorca.* Murray started taking pictures while a pilot in the Canadian Air Force, turned his hobby into a profession and started to write. The result of his first book experience was a fat file of 65 rejection slips. "One of them," he says, "was encouraging". Since then he has had published seven books about the architecture of Mallorca. Murray ransacked the press corps of Barcelona for suitable writers for this book and saw the text through its translation stage; his pictures also feature in these pages. With the assistance of **Ana Pascual** he checked the accuracy and the Catalan content of the book.

Pascual is a Mallorquine who went to university in Barcelona, from where she travelled extensively through Europe and North America. Back in Mallorca, she dedicates herself to research and journalism, sometimes in collaboration with Don Murray. She writes for national and international magazines and has been devoting much of her time in recent years to researching her book *La Casa y el Tiempo.*

Carme Riera (who writes about the Catalan language) is one of the best-known Catalan writers. Some of her prize-winning novels have run through 30 editions, and have been translated into Castilian, German, Dutch, Greek, Russian and Czechoslovakian, but only piecemeal into English. Riera teaches Spanish literature at Barcelona University, where she says she is preoccupied by the increasing youth of her students and has taken to combing her hair without looking in the mirror.

Lluís Permanyer, staff writer for the Barcelonan newspaper *La Vanguardia*, is widely considered to be the chronicler of the city. He has a law degree which he has never put into practice; instead he has written 20 books, mostly art orientated, and the libretto of an opera. He writes the football and the Olympics chapters in this book.

Like Permanyer, **Berta Caldentey** (chapters on museums and the creative city) is also

Eames   *Murray*   *Pascual*   *Permanyer*

a born and bred Barcelonan who writes for newspapers and magazines, specialising in interviews with cultural celebrities as well as holding down a full-time job with the publishers Circulo de Lectores.

For the past quarter of a century **Marcelo Aparicio** (chapters on the Plaça de Catalunya, the Gothic Quarter, the Jews, the Eixample and Shopping) has been in and out of journalism, experimenting with a hippy life in Ibiza and running his own restaurant. Although he is a believer in the Spanish proverb "the second time is never as good as the first", Aparicio has lived twice in Barcelona, twice in Rome and twice in Buenos Aires. In Barcelona he is the correspondent for Agence France Presse (AFP).

Xavier Martí was born in the Ampurias region of Catalonia, which is much affected by the cold Tramuntana wind. He says he has had the writing bug since an early age, although he has tried to cure himself of it by small doses of contributions to most of Barcelona's newspapers, and in being involved with the launch of one. Martí writes in these pages about Barcelona Today, the Ramblas, Montjuïc, the Waterfront and the Columbus Monument.

The history section of this book is the work of **Dr Felipe Fernández-Armesto**, fellow of St Antony's College, Oxford, and historian of three previous Insight Guides. Dr Fernández-Armesto is currently working on the Oxford University Press history of Spain, and his own book on Barcelona, published by Hamish Hamilton.

Three foreigners resident in Barcelona were invaluable for their contributions. **George Semler** (chapters on Around Barcelona and on the Cosmopolitan City) is an American who has been living in the city for much of his working life. His children are multi-lingual in Catalan, Castilian and English.

Geraldine Mitchell (co-author of the chapters on the Barcelonan and the Olympics) is an Irish journalist and correspondent for the *Irish Times* in Spain. **Judy Thompson** is by turns translator, public relations advisor and journalist. For this book she turned her hand to compliling the exhaustive Travel Tips section.

The Photographers

The glorious photographs are primarily the work of **Bill Wassman**, an American with a passion for Spain which he has already displayed in previous Spanish books for Apa. **George Wright**, a British photographer who works extensively for UK colour magazines, produced some of the book's best portraits.

Translation work on the Spanish texts was undertaken by **Nikki Cleugh**, the bi-lingual deputy editor on *Balearic Homes and Living* in Mallorca.

In London, the editorial centre for this book, **Jill Anderson** skilfully marshalled the text through a variety of Macintosh computers; **Berndtson & Berndtson** drew the maps; proof-reading and indexing were expertly handled by **Kate Owen**.

Caldentey

Martí

Aparicio

Armesto

CONTENTS

TRAVEL TIPS

AN INSISTENT CITY

Barcelona is the heart, lungs and legs of Catalonia, which itself is the leading economic region of Spain. Covering 6.3 percent of the country's land mass and supporting 15.5 percent of the population, Catalonia produces 19.3 percent of the nation's gross domestic product. A remarkable 71 per cent of the region's people live in the greater metropolitan area of Barcelona itself (4.2 million in the metropolis, 1.7 million in the municipal area), jammed between the hills of Tibidabo, Montjuïc and the sea. Barcelona is the largest city on the Mediterranean seaboard.

Catalonia was once a state in its own right and many Barcelonans still believe that the region deserves more autonomy from the rest of Spain than it currently has. Certainly, Barcelona is like no other Spanish city. It has its own language and its own culture and customs. The Barcelonans are unlike most other Spaniards; they are more introverted, more work-motivated, more self-conscious, more difficult to get to know.

Perhaps because of the Catalans' own insistence on separateness, their city has had a turbulent past, caught between the various powers of Europe in its allegiances against Madrid. Its growth reflects the eras of its greatest successes, from the Roman walls, through the Gothic Quarter to the palaces of the 17th century, right up to the 19th-century Eixample. In its latest phase, the city of the 1990s will reflect the work done for the Olympic Games, held in Barcelona in 1992.

The Catalan character has had to go underground so often that it expresses itself in surprising ways. The Eixample is studded with the extrovert work of Modernist architects, of whom Gaudí was one; the Barcelona football club – a sort of unofficial army – has a vociferous following which sees goals as assertions of the Catalan identity. At times the club has been virtually shut down by central government, or forced to share its best players with Madrid.

All in all, it's a city with a lot to offer, and one which has repeatedly and insistently thrust itself to the forefront of European cities. In *Don Quixote*, Miguel de Cervantes writes: "Barcelona: innately courteous, offering shelter to the travel-weary, hospitals for the poor, home for the brave, revenge for the offended, reciprocating friendship and unique in situation and beauty". This insistent city is worth getting to know.

Preceding pages: big dipper on Tibidabo hill; the port; windows on Gaudí's Casa Batlló; designer shop-window on Passeig de Gràcia. Left, Columbus directs the traffic.

Barcelona has all the amenities of a great metropolis and all the self-consciousness of a capital city, but much of its dynamism has come from always having had something to prove, and its history is very largely one of achievements incubating in frustration.

Its citizen-historians have attributed to it a myth of ancient splendour which is unjustified by the facts. In the Middle Ages it was the centre of the greatest Mediterranean empire since Roman times, but never became a sovereign city in its own right, like Venice or Genoa. Until 1716 it was the capital of the nominally sovereign Catalan state and twice fought bloody wars against the rest of Spain to defend that status; but it never became a seat of government in modern times and, with the absorption of Catalonia into the Spanish monarchy, came to be ruled from a distance by its upstart rival, Madrid, an altogether younger city.

In the 19th century, it remained the centre of an increasingly vibrant Catalan national culture, which led to further conflicts – some of them bloody – over its constitutional relationship to the rest of Spain.

City of prodigies: The Barcelonans have never reconciled themselves to living in a provincial Spanish city and have always given themselves rival identities, be they Catalan, European or Mediterranean. In the past hundred years or so, Barcelona has been a "city of prodigies" (the title of Mendoza's book on the city which charts the period between the great exhibitions of 1888 and 1929), rising in economic stature to become the heart of the biggest conurbation of the Mediterranean coastline, and culturally acknowledged as one of the liveliest artistic centres in Europe.

But the rapidity and fragility of this rise, and its dependence on Barcelona's role as a Spanish city, making or purveying goods to a protected Spanish market, have been ob-

scured by the myths of a long and glorious history of continuous greatness and of fidelity to Catalan tradition.

Roman rule: Although the Roman colony that preceded the modern city fed well off its "sea of oysters" and served rich men with such civilised amenities as porticoed baths and a forum with seven statues, it was always a small town of up to 25 to 30 acres (10 to 12 hectares) – to judge from the circuit of the walls, some of which are still standing.

These are dwarfed by those easily visited at nearby Tarragona and Empùries.

For Catalan historians, it used to be a point of honour to imagine antique greatness and "continuity" stretching back to the primeval forebears of modern Catalans. But, although the whole plain of Barcelona was well populated from neolithic times, and coins minted in the area prove the existence of a pre-Roman urban civilisation, no evidence of continuous settlement of the central site of historic Barcelona, on Mont Tàber, earlier than the first century AD has yet been found.

Pre-Roman Barkeno, a name found on

Left, 16th-century altar urn from Tarragona. **Right**, Roman walls still surround the Gothic Quarter.

early coins, may have been on the hill of Montjuïc, which the Romans inherited as a ritual centre: finds from here include an impressive Roman magistrate's seat, set ceremonially in the remains of some sort of stone enclosure.

Quiet years: For half a millennium after the end of Roman rule, Barcelona's history remains sparsely documented. Of the occupiers of those years – the Visigoths, the Moors, the Franks – only the first seem to have esteemed the city highly. According to the earliest historian of the Goths, pity for the inhabitants of Hispania, smarting under the blows of less romanised barbarians, moved

the Visigothic chief Athaulf to seize Barcelona "with his best men", leaving those "less adept in arms" to occupy the interior. This suggests that Barcelona was thought particularly desirable, or defensible, or both.

Narrators of the next century of Gothic history continue to associate Barcelona with politically important events: Athaulf was assassinated there, Amalaric was murdered in the city, and shortly after, in 540, Barcelona was the meeting-place of a synod.

Its modest growth during the Visigothic period can be detected in the excavations under the Palau Reial. Evidence here suggests that between the 4th and 6th centuries, the *intervallum* between the Roman building line and the ramparts was filled with new constructions. At the same time, streets were narrowed by building extensions. A building of noble dimensions appeared on part of the present palace site, which may have housed the royal assassination victims.

In this period the city was still without long-distance commerce and, for the Moors and Franks, seems to have been significant only as a frontier garrison or *ville-carrefour*.

Barcelona's potential for greatness only began to be realised when it was conquered, late in the 9th century, by the nascent Catalan state: a principality of regional importance, with its heartlands close by, its granary in the plain of Urgell, its defences in the mountains. Its warrior paladins adopted Barcelona as their favourite place of residence; they endowed it with religious foundations which stimulated urban growth; they kept – and sometimes spent – their treasure there; and as the state developed, they concentrated their court and counting-houses in Barcelona.

Wilfred the Hairy: Of the man acclaimed as the "founder" of the House of the Counts of Barcelona, little trace survives in the modern city: only the visitor brave enough to enter the dark alley of the Carrer d'Amargos, with its straggling balcony-plants and dangling laundry, will find the painted ceramic plaque proclaiming – almost certainly wrongly – that this was the limit of the palace of Count Wilfred the Hairy (who died in 898). The count, in a series of campaigns in the late 870s, united the hinterland of Barcelona with most of the other Frankish counties south of the Pyrenees.

By the early 10th century Barcelona was already, in a sense, the "capital" of sovereign Catalonia. In about 911, Count Wilfred II chose a house of religion outside the walls for his mausoleum. His neglected grave, marked by an inscription discovered among rubble, deserved better treatment from the Barcelonans; for it was this sort of patronage, bestowing princely status on Barcelona, that began to turn the former hick-town into a medieval metropolis.

Growth signs: For the next 200 years, Barcelona's wealth continued to come mostly from war and the agricultural produce of the plain. Its courtly status was its main source of urban character.

The first known boom happened in the late 10th century. Most historians have assumed that this must have been the result of commercially generated wealth; but there is no evidence to support that conjecture and it is at least as likely that the simple presence of the knights, the court and the growing colony of clergy were the sources of stimulation.

The growth of the cathedral chapter is the first clue to the city's growth: there were six canonries in 974, 17 by 1005. The canons were growing in sophistication as well as in

predatory vizir of Córdoba. The raid inspired traditional lamentations, with lists of buildings destroyed and martyrdoms incurred; but, except for Sant Pere de les Puelles (burned with all its inmates), real losses seem to have been slight and, by encouraging rebuilding, al-Mansur may actually have stimulated the boom.

The Moorish threat did not long survive al-Mansur's death in 1002. By 1010 a raid on Córdoba by a large expedition of Catalans dramatically illustrated how the roles of victim and prey had been reversed. The empire of Córdoba was enfeebled by politics at the centre and eroded by usurpations at the

numbers: retiring to houses of their own; acquiring a reputation for erudition; building up libraries – since disappeared – worthy, in one instance, of attracting a reader as famous for his learning as the future pope, Gerbert of Aurillac. They were not the only people building in the city, and the first satellite villages began to grow up outside the walls.

In 989 Barcelona was a target of sufficient prestige to attract a raid by al-Mansur, the

edges. In the 1030s it dissolved into small, competing successor-states. Like much of the rest of Christian Spain, Barcelona began to enjoy a bonanza on the proceeds of booty, tribute, ransom, payola and the wages of mercenaries.

An illumination in the *Liber Feudorum* (which can be seen by appointment in the Arxiu de la Corona d'Aragó, Carrer dels Comtes) shows Count Ramon Berenguer I counting out coins from a lapful of gold into his hand, for the price of the counties of Carcassonne and Béziers, which he bought. The sort of expansion his forebears could

Left, Wilfred the Hairy, credited as the founder of modern Barcelona. **Above**, Roman remains in the Plaça Vila de Madrid.

contemplate only by conquest, he could undertake by purchase.

Golden age: By the 1070s, 95 percent of transactions in Barcelona were made in gold – a level never again attained in the city's history. Some of this money was invested in a maritime enterprise which for the next 500 years supplied the city's wealth and formed its character. In 1060, although Barcelona was already a "great town", according to the fastidious chronicler al-Bakri, the Barcelonans were still hiring their galleys from Moorish ports. By 1080 the counts possessed a fleet of their own, though it may not have been based in Barcelona.

Two charters of Ramon Berenguer III (who ruled 1082–1131) mention what sounds like substantial seaborne trade. In 1104 he granted a tenth of dues paid on "all goods that come in on any ship in all my honour"; in the following year four Jews were granted a monopoly of the shipping home of ransomed Moorish slaves. That some, at least, of this trade was going through Barcelona is suggested by the terms of privileges Ramon Berenguer granted to Genoa and Pisa in 1116, easing the tolls of goods beached in Barcelona.

Despite the deficiencies of its shoaly harbour, Barcelona was the point of departure for a fleet big enough to attempt the conquest of Mallorca – 500 vessels strong, according to the undoubtedly exaggerated report of the poet of the *Liber Maidiolichinus*, who accompanied the expedition and extolled its heroic failure in epic verse.

International commerce continued to develop gradually and in 1160 Benjamin of Tudela reported vessels of "Pisa, Genoa, Sicily, Greece, Alexandria and Asia" off the beach of Barcelona.

Architectural remains: Most of the buildings of this period were replaced in later eras of even greater prosperity: only Sant Pau del Camp, Santa Llucia and the Capella de Marcús remain. For a flavour of what Catalonia was like in the 11th and 12th centuries the visitor to Barcelona has to go to the Museu de l'Art de Catalunya on Montjuïc, where the collection of murals transferred from rural churches shows the high quality of work that Catalan money could buy. The murals show the search for classical and Byzantine models by the artists: the wolf of Sant Joan de Boi bares predatory teeth as he starts around in a classical pose; the Seraphim of the apse with their feathery, eyed wings recall Byzantine mosaics.

In the streets, the explorer can match the map to documents that record the expansion of the 12th-century city. In 1160, Ramon Berenguer IV gave permission for a new public bath outside the city wall, where today the Carrer dels Banys Nous (literally "street of the new baths") curves in the spectral shadow of lost ramparts: the profits of this enterprise were to be divided equally between the count and the Jewish investor.

Merits of conquest: The winds and currents of the western Mediterranean meant that Barcelona had to solve its problem of access to the Balearic Islands, to become a great centre of long-distance commerce, rivalling Genoa and Pisa. An illumination in Barcelona University library shows a leading merchant of the city, entertaining the count-king "and the greater part of the nobles of Catalonia" in November or December 1228, and persuading them of the merits of conquering the islands.

In his extraordinary *Book of Deeds*, Jaume I (who reigned between 1213–76) identified his own motives for launching the conquest of the Balearics as essentially chivalric: there was more honour in conquering a single kingdom "in the midst of the sea, where God has been pleased to put it" than three on dry land. To chivalric and crusading satisfactions, the nobles who took part added substantial territorial rewards. The Barcelonans, however, and the other merchant-communities of the Catalan and Provençal worlds, needed little inducement. Their participation is explained by commercial motives: the anxiety to break the entrenched position of Moorish traders and their privileged partners from Genoa and Pisa.

Signs of glory: Like so many imperial adventures, Barcelona's acquisition of a Mediterranean empire, beginning in the Balearics, marked the apogee of its achievement and sowed the seeds of its decline. The marks of both are everywhere in the old city today, in the form of great churches begun in the

13th or 14th centuries; in vast ritual and even industrial spaces that survive from that time; in building works slowed or halted in the 15th century and in decayed aristocratic streets of the late Middle Ages. The new walls of the reign of Jaume I enclosed an area more than 10 times greater than those they replaced.

The cathedral is the dominant monument of the 13th century: the cloister portal, with its obscure carving of harpies and wild men dragging a half-naked, pudge-faced warrior, contrasts with the elegant High Gothic of the west front and the interior.

The early 14th century, when the profits of magistrates, could dent the city's confidence or interrupt the building boom. Never was the city so spectacularly embellished as in the reign of Pere III (1336–87); he built the vaulted halls – more reminiscent of Italy than Spain – of the Saló de Cent (Plaça de Sant Jaume) and the Saló de Tinell, with its martial wall-paintings, in the palace of the Plaça del Rei. Pere III also rebuilt the shipyards on a larger scale, where galleys for the Mediterranean war effort had been built since the reign of Pere II (1276–85): the eight great bays of the Drassanes at the foot of the Ramblas can still be visited, and now house the Maritime Museum.

empire were perhaps at their height, was a time of frenzied building. The chapel of San Agata, in the count-kings' palace (the Palau Reial in the Plaça del Rei), was built by Jaume II (who died in 1327). The first stone of the church of El Pi was laid in 1322, that of Santa Maria del Mar, which still has its medieval glazing largely intact, in 1329.

Not even the Black Death – which killed half the city council and four of the five chief

Above, Ramon Berenguer, who presided over Barcelona's hyperactive trading period in the 12th century.

Private builders were also active. An example of late medieval urbanisation, the Carrer de Montcada was driven through the old town in a broad, straight line and promptly colonised by the aristocracy: the modern visitor, seeking the street for the sake of the Picasso Museum, runs the risk of being more impressed by the medieval architecture of the street's palaces.

Price of conquest: The trading empire which paid for this was essentially a western Mediterranean affair. The deeds of Catalans in the east – of mercenaries in Thrace and Athens, of merchants in Alexandria and

Constantinople – are justly renowned. But they took place in the wings of the main theatre. The conquest by Barcelona's count-kings, or their subjects, of Mallorca (1229), Ibiza (1235), Sicily (1282), Menorca (1287) and Sardinia (1324), and the territorial extension by a series of treaties from 1271 gave the count-kings something like a protectorate over a number of Maghribi ports: these were the landmarks of an empire of grain and gold, of silver and salt.

As the empire grew, its costs came to exceed its benefits. Mallorca proved a thankless daughter, sustaining a turbulent political relationship with the count-kings and using

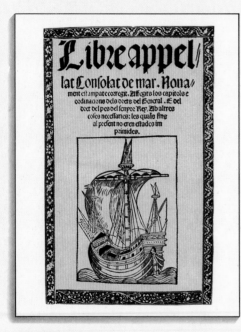

Catalan knowledge to set up shipping, arms and textile industries in competition with Barcelona's own. The ambition to control the western Mediterranean sea lanes caused wars with Genoa which were wasteful because Barcelona never had sufficient resources to exploit its victories. Above all, Sardinia was Barcelona's "Spanish ulcer"; the city seems largely to have borne the costs of conquest of the island by itself, with little support from the count-kings' other realms, while Sardinian resistance lasted, intermittently, for a hundred years, and exhausted the over-committed conquerors.

The empire which made a metropolis of Barcelona also sucked the rural life-blood out of Catalonia: as the centre of gravity of the count-kings' realms moved towards the city, the balance of population shifted. On the eve of the Black Death, Barcelona contained 20 percent of the population of Catalonia. The countryside could no longer keep the armies supplied with men or, perhaps, the city with food. In 1330 Barcelona experienced its first serious famine.

Never was a city more obviously the victim of its own success. Barcelona evinced the classic symptoms of the monster: corpulence induced by overfeeding, tentacles grown to uncontrollable lengths. Yet resolute civic spirit remains etched into the faces of the élite depicted, for instance, in Lluís Dalmau's *La Verge dels Consellers*, painted in 1443 to project a magnificent image of the city magistracy in the intimate company of heavenly protectors. Today the painting can be seen in the Museu de l'Art de Catalunya in the Palau Nacional on Montjuïc.

The passing of glory: Like the similar problem of the "decline" of Spain in the 17th century, that of the decline of Catalonia in the 15th has to be treated cautiously. Though it appears with hindsight that by the end of the century the gravity of power in the Iberian peninsula had shifted forever towards the centre, the experience in Catalonia seems too mottled with short-term checks, leaps and lurches to justify the use of a sweeping term like "decline", except in a relative sense: especially in the late 15th century, the neighbouring kingdoms of France and Castile were developing the means to mobilise unprecedented strength. Barcelona's 15th century, however, was at best an "era of difficulties" involving progressive exhaustion to ultimate prostration, redeemed only by the extraordinary mental resilience of an indomitably optimistic ruling class.

The city's predicament was a mixture of social violence, demographic stagnation and economic constraint. In the century after 1360, not a decade went by without a recurrence of plague, sometimes accompanied by famine; from 1426, the yield of the customs and wool tax plummeted and did not recover until the next century. Hearth-counts suggest a modest increase in population until the cataclysmic civil war of the 1460s: the count of 1500, showing 5,765 hearths, probably represents the lowest tally of households since the Black Death.

The protracted insecurity of this era of difficulties was bound to cause social tension. The first uncontrollable outburst was the pogrom of 1391, when the authorities were powerless to protect the Jews from massacre. In 1436 and 1437 popular agitations were effectively suppressed, but by the mid-century the failures of the city's natural rulers had attracted the sympathy of the city governor for a movement to democratise the

long run unseat the traditional ruling élite, but left it enfeebled and embittered against the count-king Joan II. His unpopularity grew as he tried to exploit Catalonia in what was felt to be a private attempt to meddle in Castile; he exacerbated his relations with his subjects by attempting to exclude his son and one of his daughters from succession to the throne. By appealing to popular elements in the towns and the peasants in the country, he alienated urban patricians and rural aristocrats alike.

As a result, no part of the realm entered the rebellion of 1462 more wholeheartedly than Barcelona; none suffered so much from the

municipal institutions or – at least – to enlarge the élite. The name of the incumbent party, the *Biga*, probably signifies a large beam used in the construction of a building; that of the challengers, the *Busca*, a piece of tinder or bunch of kindling. The names evoke the natures of the parties: the solidity of the establishment, the incendiary menace of its opponents.

Their conflict in the 1450s did not in the

Left, trade agreements were the city's major concern. **Above**, tomb of Jaume I, the conqueror-king who invaded the Balearics.

results. The insurgents' cause, never very promising, became desperate as each of the pretenders they put up to challenge the king died or dropped out in turn.

The siege that ended resistance in 1473, followed by punitive measures, left Barcelona devastated. "Today no trade at all is practised in this city," the *consellers* wrote. "Not a bolt of cloth is seen. The workers are unemployed and the men of property are deprived of their rents and goods… And of all our troubles, the worst is this: for we see our city turning into something no bigger than a village on the road to Vic."

BARC

No visitor to Barcelona can fail to be struck by the relative dearth of great Renaissance and baroque buildings. There are examples of grandeur, but they are elusive: the Palau de la Generalitat hides its medieval core behind a Renaissance facade. Most of what survives in the city from the 16th and 17th centuries reflects private effort, rather than public wealth, and a history of slow recovery until 1640, before the terrible era of war and unrest which lasted until 1714.

Ports and palaces: In the 16th century Barcelona kept closely enough in touch with fashion to earn praise from almost every visitor who left an account of the city. With the unremitting confidence that has characterised them in every age, the city fathers poured money into the creation of an artificial port in an attempt to recover lost trade: the task would remain incomplete for 300 years, but was never abandoned.

Private patrons like the Fivaller family could build splendid new palaces – theirs still stands in the Plaça de Sant Josep Oriol, where it now serves as an agricultural college; and the Carrer Ample, a conspicuous straight gash across Anton van Wyngaerde's view of the town, was opened as a gesture to Renaissance town planning.

At the beginning of the century, Guicciardini commended the city for its beauty while lamenting the decline of its commerce; by the end, a measure of recovery can be detected in the terms of Lope de Vega's praise: "Just as a splendid facade enhances the value of a building, so great Barcelona stands at the entrance to Spain, like a portico framing a famous threshold."

Royal neglect: Barcelona's decline in the 16th century coincided with the progressive loss of the courtly status which, before the rise of the city's commercial importance, had been the foundation of its fortune. After

the extinction of the ruling House of Barcelona in 1412, it had been governed by a series of kings whose main interests were in Castile or Naples and who spent ever less time in Barcelona. For a while from 1479 and continuously from 1516, her counts were also kings of Castile and were mainly concerned with the affairs of that larger and fiscally more productive country.

Yet the patriciate never lost their sense of ruling the capital of a sovereign principality – or even a quasi-polis, a city with the potential, at least, to be a city-state like Genoa or Venice. From inside the Spanish monarchy, Barcelona affected the status of a foreign power and its representatives swaggered like the emissaries of foreign potentates.

When, for instance, a new viceroy of Catalonia was appointed in 1622, the congratulations of Barcelona were tendered by an ambassador, attended by 200 carriages, in what was rumoured to be the most magnificent procession ever seen in Madrid.

Twenty years earlier, the city's representative at court was honoured with so much

Preceding pages: Columbus presents the riches of his first voyage of discovery. Left, detail from the Romanesque collection in the Palau Nacional. Right, the shield of a city-state.

pomp that "even the leading nobles of this court," he reported, "say that neither the nuncio of His Holiness himself, nor the envoy of the Emperor has ever been given such a reception… and the Castilians are all amazed that an ambassador who is a vassal of the king should be received with so much honour". A similar war of protocol was carried on inside the city, where leading magistrates demanded the right to remain hatted in the king's presence and disputed seats of honour in church with the viceroy's wife.

This was more than play-acting. The privileges (*privilegis*) and liberties (*furs*) which meant so much to Barcelona were never systematically codified and are difficult to define. The Castilian models, and the different nuances of Castilian thinking, which could not be translated into Catalan, tended to mislead policy makers in Madrid into misunderstandings about the sort of traditions they had to deal with in relations with Barcelona. In Castile, civic liberties normally rested in a charter granted by the king: they were a negotiable commodity, revered but not written in stone.

Private laws: Barcelona's identity, however, was bound up with the status in law of the principality of Catalonia as a distinct and equal partner in the Spanish monarchy. It had liberties not granted by the Prince as an act of grace, but governed by the *constitucions* – the statutes irrevocable except by the representative parliamentary assembly of Catalonia (the *corts*), which limited royal authority in the principality.

During the early 17th century, when the Spanish monarchy was tottering from the inevitable effects of immoderate greatness, the growing need for money and manpower made the Catalans fearful for their immunities. At a time when to be a very good Catalan was to be "jealous of the country's privileges", the implicit constitutional conflict between the interests of Spain and Catalonia was bound to be noticed in Barcelona, where all the institutions of the statehood of Catalonia, inherited from the Middle Ages, were concentrated, and where a large body of professional lawyers more or less lived by watching the *constitucions*.

The cost of the Thirty Years' War, and direct hostilities with France from 1635, brought the demands of the monarchy for money and men to a peak and the differences with the principality to a head. When Catalonia rose in revolt in 1640, and the rebels transferred their allegiance to Louis XIII of France, Barcelona was the head and heart of the rebellion.

Disaster: Like the roughly contemporary rebellion in England, Catalonia's was reluctantly supported elsewhere. An anonymous but representative diarist in Barcelona blamed the king's bad counsel for "the greatest sorrow this Principality of Catalonia has suffered" which was "to have been obliged to rely upon a foreign prince, moved by necessity, and to have had no other recourse… May God and most holy Mary be pleased to return us to the grace of our father and lord, Felipe".

But, like the English war, the Catalan juggernaut rolled out of control. The élite of Barcelona had to share power with popular elements and 16 years of war devastated its land, depopulated its towns and despoiled its wealth. The siege of Barcelona in 1652 was one of the most desperate episodes of the war and it ended only when the citizens were "reduced to eating grass".

However, the successful army commander, Don Juan José of Austria, was the architect of a remarkable restoration of the broken city and of Catalonia's national pride. His very success raised the danger of another round of similar conflict.

In the second half of the 17th century, Barcelona had little respite. Civic-minded optimists like Feliu de la Penya had hardly begun to revive all things Catalan before the French wars of the 1680s and 1690s exposed her lands to more campaigns and the city to another siege.

Nationalist instincts: Then the War of the Spanish Succession plunged the entire monarchy into crisis. The Bourbon claimant, Felipe V, arrived in 1702, scattering rewards and promises with a lavish hand; but he was suspected of an arbitrary disposition and absolutist plans – an impression confirmed in Catalan eyes by his failure to invite the chief magistrates to cover their heads in his presence. His insensitive viceroy, Francisco

Fernández de Velasco, blundered into other infringements of the *constitucions*.

Despite the naturally peaceful inclinations of a mercantile élite, many of the leading members of Barcelonan society were willing to respond to Velasco's tactless rule with violence. Psychologically inclined to fight, they were also ideologically equipped. It was an almost unquestioned assumption that Catalonia was a sovereign state with a right, in principle, to secede from a monarchy which had ambitions to control the whole country.

Catalans' reading of their own history represented theirs as a contractual monar-

chy, in which the contract between people and prince, once broken, could be repudiated. By the end of the war, when Barcelona was left to fight on alone, the inhabitants were inclined to blame the English for inveigling them into the fight with promises: the trick was performed, almost equally, with implicit threats. On 20 June 1705, when representatives of "the most Illustrious, Famous and Renowned Principality of Cata-

Above, Felipe V, who made himself unpopular in Catalonia by not respecting the Catalan *constitucions* or statutes.

lonia" signed a treaty with England in Genoa, the guns of British ships could be heard in local waters.

Catalans came to see the episode as a typical instance of England's habit of acquiring by bribery or intimidation an ally whom she would later abandon. From their point of view, the sixth clause of the treaty was the most important, by which England guaranteed that "now and in the future the Principality of Catalonia shall keep all the graces, privileges, laws and customs which severally and in common her people have enjoyed and do enjoy".

Defeat: In Barcelona it seems, appetite for war *vient en mangeant* (grew with eating), and the Barcelonans, after their shy start, became the most committed opponents of the Bourbon claimant, Felipe V. They joined the allied cause in a calculating spirit but clung on when all the other allies had withdrawn. They dared beyond hope, endured beyond reason and reaped the usual reward of that sort of heroism: defeat.

The previous recovery of 1652 was fatally misleading: it encouraged the Barcelonans to believe that their liberties could be ventured again and that a hopeless resistance would save them. The final siege lasted from August 1713 until November 1714, when the city capitulated (a date now celebrated by the Diada de Catalunya – Catalonia's national day).

The repression denounced by Catalan historians after Felipe's victory was really rather mild: clerics and generals were its only individually targeted victims. But the *constitucions* were abolished; Barcelona was reduced to the rank of a provincial city and subjected to the indignity of a permanent garrison – an army of occupation was billeted in what is now the Ciutadella Park.

Drive to be rich: Defeat turned the energies of the citizens to a mood of *enrichissez-vous*. Though the city was prostrate and revival slow, the 18th century as a whole was an era of forward-looking prosperity in which sustained economic growth began, thanks to new activities such as direct trade with the Americas and the beginnings of industrialisation based on imports of American cotton. Some of the palaces and villas of the Bourbon collaborators can still be seen: the finest of them, the Palau de Comillas, houses the Generalitat bookshop in the Ramblas; around the corner, the palace of the Comte de Fonallar enhances the grandeur of the expensive shops in the Carrer de Portaferrissa.

The ensemble which has most to say about Barcelona's 18th century is the Barceloneta district, the first industrial suburb, begun in 1753 to house a population then beginning to burst out of the diminished city. The tight, neat grid of its streets, the contrast with the traditional cityscape of Barcelona, make it one of the earliest surviving examples of "enlightened" town planning in Europe.

Factories and guilds: In pre-industrial Barcelona manufacturing was a mainstay of the economy, but it was confined to the intimate society of the workshop and the master's home, regulated not by the impersonal market but by the powerful guilds. A visitor to the Museu de l'Història de la Ciutat in the Carrer del Veguer can see the sort of images which dominated the mental world of the guilds: their art reflected professional pride and devotion to their patron saints.

The book of privileges of the shoemakers is decorated with a huge but elegant gilt-bronze slipper with tapering toe; the silver-smiths' pattern books record, in meticulous detail, the masters' copyright to thousands of intricate designs. The market-gardeners' book of privileges, begun in 1453, is flanked by busts of their otherwise obscure patrons, saints Abdó and Senen, and the gaudily painted coffer in which their relics were preserved.

Everywhere the images of saints are reminders that the guilds doubled as devotional confraternities. Evidence of their prestige and wealth can be found around the city today: the shoemakers' palatial hall, for instance, in the Plaça de Sant Felip Neri, decorated with the lion of St Mark, who converted the first Christian shoemaker; the graves of the masters in the cathedral cloister, bearing the same emblem; the sumptuous premises of the silk weavers' guild in the Via Laietana.

The beginnings of the transformation of Barcelona's economy to an industrial basis can be traced in the decline of the guilds. The 18th-century immigrants – most of them from communities in southern France, where languages similar to Catalan were spoken – "preferred factory life to subjection under the oligarchy of guild-masters".

The bridle-makers had 108 members in 1729, 47 in 1808 and 27 in 1814; the decline occurred during a period when the population of the city trebled and was at its most acute at a time of war and high demand for harnesses. In the textile industry, which was directly affected by reorganisation into factories, the decline was even more spectacular. By 1825, the cloth-dressers had only three members left, who had neither studios nor workshops and were too old to work.

In the last quarter of the 18th century a number of economic indicators seem to have accelerated. The rate of increase in wages between 1780 and 1797, for instance, was double that of Madrid. Manufacturers' profits, which had already doubled between 1720 and 1775, more than kept pace. When an English traveller visited in 1786, he was particularly impressed by the Bernis factory, which employed 350 operatives making woollen cloth for America; the following year, the famous English economist and agrarian reformer, Arthur Young, could hear "the noise of business" everywhere.

The Napoleonic wars and their aftermath interrupted progress. Amid post-war unemployment, after a terrible yellow fever epidemic in 1821, the city council of Barcelona lost its habitual optimism and publicly doubted whether the city would ever recover. In fact, though recovery was socially painful, it was complete: in 1836, the first steamship rolled off the slipway of Barceloneta; in 1848 Spain's first railway linked Barcelona to Mataró.

Social side-effects: Working-class degradation and unrest accompanied economic change. The pattern of life in Barcelona in the mid-19th century was of fitful mass vio-

Disorder incubated with disease and riots were a regular feature of the long, hot summer of 1854. With increasing frequency these took on revolutionary proportions. The rioters' targets gradually changed: there had been disturbances in the 18th century – in 1766, 1773 and 1789, when the targets had been grain speculators and the military service quotas. The insurgents of 1835 also attacked steam-powered factories, representatives of the government, and houses of religion; the disturbances of 1840–42 culminated in a political revolution by a coalition of the disaffected whose only rallying point was the call for protective tariffs: it was sup-

lence and intermittent plague.

Ildefons Cerdà (the urban planner who was to create the Eixample and transform Barcelona) surveyed the working-class way of life in the 1850s and found that a diet of bread and potatoes, enhanced with the odd sardine, was all an average family could afford. Observers blamed the cholera epidemic of 1854, which claimed 6,000 lives, on overcrowding in insanitary conditions.

Left, the Ramblas, where the successful paraded their wealth. **Above**, workers from a textile factory, breeding grounds of discontent.

pressed by force.

In 1854 a long series of strikes and Luddite outrages began in defiance of the spectacularly fast automation of the textile industry. The riots were soon deflected into political channels by the fall of a "progressive" ministry in Madrid; respectable radicals joined the mob in resistance. The barricades of Barcelona had to be reconquered bloodily, in the worst scenes the city had witnessed since 1714. A conservative observer noted with satisfaction: "The rebels were massacred as they were captured… The spectacle was magnificent."

40

The bloodshed of the mid-19th century was a shock to the sensibilities of the bourgeoisie; but the authorities' confidence that they would soon recover proved justified. The optimism of the burgeoning city was displayed in the competition, held in 1859, for a design for the expansion (*eixample*) of the city beyond the walls.

The public exhibition attracted huge crowds. Antoni Rovira i Trias submitted a popular plan, sympathetically integrating the old town; Ildefons Cerdà's proposal looked more rigidly modern. He made only minimal use of nodal *piazze* and masked the old town with a grid-plan of boulevards and public gardens. Political controversy, caused by the Madrid government's determination to impose Cerdà's solution, delayed work while the situation grew desperately urgent: in 1863, for instance, the rate of growth of the population of Barcelona was 27.42 percent, three times the Spanish national average.

The Spanish revolution of 1868, which swept the Bourbons from the throne, temporarily abated the differences between Barcelona and Madrid and in 1869 the laying out of the Eixample proceeded along the lines of the Cerdà plan.

Despite the delayed start and the slow initial growth, Barcelona's boom in the late 19th century was so rapid that the expectations of the plan were exceeded. In-filling robbed it of its best feature, the expansive parks and garden squares. The sudden grafting of a criss-cross of 19th-century branches on to the trunk of an ancient town created the view from Montjuïc – the image which defines the city's character, despite the subsequent (even greater) growth, to this day.

Political peace: The era of the Eixample was accompanied by relative social peace. The political energies of most of the Barcelonans were deflected into Catalanism, the movement for the recognition of Catalonia's distinctive institutions and the conservation of its language and cultural heritage. Bourgeois life moved out of the cafés on to pavement terraces and out of the house into the gas-lit streets that so dazzled Hans Christian Andersen when he visited in 1862.

One novelist called this the "gold fever era" when the industrialisation of Barcelona swallowed up huge amounts of capital, scattered among too many under-funded firms.

The "gamblers' synagogue" – the unofficial Bourse or stock exchange – began in 1858. Slack money and new money created a market for art and architecture that has given Barcelona the rather showy, experimental look that has characterised *le style barcelonais* ever since.

The symbol of this era of self-assurance was the Universal Exhibition of 1888. The idea originated with a Galician entrepreneur who had seen the Paris and Vienna exhibitions and it was taken up by Barcelona's Mayor Rius i Taulat after he came to office in city hall in 1885.

Left, the Right exploits regional feeling in a Civil War propaganda poster. **Right**, workers discussing strike action on the Ramblas.

When he summoned the world to Barcelona on 13 June 1887, everything had still to be extemporised with less than a year to go. But not only did the citizens build on time the exhibition ground that cynics had deemed impossible, they also planted the Plaça de Colom with palms and drove the Rambla de Catalunya and the Paral.lel through suburbs where they had previously been stymied. The Hotel Internacional was built in only 60 days and its five floors proved unequal to the demand.

The exhibition opened 10 days late, but despite this it drew exhibitors from 20 countries and attracted well over two million

Social conflict could hardly be avoided.

When the rail link was completed young French anarchists took the Barcelona Express and were shocked on arrival by the prostitutes: this was the character of the revolutionary anarchism that became the most potent force of Barcelona's political underworld: naïve and puritanical. In the 1890s, Barcelona was the "city of bombs", symbolised by Ramon Casas's restrained painting of the Corpus Christi procession that was attacked in 1896 (in the Museu d'Art Modern in Ciutadella Park).

In the early 1900s, while terrorism collapsed, the workers' movement was infused

visitors. The young Josep Puig i Cadafalch (who would become a major influence in the architecture, letters and politics of Barcelona) was inspired with a vision of a great Barcelona. With the exhibition the idea of Barcelona as a model of go-ahead hard work entered popular fiction.

Anarchy: But rapid growth never happens painlessly. In 1860, Barcelona had less than 200,000 inhabitants. By 1897, when the city limits were redefined to incorporate the towns of the immediate hinterland, the official figure was 383,908. By 1930, the conurbation contained well over a million people.

with anarchism. There was a general strike in 1901–2; the Setmana Tràgica of 1909, when a strangely self-disciplined mob systematically destroyed 70 buildings of religious orders while sparing other targets, was attributed to anarcho-syndicalism; the movement's spokesman, Francesc Ferrer, was executed for presumed complicity after a show trial which shocked the world.

Art from chaos: Some of these tensions were reflected in the work of the modernist artists who gathered in the Quatre Gats café (today expensively restored in the Carrer Montsió). The most representative figure was Ramon

Casas, whose father had made a fortune in the Indies and who, on his mother's side, was the heir to a textile mill. His inheritance thus combined two typical sources of the wealth of Barcelona in his day.

Casas's best works were problematical genre scenes, but his most memorable canvases, (many of which can be seen in the Museu d'Art Modern) are those in which the social commentary is most overt. *Barcelona 1902* is an extraordinarily dynamic composition, in which a mounted civil guard is about to trample a sprawling, dramatically foreshortened worker in the foreground, while the crowd is cleared by the cavalry

conical caps prod towards the centre of the canvas like pitchfork-prongs.

The public loved the engaging horror more than they feared the social import; horror-paintings in Barcelona were always popular and frequently connected with the traditions of public scourging – common until the early 19th century – and public execution, which continued until 1908.

A state of confusion existed throughout Spain in the first three decades of the 20th century. Eventually, in 1931, the Left won a resounding election victory and King Alfonso XIII was forced to leave Spain without formally abdicating. The Second Republic

from a space which seems to grow before the onlooker's eyes.

Casas's most famous work was *Garrote Vil,* of 1893, recording the public execution of a 19-year-old who had cut the throats of his victim and his own accomplice for a gold watch. Some aspects seem ironic: the clergy are a corpulent contingent, under an enormous crucifix; the penitents' black

Left, demonstrators for independence in 1936. **Above**, separatist tendencies were soon squashed by the Civil War: show of strength by Nationalist troops in Plaça de Catalunya in 1939.

was proclaimed. To the Barcelonans' delight, the exiled socialist leader Francesc Macià returned from Paris to become president of the Barcelona Generalitat.

The Macià plan was an ambitious project to expand and develop the city, but its life was as shortlived as that of the Republic. The Right struck back, and the Civil War erupted before any major works could be completed.

In Barcelona the anarchist revolution of 1936 had made an enemy of anyone who wore a tie in the street. So when Franco's troops marched in with the slogan "Spain has arrived", a collaborationist bourgeoisie came out of the woodwork. Catalan culture went deeper underground than under the dictatorship of General Primo de Rivera. Josep Viladomat's monumental sculptured allegory, *La República*, found an ignominious refuge among the packing-cases of the municipal storehouse.

Immigrant flood: The big threat to Barcelona's identity under Franco came, however, not from repression but from economic growth. Three-quarters of a million immigrants, mostly from southern Spain, came to the city between 1950 and 1970, selling up their homes elsewhere to live in dreadful accommodation in the city. They

were attracted by the employment possibilities in Catalonia, which had established itself as the economic powerhouse of the Spanish peninsula.

It was easy for Francoism to buy these people with job security and modest economic rewards, hard for Catalanism to win them with the blandishments of an alien tongue, an inhospitable culture and a mandarin creed. Yet when the exiled Catalan leader, Josep Taradellas, appeared after Franco's death on the balcony of the Generalitat in the Plaça de Sant Jaume, he found the immigrants willing to vote for autonomy.

His cry, *Ja soc aqui*! (Here I am at last!) contrasted with the "Spain has arrived" of the Francoists. A survey found that many *soi-disant* Andalucíans also considered themselves Catalans: but the main reason for favouring autonomy was rejection of Francoism, not Catalanist sentiment.

The dictatorship's other legacy was a proletariat with drawn fangs. Communists took the lead in organising a clandestine union movement from 1963: by the 1970s it was strong enough to attempt political strikes. But, as it grew in numbers, it became ideologically diluted. The union elections of 1975 put apolitical leaders in control of most branches, and "responsible" unionism has been dominant ever since. In partial consequence, investment has poured into what is now the biggest city of any along the Mediterranean coast.

Changing city: Walking in the streets today, one can stumble across contrasts which encapsulate the whole history of Barcelona, from country town to industrial wen. A *masia* – a farmhouse of the prosperous early-modern peasantry – still stands in the Plaça de Málaga, close to the main railway station; another, rather grand, occupies the corner of the Passeig Maragall with the Carrer de Frederic Ramola. The remains of the villages of Santa Eulàlia de Vilapicina and Sant Martí dels Provençals survive among the tower blocks.

The latest changes in the cityscape, where recent works have opened up the seafront to diners and promenaders, have re-established a link with the more glorious maritime chapter of Barcelona's past.

This is, perhaps, more evidence of continuity than one might expect in such a brash and dynamic city. But Barcelona will cease to be Barcelona if the immigrants of the exclusively Spanish-speaking districts of the industrial *barris* remain unassimilated. When the Olympic Village is finished, the Catalanisation of the masses will once again be the administration's most urgent task.

Left, the bombing of Barcelona port during the Civil War by Italian aircraft loyal to Franco. **Right**, Francesc Macià, leader of the Generalitat during the short-lived Republic.

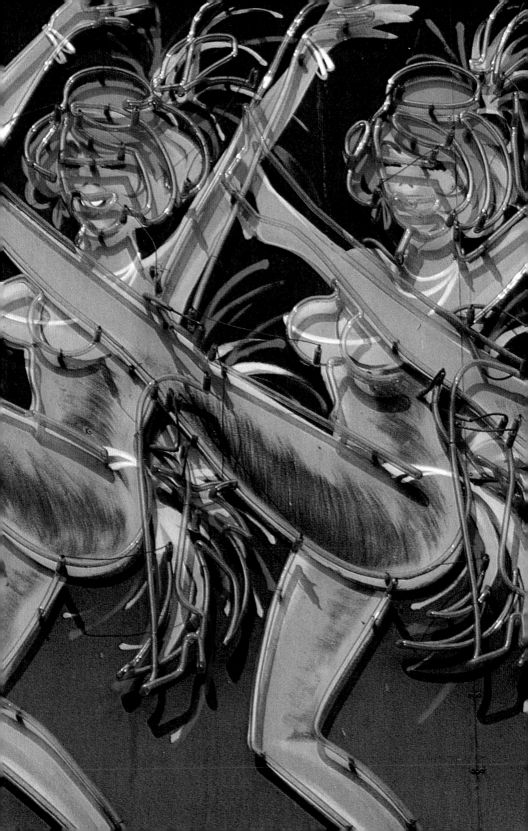

Despite the millions of words written about Barcelona, nobody has managed to capture the city completely in all its complexity. From the "city of the prodigals", as it was called by Eduardo Mendoza, it has subsequently been called "the Spanish Paris", "capital of the future", "territory of illusions" and "city of symbols".

Aurèlia Capmany, author and City Hall councillor, has recently written: "It is now no longer possible to see Barcelona at a glance. If we arrive by sea, the city greets us with all the splendour of the dawn, of thousands of city lights. If we arrive from the south, leaving to our right the banner of Montjuïc, we are greeted by an elegant avenue, slightly unkempt, as if it had not had the time to smarten up a little. Coming down from the north, we are stopped by the walls of skyscrapers and factories. Here is a city that is too large, some say, that has grown in a disorderly fashion stemming from the greed of a small village with a glorious past."

To every piece of descriptive writing you could add as many contradictory adjectives as you please: welcoming, harsh, charming and abrupt; faithful and hypocritical, sordid and sophisticated. Barcelona also claims to be a fashion-leader, but eternally up to date may be a better description.

Today's city, with 680 miles (1,100 km) of streets and an estimated 750,000 vehicles, is dense, crowded, noisy, with a covering of smog – but within this smog it is regenerating itself. Barcelona seems to have stopped momentarily to lick its wounds, powder its face again and clean the treasures that have become dirty through lack of care, through idleness and too much introspection.

Vital statistics: In the year 1900 the city of Barcelona had a population of 537,354. Thirty years later it reached one million and by 1986 the population stood at 1,701,812.

Preceding pages: neon on Arnau's Music Hall; supporters in full cry; opera fans. **Left,** keeping up with the Barcelona edition. **Right,** Maragall, Barcelona's Mayor.

The rhythm of growth indicates that by the year 2000 this figure will not even reach 1.8 million, but this is not to say that the city does not have problems similar to those of any other, larger, European metropolis. The city grew alarmingly during the 1950s and 1960s due, fundamentally, to the influx of immigrants who arrived from outlying rural areas.

Recent history has reversed that trend, with numbers of people leaving Barcelona to go and live elsewhere because of the nega-

tive ambience of city life and severe housing problems (poor quality, small and an almost total lack of first homes).

Barcelona's dynamism depends on maintaining the flow of the city's enormous surface transport. Even along the Diagonal – its greatest avenue – traffic crawls at an average of 9 mph (14 kph).

The Barcelona of the late 1980s and early 1990s has had to cope with a disconcerting paradox, in that its focal point has been located in the future: the day after the closing of the XXV Summer Olympic Games in 1992. The city, bristling with signs date-stamped with 1992 or 1993 logos, grows at a discordant pace, driven by resources far beyond those usually available to a city of its size. Isabel Gómez Melenchón, writing in *La Vanguardia*, the city's highest circulation newspaper, said that: "Barcelona is, according to the opinions of some of its inhabitants and many of its casual residents, a city of masochists that constantly asks to be pardoned for its successes, that grows with its failures and feeds on criticism… Barcelona needs excuses to continue to grow, to reaffirm itself, and it needs to complete this growth in leaps and bounds. The last of these acrobatic exercises was to request, and ob-

even a decent second-hand apartment.

Dual personality: There are many cities within this city. All major conurbations have a dual personality, presenting one face to the visitor or foreigner and another to the long-suffering citizen. Barcelona has been described either as a southern city of the north or as a northern city of the south. It is a Spanish city for the inhabitants of the Mediterranean region and a Mediterranean city to the Spaniards. For the British, it is the Catalan Manchester.

Between the city discovered by Gide and the city of Gaudí, there is a side of Barcelona that, though unwelcome, will not go away

tain, the 1992 Olympic Games."

An X-ray of the city of the future shows that, three years after that magic date of 1992, Barcelona will have almost 50,000 fewer inhabitants; restoration works will have created chaos but there will be more parks, more green zones; unemployment will have been reduced by eight points while the average income will have increased by two points; the poor and the homeless will still be poor and still homeless; the traffic will be unbearable, with more cars, more noise than ever and the wallets of the Barcelonans will not contain enough money to buy

despite renovation. It emerges on the disaster pages of the newspapers, where the process of degradation is frightening, steeped in drugs and poverty. This is a Barcelona – perhaps the essence is common to every major port city – that escapes the control of its rulers, a ghetto of misery and delinquency that does not match the new image of a happy and confident city that is being sold to the world for the Olympic Games. Efforts have been made, such as in the renovation of the Plaça Reial or the Ramblas, to stop the degradation. But the truth contaminates the dream, the drunks and addicts still crowd into the Plaça and the prostitutes on to the foot of the Ramblas, the tree-lined street that is the spinal cord of the older quarters.

Ingrowing city: Where Barcelona has changed most of all is in the ambience of the city itself. Forced by a series of barriers, some natural and some man-made, to grow in upon itself, the city has rediscovered its own spaces and has learnt to make use of them. The use of space and sculpture has spearheaded these new designs over the past few years, backed up by careful quality control of all new architecture.

A new attitude, a new hunger for aesthetic pleasure, is becoming more apparent among

architects, engineers and artists involved in the design and construction of urban areas. In addition, now that the administration has finally accepted that it is directly responsible for the construction and maintenance of public areas, some surprisingly spectacular parks, squares and roads have been built.

Undoubtedly this current phenomenon will be the subject of careful study in the future, for this is a city that has converted its

Left, the Communist party endorses self-government on a Barcelona wall. **Above**, the cathedral, at the centre of the old city.

streets into museums and its factories into leisure centres. The architectural critic Robert Hughes has written: "The programme of parks and sculptures with which Barcelona has been endowed constitutes the most ambitious project of its kind to be undertaken by the Town Hall of any city in the 20th century." And he adds: "The effort to meticulously integrate contemporary sculptures within the very fabric of the city is not only an unusual one, it is unique."

Art spaces: The Parc de l'Espanya Industrial is a good example of this redevelopment: once the site of the old "Vapor Nou" factory, one of the first to be built on the Pla (plain) of Barcelona, the park's basic design is a copy of modern Roman hot springs, with a navigable lake as a central feature, bordered by tiers and dominated by 10 towers which function as both viewing points and lighting supports. The whole area is decorated with a variety of artworks such as the grand dragon with interior water chutes designed by Andrés Nagel, or the works of Anthony Caro and Pablo Palazuelo.

Very close by is the daring and controversial Plaça dels Països Catalans, opposite the Sants railway station. A space created by Helio Piñón and Albert Viaplana, it follows the norms of ultimate modernism, converting an already unusual area into a space that appears to be defined, not by its own limits, but by the objects that it contains: an enormous, 50-ft (15-metre) high canopy; a sinuous covered pagoda; a double row of water jets that spray both passers-by and part of the granite paving; podiums with no statues; billboards with no advertisements; and children's play areas.

Sculpture is everywhere: the Parc de Joan Miró, also known as the Escorxador, which occupies a whole block not far from the Plaça dels Països Catalans, is presided over by an esplanade from which emerges the spectacular Miró sculpture *Dona i ocell* (woman and bird).

In the Sagrera district, the Parc de la Pegasso occupies land left vacant by the company of the same name. The project, carried out by Joan Roig and Enric Batlle, boasts a paved square with a sculpture by Ellsworth Kelly, woodland areas and a small lake.

In the Plaça de la Palmera the conceptual artist Richard Serra conceived a giant sculpture made from two concentric blocks of cement, each one 170 ft long by 10 ft high (52 by 3 metres). The idea was to create a psychological tension suggested by the sight of these two gigantic forms.

An impressive hanging sculpture is Eduardo Chillida's *Elogi de l'aigua*, suspended over the pond that forms part of the Parc de la Creueta del Coll (in the shadow of Tibidabo). This is one of the most successful of recent enterprises. It was designed by the architects Martorell and Mackay, who reclaimed an absolutely useless space which

including bars and shops. Even the design of the toilets has become a talking point. Design fever reaches its peak in the many discotheques scattered throughout the city: Zeleste (next to the Olympic Village), K.G.B., Nick Havanna, Velvet, Network, Sisisi, Ticktactoe, Snooker, Universal, Diametro 77, Prosit, Bijou, Metropol or Speed: each tries to outdo the others in creating new images and new venues.

Once the Olympic Games are over, the Barcelonans will live in a renovated city that has had to cope with some extremely difficult demands. The Games will not only leave a series of high-quality sports facilities, there

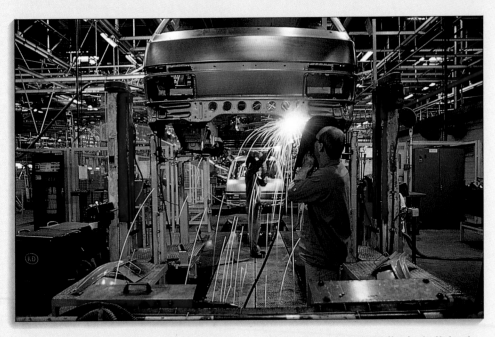

was once the site of an old quarry; in its stead, a small artificial beach has been created. The park is adorned with sculptures by Ellsworth Kelly and Roy Lichtenstein.

On the other hand, there are those who consider the bridge, Pont Felip II-Bac de Roda, measuring 420 ft (128 metres), to be the greatest sculpture of recent times. Based on a project by the civil engineer Santiago Calatrava, the bridge joins the Bac de Roda and Carrer de Felip II in the north.

Design fever: The emphasis on aesthetic appeal is evident also in the decoration and interior architecture of public buildings,

will also be a whole new district built by the sea, a splendid port on the site of the old commercial docks, a futuristic airport, an impressive network of communications, modern cultural complexes and high-technology communications systems.

New development areas have been established throughout the outlying Eixample, to provide for the harmonious and well-planned development of vast city projects with a marked tendency towards decentralisation. Most of these are located in the east of Barcelona, from Nou Barris to Poble Nou. These areas will also be converted into space

56

for tertiary activities (particularly leisure activities) which now have no space within the confines of the rigid Eixample.

Waterfront work: The Barcelona of 1993 will turn once again to the sea. The redevelopment of the waterfront represents the greatest expenditure of effort within the 1992 programme, with the creation of a city sea promenade that will start in Montjuïc and continue up to Ciutadella Park, incorporating the Moll de la Fusta. Much of the *barri* Xinès (otherwise known as the *barrio* Chino or the red-light district) has been bulldozed and the daylight let in.

In the port itself, planners hope to integrate

Nor has the city's cultural side been forgotten in this overall improvement in the quality of city life. The Museu d'Art de Catalunya is being remodelled to become the Museu d'Art Modern, based on a project drawn up by the architect Gae Aulenti. An enormous contemporary cultural centre featuring the Museu d'Art Contemporani is being created, together with an extensive complex of the Casa de la Caritat by Richard Meier and the designs for the so-called "Plaça Culta".

Adjoining the Plaça de las Glòries, another authentic cultural centre will be built, combining the Teatre Nacional de Cata-

into the city's life those areas which are no longer vital to commercial activities. With the construction of the Olympic Village in the new district of Nova Icaria, the area situated between La Barceloneta and Poble Nou will undergo radical changes. The areas previously occupied by the old industries (the heart of the "Catalan Manchester") will be transformed, together with their access routes and facilities.

Left, production line in the Nissan factory. **Above**, hosting the Olympics is a matter of great pride to the city.

lunya, designed by Ricard Bofill, and Rafael Moneo's Auditori Municipal. The former will have two auditoriums in a building constructed in the form of a classical temple, composed of metallic structures and massive glass windows. The latter, larger but also with two auditoriums, combines the elements of new designs and classical tradition.

The 1992 Olympic Games have proved the ideal catalyst for the redesign and redevelopment of the city. When the last race has been run and the last javelin thrown, the athletes will leave a city that is already reaching out to embrace the 21st century.

Barcelona is a city within a city within a city, like a set of Russian dolls. Each layer the visitor peels away reveals more: museums and galleries, street musicians and entertainers, dimly lit port bars or backstreet pubs, and layer upon layer of history like several coats of paint on a wall.

Animating this rich tapestry are the Barcelonans, running around the city like ants over a carpet. Thanks to their city's excessively turbulent and varied history, they are ambiguous people, not easy to get to know. They are creative, serious and industrious. They are unorthodox in their tastes, equally at home with an *avant-garde* sculpture by Chillida or with the medieval ambience of the Plaça del Reial: what strikes the visitor as an extraordinary contrast seems perfectly natural to the Barcelonan.

Those who believe that the best short cut to determining a people's character is to ask a taxi driver will be out of luck in Barcelona. Many of the city's *taxistes* are from the south of Spain, having been driven out of their native Andalucía by hunger in the lean years of the 1950s and 1960s. Because their experience as immigrants has not been a happy one, they tend to repeat every cliché ever coined about the Catalan character.

Juan Manuel is a good example. He is from Albacete, 350 miles (560 km) southwest of Barcelona and has been living in the Catalan capital for 35 years. He drives a cab which, like its owner, has seen better days. He even has a Catalan wife. He doesn't beat about the bush when asked what he makes of the Barcelonans. "I can't stand them!" he spits. "They're cold, mean and tight-fisted. Invite them for a meal in your house and afterwards go for a coffee and brandy in the bar down the road: you can be sure they'll pay for their own drink and not even offer to get yours." Even his wife doesn't escape his harsh judgement. On the contrary: Juan Manuel

apparently can't stand her either and resents her Catalan-ness.

"One Christmas she won a hamper at the textile factory where she worked. I could never understand what happened to those bottles of *cava* and the biscuits that were in it. Then one day I was looking for something in the back of a cupboard," says Juan Manuel, the bitterness growing in his voice, "and what do you think I found? I'm damned if she hadn't stashed the whole lot away!"

Work ethic: And there you have the core of an old platitude about the Barcelonan which is still tossed around today: he's stingy and unfriendly, puts his own interests first and is distrustful of outsiders. "Of course there's another side to the coin," says Milagros Perez Oliva, who is not a Barcelonan but reckons that she knows how they tick after 10 years of living among them as a journalist. "They're workers, they like things to run efficiently and they aren't afraid of putting in the necessary effort to make it that way. If you have children and you and your spouse both work hard, it's difficult not to appear

Preceding pages: Rosa Maria Malet, director of the Miró Foundation. **Left**, Xavier Güell, conductor. **Right**, street musician.

'cold' or 'unfriendly' to the outsider. But it doesn't mean you *are* that way. The Andaluz who spends his day in the bar is open and friendly, no doubt about that, but he doesn't get much done, does he?"

The most characteristic trait of the Barcelonans, and that of Catalans in general, is their passion for work, for economy, and, above all, for their famous *seny català* (prudence) in business. The *mañana* attitude so often referred to in reference to business with other parts of Spain scarcely exists here.

The Catalans' work ethic – they've been referred to as the Protestants of southern Europe – is especially noticeable if you come to Phoenicians and the Romans. Business has always been business; if you don't clinch the deal, your neighbour will – and that's no good for the bank balance. Barcelona has been built up through family enterprises, such as the legendary textile factories where sons and daughters have always knuckled down to the job regardless of gender, with everyone feeling personally involved.

The Barcelonans adhere fiercely to their traditions, but they are essentially a private people. Their social life is wrapped in discretion and they rigorously respect the established social classes – although you are unlikely to find as much obsession with the

Barcelona after visiting the rest of Spain. It is perhaps less striking for someone who has flown in from Bonn or Tokyo. You can see it in the comparatively early closing of bars and restaurants ("early to bed, early to rise…"), shop opening hours which are the longest in Spain (just in case they missed a customer or two), and a respect for the clock which is bliss for anyone who has tried to make business appointments anywhere south of Madrid. In Barcelona, 10 o'clock means 10 o'clock, not half past 11.

But then Barcelona's background is purely mercantile, reaching right back to the aristocracy and with petty titles here as in other parts of the country.

An integral part of the Catalan temperament is the longstanding rivalry with Madrid. The history of Catalonia and the character of the Barcelonans are inextricably connected to the defence of their autonomous identity as a separate people and – once – as a nation. The anti-central government sentiment is taken very seriously, although it is not without a touch of humour at times. Refer in passing to the city of Madrid and likely as not a Barcelonan will interject: "Someone told me that Madrid has once again become the capital of Spain."

Even during the repressive Franco regime, Barcelona retained its air of excitement and vitality. While the rest of Spain has changed enormously and extrovertedly since the death of the dictator, Barcelona's changes have not been so marked: the city is well used to centuries of changes of fortune, and Franco was just another of many.

Pitch battles: Football, the "passion of the masses", forms an important part of the duel between Barcelona and Madrid. When the city's football team, the venerated "Barça", wins a match the work ethic is drowned in a delirium of nationalistic fervour because

defence of their Catalan identity. The patriotic fervour for Catalonia and Barcelona generated in the stadium – particularly in the matches against Madrid – has been channelled by politicians into their political campaigns. During the transition to democracy the phrase "The Barça is much more than just a club" was used frequently. Today the slogan has lost much of its strength with Catalonia's return to autonomous government – and with the recent dog-days for the fortunes of the club.

A telling example of this partisan spirit can be found in the incidents surrounding a match between Real Madrid and the Italian

"our boys" have shown them once again. The red and gold of the Catalan colours combine with the blue and maroon ("*blau grana*") of the football club in a swirling mass down the Ramblas, and woe betide the joker who mentions the word "Madrid" in anything above a whisper.

At times, the Barcelona Football Club has even become the springboard for the local population's claims against the ruling classes and it has also been a bulwark in the

Left, on the streets with a Catalan hat. **Above**, the top hat of authority.

team from Milan, recently staged in the Barça stadium. Every goal scored by the Italians was greeted with a barrage of victorious firecrackers from the Catalan crowd and the entire city of Barcelona exulted in the overwhelming victory of the foreign team.

Famous people: Many personalities from Barcelona have achieved prestige and international acclaim in all areas of the arts: Gaudí, Sert, Picasso, Tàpies, Espriu, Mendoza, Miró and Casals are just a few, although it is true that their talents have not always been readily recognised by their fellow Barcelonans.

COSMOPOLITAN CITY

Barcelona has always been a haven for foreigners. Traders from all over the Mediterranean – Greeks, Phoenicians, Carthaginians, Romans – have been part of Barcelona's busy port life since well before the Roman conquest in 133 BC.

Situated near the Crusade routes from western Europe, Barcelona continued to collect a foreign community during the Middle Ages, and when "infidels" (citizens of Muslim and Judaic faiths) were officially expelled from Spain in 1492, thousands of Barcelona residents became "new Christians". George Orwell, in his Spanish Civil War memoir *Homage to Catalonia*, chronicled the ideologically boiling Barcelona of 1936, filled with young foreigners from all over the world who had come to defend democracy in what had become a workers' city.

Later, during the four decades of the Franco regime, Barcelona was Spain's most cosmopolitan city, a relief from the claustrophobic social, intellectual and artistic aspects of Franco's isolationist Movimiento Nacional.

In the later years of Franco's rule, Barcelona became something of an ersatz Paris with its own Montmartre and Arc de Triomphe, or a Mediterranean Manhattan, with one foot in Europe and the other in the Hispanic world. Gabriel García Marquez, Mario Vargas Llosa and other international writers lived here during the 1960s and early 1970s in search of a combination of Europe, Spain and America: metropolitan energy and diversity at a survivable price and pace.

In the 15 years since Franco's death, the city's foreign community has continued to grow, and is now estimated at 150,000. But official and unofficial figures are wildly divergent. The French colony, for example, is officially reported at 5,000, while the French Institute estimates 15,000 and long-time resident French citizens suggest that 30,000 may be more realistic.

The West German consulate reports 16,000 countrymen in the Barcelona area, a figure which has the advantage of being an unofficial estimate,

as West German citizens are not required to register with consular authorities. The American colony, officially estimated at 5,000, is unofficially put at twice that figure. The British presence in Barcelona, estimated at 6,000, goes back to the beginning of the century and includes one of the founders of the local football club. The Italian colony, like the French, is large but linguistically and socially assimilated.

Barcelona's Lycée Français has long been one of the top preparatory schools, partly as an alternative to church and state-dominated education under Franco and partly as a result of the proximity of Catalan and French, linguistically more similar than Catalan and Spanish. The German School has flourished for decades, as have the Swiss, Italian, British and American Schools.

Foreigners come to Barcelona for a variety of reasons, all revolving around the basic formula of exciting, civilised living at unterrifying prices (although the latter is not quite so true now). Germans are frequently retired; French and Italians are usually married to Catalans; English, Irish and Americans are often English teachers, writers and translators; Scandinavians may be entrepreneurs looking for a more rewarding tax structure.

The foreign business community is increasingly important in Barcelona as Spain's economy gains momentum. Foreign painters, sculptors, writers, actors, dancers, singers and artists are all attracted by the opportunity for personal and professional survival.

Barcelona is Spain, but it is partly removed from Celtiberia and the Hispanic world by its own language and culture. It is mainstream Europe, yet part of the passionate Mediterranean. It is only a short flight from Rome, Zurich, Munich, Paris, London, Madrid or Lisbon. Beaches as well as ski slopes are within easy reach. The city is bilingual in Catalan and Spanish, with French a closely related third language and English becoming a professionally necessary fourth.

Foreigners, all in all, do well in Barcelona. Xenophilia, not xenophobia, is the rule, while passion, inspiration, civilisation, ambition and pleasure co-exist peacefully in this ancient Catalan capital, a stone's throw from everywhere.

Music is particularly important. The streets and plaças hum with the rhythm of the city's occupants, beginning with the haunting sounds of the *cobles* (wind instruments) which accompany the unhurried movements of the traditional *sardana*. The *cançó catalana* (Catalan folk singing) has been revived by Joan Manuel Serrat, Lluís Llach and Mallorcan folk singer Maria del Mar Bonet.

The long lines of ticket buyers outside the Liceu Theatre attest to the fact that the theatre's 19th-century creators were only doing the people's bidding – as does the glory of the Palau de la Música Catalana, which was inaugurated in 1908 by the Berlin

[Barcelona province], which in 1900 had a population of 2,269,406, reached the figure of 3,116,037 in 1930." In 1936 a quarter of the citizens living in Barcelona itself were not native Barcelonans. Immigration reached massive proportions throughout the 1950s and 1960s.

The *Ciutat Condal* (city state) has always been a promised land, not only for Spaniards but also for foreigners. During the 18th century the number of French immigrants was greater even than the number who arrived from Spain, and it is perhaps partly for this reason and partly because of hostility towards Madrid that a Catalan-speaking

Philharmonic Orchestra.

Immigrant influence: One of the first consequences of the new-found economic strength of the 19th century, when Barcelona became a manufacturing powerhouse, was a marked increase in the city's population. The first to arrive were the skilled labourers from the surrounding areas of Catalonia; they provided an important economic bedrock. According to Albert Balcells in his *Cataluña Contemporánea*: "The Principado

Above, young and beautiful and up all hours of the night.

Barcelonan is as happy to converse with a foreigner in English or French as in Castilian. Today it is the South Americans who form the latest flourishing and expanding immigrant community.

The health and the use of the Catalan language has always been a key concern for Barcelonans. All in all, some six million people worldwide speak Catalan as their mother tongue. Today there is a large Catalan media, including books, newspapers, television and radio stations, all centred on Barcelona. There have been times in the past when the language has been forced to go underground, particularly during the Franco regime. After Franco's death, the Spanish Constitution of 1978 re-established Catalan as one of Spain's official languages.

In recent years the Generalitat's Department of Linguistic Policy has been active in the normalisation of Catalan, concentrating its efforts on the teaching of the language in schools from first grade through to university level; students can now choose whether to study in Catalan or Castilian, and Catalan is recognised as an official language of the 1992 Olympic Games.

Personal freedom: The Barcelonans are far from being the staid, unimaginative and

convention-bound people that one might imagine, given all that work weighing heavily on their minds. (Just look what they let Gaudí do, for heaven's sake!) There's room in the city for creativity and risk-taking without attracting social reprobation. "A sense of initiative is essential in order to get on probably because everyone is working so hard," says Montse, a partner in a group of graphic designers. "Barcelona has always been tolerant of difference and it's a place where women don't have to fight for their place professionally. There's a wonderful freedom from silly conventions which allows

you to go ahead and do your own thing if you want to."

It is easy to believe in the prosperity of this stylish city where the modernist facades have been renovated and treated with care (after some decades of neglect), where the shop windows gleam with luxury and suggest an affluent consumer society. Citizens of Barcelona today walk with their heads held high, proud of the progress, avidly approving the smallest signs of renewal. Modern boutiques, traditional pastry shops and old-fashioned grocery stores live side by side with old garages converted into shops for yuppies and branch offices of international enterprises. No day goes by without a new business being opened, nor a night when a new bar, restaurant or risqué night club doesn't make its first appearance.

Barcelona is probably the only place in Spain where you can declare yourself a vegetarian, an ecologist, a gay, a pacifist or even all four at once without provoking withering looks or worse.

Finally, good humour is an unexpected element of the Barcelonan character. Hard work hasn't killed off warmth and civility. However much part of a sales technique, it does a person good to be hailed as *reina* (queen) or *guapísima* (very pretty) – terms of endearment used on women of all ages, from eight to eighty, in markets and bread shops especially. "But you're our customer," you will be told if you show gratitude for what could be mistaken for nascent friendship. Never mind: to be able to buy freshly cooked lentils or chick-peas from a smiling old man who's been up at 3.30 a.m. to start cooking them and who still has the vitality to crack a joke with you at midday is worth a lot more than money.

In Barcelona on Midsummer's Day (*Nit de San Joan* or St John's Day, 24 June), fire-crackers and fireworks never stop – in fact, they started weeks before – and bonfires are lit all over the city. The Barcelonans know that all work and no play would make them very dull indeed and that's something they have no desire to be.

Left, **Bigas Luna**, film director. **Right**, **Richard Boffil**, **architect**, at Gaudí's La Pedrera.

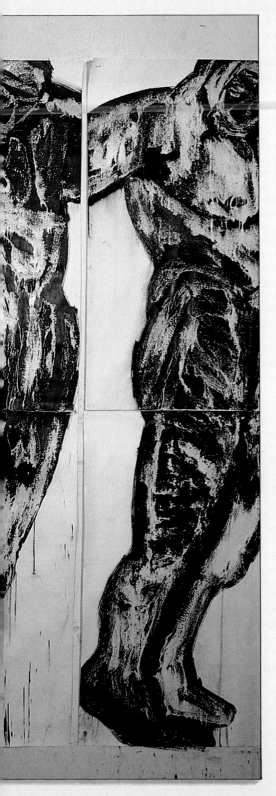

Left, Tomas Gomez, painter.

Barcelona is like a magnet, attracting various artistic influences from every form of creative expression. It's a place where ideas from other parts of the world are sifted and recombined in new and original ways. This is the city of Miró, of Picasso and of Gaudí; it is also the city of "Supermerc'art", an annual artistic supermarket where artists of all styles sell their paintings and drawings at three different set price levels. The buyers stroll through, filling up supermarket trolleys from each stack as if they were stocking up with groceries.

Barcelona's nomination as the Olympic city has seemingly prompted a new surge of creative activity, although in reality this is largely the result of an increase in media attention on what already exists. In Barcelona, art and urban planning overlap: not only is the city carrying out projects of reconstruction and architectural restoration, but in the redesigning of both new and old interiors an increasingly praiseworthy touch of personality is being sought.

Jordi Bieto, president of IFAD (Interioristes del Foment de les Arts Decoratives), claims that in the field of interior design, where improvisation is very hard to achieve, a tradition is being established which will make its presence felt more and more strongly over the coming years, and that the standard and quality of work in Barcelona is on a par with that in Italy.

Creative cafés: Originality is not just reserved for the homes of the rich. There is ample evidence of creative interior design even in the city's day-to-day venues. Barcelona is a city of restaurants, shops and, above all, bars. Noteworthy among the bars of design interest are the expensive and modern restaurant Neichel (Avinguda de Pedralbes, 16 bis), the Café de Colombia, which was designed by Alicia Muñoz (Carrer de Iradier), the Azulete (in Via Augusta, on the corner with Carrer de Doctor Roux) complete with terrace, the modernised Chinese

Pekin (Carrer de Roselló) and La Vaqueira (Carrer de Mata), an opulent place which combines classical and modern décor.

As far as shops are concerned, heading the list are the three shopping malls named Bulevar Rosa (the first of which was opened on Passeig de Gràcia, between Carrer de València and Carrer d'Aragó; the second on the Diagonal close to Vía Augusta, and the third, also in the Avinguda de Diagonal, next to the department store El Corte Inglés). Then there are all the shops around Plaça Francesc Maciá and the streets Diagonal and Ganduxer, as well as those along the Rambla de Catalunya and Passeig de Gràcia.

table was ever installed. Merbeye and Mirablau are both at the end of the Tranvia Blau route at the top of Tibidabo and therefore have spectacular views.

The top three fashionable nightspots are KGB (Carrer d'Alegre de Dalt), a postmodernist venue with a mobile bar; Nick Havanna (Carrer de Roselló, between Carrer de Balmes and the Rambla de Catalunya), which is renowned for its waterfalls in the men's toilet and a swinging pendulum among the video screens; and the unbeatable Otto Zultz (Carrer de Lincoln), a spectacular New York-style modern disco with excellent music, *the* place to end the night.

Barcelona's nightspots and key bars give an even better idea of the city's progress in architectural and interior design, but you need stamina to see them. Start the evening at Zig Zag (Carrer de Plató), a bar that leads the field of innovative design with its cold and functional décor, continue on to the two-storey Universal (Carrer de Mariano Cubí near Carrer de Calvet), and the ultra-modern restaurant-bar Network (Diagonal/Ganduxer). An old friend for the less fashionable crowd is Gimlet (Carrer de Santaló). Snooker (Carrer de Roger de Llúria, near the Gran Via) got its name long before a snooker

Literary worlds: Venues like these are not just hotspots for teenage boppers. They are meeting points, neutral ground, where a large proportion of the city's intelligentsia congregate – particularly writers. Here, the barrier that divides Barcelona's literary world between those who write in Catalan and those who write in Castilian is overcome. Outside these premises they stick exclusively to their own linguistic group.

More literary works than ever are being published today and, strangely enough, it is the short story – that genre of writing always considered to be commercially unviable –

that is finding greater acceptance amongst the reading public. Maybe this has something to do with the unceasing labour carried out by publishing groups such as Anagrama or Quaderns Crema, a modest company that publishes in both languages and to whom we owe, amongst others, the discovery of the Catalan storyteller Quim Monzó.

Alongside Monzó, notable figures of Catalan literature are Sergi Pàmies and Ramon Solsona for prose, Carme Riera for her novels, Aurèlia Capmany for her novels and intellectual guidance for Barcelona from City Hall, and novelist Baltasar Porcel.

On the opposing side, current Castilian Barcelona at a frenetic, almost feverish pace.

Popular in poetry is the growing satirical and ironic work of the Catalans Jordi Cornudella and Salvador Oliva; among those writing in Castilian are Angel Crespo, the young critic José Angel Cilleruelo, Concha García and Feliu Formosa.

Art works: Barcelona's tradition of constant change continues to produce top-quality art and sculpture, and many new art galleries open every year. Carlos Velilla, artist and Professor of Fine Arts at Barcelona University, suggests that the tempo has increased recently because the higher income bracket social classes have started to treat modern art

literature written in Barcelona comes from Eduardo Mendoza (serious fiction, and author of *City of Prodigies*, the best-known book about Barcelona), Félix de Azúa (fashionable novels), M. Vázquez Montalbán ("black" fiction), Javier Tomeo (a new novelist particularly successful in Germany), the increasingly powerful J. García Sánchez and the storyteller Martínez de Pisón. The list goes on, and books are being published in

as something worth collecting and paying for. As their understanding and appreciation of contemporary art and sculpture has improved, so they have begun to value the investment potential of such works. The result is that new young artists in Barcelona can sell their work for high prices, even while still teenagers.

The traditional art galleries are largely located along the Carrer de Consell de Cent (more or less between the streets Balmes and Pau Claris), but more recently a new genre of exhibitions has opened up in the galleries located in the Born, towards Ciutadella Park.

Far left, Miró's *Dona i Ocell* (woman with bird).
Left, *Núvol i Cadira* (cloud and chair) by Tàpies.
Above, metal beast on the Diagonal.

Along the Carrer de Consell de Cent are the galleries of Gaspar, Dude, Carles Tache (where works of Plensa and Tàpies predominate), Metras, Dau Al Set, Ciento, Génesis, Ambit and Gaudí, and to this group must be added the Joan Prats and Alcolea galleries (both in the Rambla de Catalunya, close to those previously mentioned).

The Born group has emerged as a counterbalance to the group on the Consell de Cent, and it is from here that many of today's young artists are launched. The Metrònom gallery (Carrer Fusina, 9) was the first to open on the Born. It is an endowed institution founded by the collector Rafael Tous and

has, in addition to the art gallery, one of Spain's most extensive art libraries. This gallery-institution is particularly strong on the encouragement and promotion of new artists, focusing on "marginal" art, conceptual art and *arte povera*. Also in this area are the Ferran Cano, Maeght, Berini and Benet Costa galleries.

New artists who have been launched by exhibitions here include Xavier Grau, J.M. Broto, Viladecans, Velilla, Albert Gonzalo and Miquel Barceló, who was born on Mallorca but started his career from the Catalan capital. Among the sculptors are Susana

Solana, who has made an international reputation, as well as Navarro and Plensa.

Sometimes, with all this art being produced and all this money changing hands, one gets the feeling that professionalism and turnover of production and therefore income are being over-emphasised, to the detriment of the creative process. For the best quality results, should not a true artist put love of art above economic considerations? Shouldn't artists be poor? Increasingly, local artists and designers are returning to this traditional view, and the urge to make their fortunes early is less overwhelming.

Beat routes: A survey of Barcelona's originality would not be complete without mentioning the musical pulse that beats within the city. The Taller Musical or musical workshop (Carrer de Requesens, 1–3) is dedicated to the constant training of professional musicians, with particular emphasis on jazz. The workshop organises musical seminars which contribute towards keeping Barcelona at the pinnacle of the musical world. The workshop is a focal point for most of the city's professional musicians and even has its own record label. Among the city's prominent jazz groups are Tete Montoliu and his Big Band, the C. Eduardo Unit, Hermanos Rossy and Jordi Bonell.

Jazz lovers are assiduous visitors to La Cova del Drac (Carrer de Tusset, 30), the Harlem Jazz Club (Carrer de Comtessa de Sobradiel, 8), L'Eixample (Carrer de Diputació) or Up and Down (Carrer de Numància) every Tuesday. Barcelona also hosts an annual International Jazz Festival.

Cartoons: In commercial art – as a by-product of design – Barcelona dominates Spain's comic strip industry, producing 80 percent of the total national output. Some of the country's most prestigious draughtsmen live in Barcelona, which hosts the Salón Internacional del Cómic, and their acceptance beyond the city limits has increased enormously. Today the best comic series are published in albums; try the small comic shop in the Placeta del Pi for samples.

Left, ancient and modern design in synthesis.
Right, Barcelona is responsible for 80 percent of Spain's comic strip industry.

ALS INFANTS

EL FEIXISME
US LLENÇA
BOMBES

CATALUNYA
US OFRENA
JOGUINES

C.N.T. - U.G.T.

Conselleria de Sanitat
i Assistència Social
(Secció de Propaganda)

GENERALITAT DE CATALUNYA

Tim.-

SETMANA DE L'INFANT
1 A 7 GENER

GRÁFOS COLECTIVIZADA BARNA

74

A History Of The Catalan Language

In the modern world at least 6 million people use the Catalan language as their mother tongue. As well as being spoken in the city of Barcelona and the rest of northeast Spain, Catalan is also commonly used in the south of France, in Andorra, where it is the only official language, and, surprisingly, in the city of Alguer in Sardinia.

The Catalan-speaking area of Spain covers the four Catalan provinces of Barcelona, Tarragona, Lléida and Girona, the Balearic Islands (Mallorca, Menorca, Ibiza and Formentera), the community of València, which also includes Alicante and Castellón, and the three small border areas of Iecla, Jumella and Favanella, which lie within the province of Murcia. Within Catalonia the only exception is the mountainous Val d'Aran, where the people speak Arense, a language like Gascon.

Catalan is derived from Latin as used in the eastern part of the Pyrenees and shares characteristics with French, Italian and Castilian – particularly the dialects of Occitane and Aragón. To the linguist, modern Catalan seems a polyglot language, comprising something of everything on paper, but with a very individual sound when spoken.

The spread of the language outside Catalonia followed in the wake of the conquests of the kings of Catalunya and Aragón, particularly of Jaume I. In order to ensure his control of the land he distributed the new territory amongst his nobles on the condition that they repopulated it with Christian subjects. Consequently, after the conquest of Mallorca in 1229, the island was repopulated by Catalans, as was Ibiza in 1235. The differences in dialects that developed throughout both islands are the result of the differing origins of the new colonialists.

València, which was also conquered and repopulated by Jaume I between 1233 and 1238, was colonialised by Castilian-speak-

ing people from Aragón, but the Catalan language implanted itself only along the coast. Murcia too was conquered and colonised by Catalans. Ramon Muntaner, author of *Cronica*, one of the most brilliant works of Spanish medieval literature, refers to these Catalans, saying that they speak *del bell catalanesc del món* – the most beautiful Catalan in the world.

Literature: The first written words of Catalan appeared around the 9th century in Latin

texts. Although more extended texts have been found dating from the 11th century, it was not until the 12th century that the first complete manuscripts are found – translated fragments of *Forum Iudicorum* and *Homilies d'Organya*. Then, from the 13th century onwards, Catalan gradually began to replace Latin in legal and administrative documents.

It was a Mallorcan, Ramon Llull (1232–1315), who produced the first major work in Catalan: a vast encyclopedia of more than 200 volumes. The chroniclers of the time – Jaume I, Muntaner, Desclot and Pere III – all helped further to establish Catalan as

Left, the Catalan language has always been a political issue, used here in anti-fascist propaganda. **Right**, reading matter.

a written language. The period from the end of the 14th century until the beginning of the 16th century was the Golden Century of Catalan literature, with the emergence of such names as Valencian-born Ausias March (1397–1459), who incorporated many of Petrarch's innovations in one of the best-ever examples of lyrical Catalan; or Joanot Martorell (1413–68), also from València, whose novel *Tirant lo blanc* was praised by Cervantes in *Don Quixote*.

With the coming to power of the House of Austria in 1516, the Castilianisation of Spain gained enormous strength, to the detriment of Catalan. At the end of the War of Succes-

possible without the triumph of the industrial revolution and the birth of a dynamic middle class. In the poem *La Pàtria*, written by Bonaventura Carles Aribau in 1833, a new period of language development began, albeit not without a certain amount of controversy. Some believed that the purest Catalan belonged to the year 1500, or even before, even though this would mean a massive use of archaic words and terminology which have long since fallen into disuse.

For others, the language should have been taken exclusively from that spoken at the day, even though it was replete with Castilianisations. From 1859, the celebration of *Els*

sion the Catalans were punished for having defended the Archduke Carlos against the pretensions of Felipe V and were made to accept the Castilian language. From this time literary works were scarce and relegated to a popular or religious standing.

Renaissance: But with the literary and social upheaval that resulted from the Romantic movement, the Catalans took a renewed interest in their medieval past and began the slow revitalisation of their language. In Catalonia "Romanticism" is known as the "Renaixença" (Renaissance). The Renaixença would not have been

Jocs Florals (the Floral Games, a poetry competition which derived from troubadour days with prizes of bouquets of flowers) acted as a spur to the updating of the written language, which still retained its medieval tendencies. The competition's motto, "Faith, Country and Love", was to be interpreted within the compositions entered.

Amalgam of influences: In the end, cultural, economic and demographic factors finally decided the parameters of the written language, and it accepted the modernisations and Castilianisations which had crept into the spoken form. The unifying work of

Pompeu Fabra (1868–1948) set about establishing grammatical unity. Through the Institut d'Etudis Catalans a number of orthographic rules were drawn up in 1913. They were followed in 1917 by the *Diccionari Ortogràfic* and, finally, the *Diccionari General* in 1932.

At the beginning of the 20th century Catalonia became involved with the literary movements of the day, first through the modernism movement and later with "Noucentisme", a more conservative arts movement. Illustrious figures such as Joan Maragall (1860–1911) and Santiago Rusiñol (1861–1931) and Noucentistes such as

Spanish Civil War (1936–39), the use of Catalan was forbidden and anyone heard speaking it in public could be fined. Towards the middle of the 1940s a certain tolerance had crept into this edict, but it was not until 1946 that magazines and books could once again be published in Catalan.

During this period many notable figures within the world of Catalan literature went into exile, from where they continued silently to "write (their) ill-treated language to save the word from such ignominy". The poem *Inici de Càntic en el Temple* by Salvador Espriu is representative of this period.

After the death of Franco, Josep Tarradel-

poets Josep Carner (1884–1970), Guerau de Liost (pseudonym of Jaume Bofill i Matas, 1878–1933) and Josep Maria Lopez Picó (1886–1959), along with essayist Eugeni d'Ors (1881–1954), all contributed to this period of prosperity. But it was not until the establishment of the Generalitat, in 1931, and the announcement of the "Estatut de Catalunya" in 1939, that Catalan achieved the rank of official language.

Word unheard: However, following the

Left, independence stickers. **Above**, Jesus Ferrero, one of a new generation of writers.

las, the exiled President of the Generalitat, returned and the modern "Statute of Autonomy" was created. The Spanish constitution of 1978 re-established Catalan as one of the official languages in Spain.

Today, schools, universities, newspapers, magazines, books, theatre and television in Barcelona all operate in both languages. Most street names have been converted to Catalan, although some maps and even some Catalans continue to refer to places by their Castilian names. Moreover, Catalan is an official language of the 1992 Olympic Games.

The French novelist Gustav Flaubert once stated that "bad taste is always the taste of the preceding epoch". In the years following its heyday, modernism in Barcelona was not only considered a style in bad taste, it was widely despised. The description "modernist" was intended to be deprecatory; it was used to ridicule anyone and anything which, in their turn, mocked what were considered to be traditional values. History, of course, was repeating itself: in earlier epochs, the words Gothic, baroque and Cubism were originally intended to be pejorative.

Shortly after the modernist era, the style was considered embarrassing by everyone, up to and including many of the participating architects. In 1929, the year of the second World Fair, a guide was published called *The Art of Showing Barcelona*. The text explained to any guide or citizen accompanying a tourist that he or she must explain "that the city had the *desgracia* (disgrace) of having a large part of the Eixample built in the modernist style".

Today it is no longer a disgrace: modernism is *the* architecture of Barcelona. Avoiding it would be tantamount to visiting Paris without seeing the Eiffel Tower or going to Athens and by-passing the Acropolis.

Way of life: "Modernism" was the Catalan response to a variety of artistic currents running throughout Europe at the end of the 19th century. In Britain its equivalent was called "Modern Style". The Belgians named it the "Style 1900", while Germany, Austria and Italy knew it as "Jugend-stil", "Sezessionstil" and "Liberty". Since then it has become known almost universally by its French designation of "Art Nouveau".

But modernism in Catalonia, unlike its counterparts in the rest of Europe, became far more than a bizarre artistic style. It became a way of life. According to authors Cristina and Eduardo Mendoza, in their re-

cent book *Barcelona Modernist*, "...the Barcelonans, and especially the bourgeoisie, lived immersed in modernism: from the architecture of their houses to the most insignificant object; from the office in which (the man) passed the hours of his day to the café in which were held his *tertulias* (social chats); from his birth to his grave."

The fashion, which began as an anti-establishment art and ended up being the art of the establishment, was "too anarchic" to its

many critics. It was an epoch preoccupied with the decorative. Those most loyal to this new social wave were architects and decorators, a group which included furniture makers, makers of mosaics, ceramicists, jewellers and ironworkers. The least faithful to the trend were painters and writers, who continued doing their own thing. Today the most obvious remnants of this period, which ended in the mid-1920s, are the myriad houses scattered through the Eixample.

"When one contemplates a building, a sculpture, or a painting, that which is most noticeable is its decorative content," wrote

Preceding pages: extreme decoration is the common thread to all modernist works. Left, breath-catching detail in Montaner's Palau de la Música Catalana. Right, modernist delicacies.

A. Cirici Pellicer, one of the first of modernism's academics. For the modernists themselves, decoration of even the smallest detail became an obsession. The complexity of the detail of the facades is quite stunning, particularly on buildings such as the Palau de la Música Catalana, by Lluís Domènech i Montaner, which is considered to be the most remarkable of the modernist buildings.

Most visitors will see modernism from the outside, unaware that the interior continues the ornamental theme to even greater lengths. The Palau de la Música, open to visitors, is evidence of this. With gigantic winged Pegasuses "flying" from the upper

architecture, of which there are numerous fine examples in the Gothic Quarter). Neo-Gothic design was a reminder to the scholars and the public that their predecessors had been among the most daring in Europe.

But alongside this hearkening back to the past, a period of cultural and political nationalism had begun to develop within Catalonia. Wealthy flag-waving patrons such as Eusebi Güell and the Marquès de Comillas wanted to show their commitment to a new order of Catalan originality; a second "golden age". They invested huge sums to patronise the unknown talents of architects such as Gaudí and Domènech i Montaner.

balcony columns, a stained-glass ceiling which will leave the visitor with a stiff neck, and a long roll-call of sculptures and ceramics dedicated to musical muses, it is hard to imagine that a first-timer could concentrate on the concert for which he has paid.

Origins: Catalonian modernism was the sum of a series of reflections of foreign currents in art and design. At the time, local students of architecture were taught from a strongly neo-Gothic standpoint which emphasised the importance of Catalan power and ingenuity during its "golden age" at the end of the Middle Ages (thus Catalan Gothic

The movement took its roots in medievalism, a Gothic return to the Middle Ages, and in pre-Raphaelite ingenuity called primitivism. Into the pot was thrown a bit of Moorish orientalism, which had been in fashion in Catalonia since the middle of the 19th century. Neo-*mudéjar* decorative trends and techniques can be seen in many of the earliest examples, including what is considered to be the first modernist building, Casa Viçens (Carrer de les Carolines, 18–24). The brick-and-tile building, which Antoni Gaudí completed in 1878, shows strong Moorish influence which was soon to evaporate from the movement because of its obvious association with the rest of Spain and its contradiction of the very *raison d'être* of Catalan modernism's spirit of "rebellion".

William Morris, the English pre-Raphaelite artist and writer, who was instrumental in Britain in reviving traditional artisan skills in his Arts and Crafts movement, was also admired by Catalan modernists.

Big names: But while there was a synthesis of ideas among Catalan modernists, the three big names of the time, Lluís Domènech i Montaner, Josep Puig i Cadafalch and Antoni Gaudí, were extremely diverse in their personal interpretations of the style. While

"his genius permitted him to live in a world populated exclusively with his own fantasies. His life and his works coincided with the general characteristics of a period which, in its fervour for renovation, was fertile ground for his immeasurable creativity."

The three architects and their individual and conflicting interpretations of the modernist theme come together in the so-called "Manzana de la Discòrdia" (the Block of Discord) on the Passeig de Gràcia between Carrer d'Aragó and Carrer Consell de Cent. Almost side by side stand what are among the best works of the three most celebrated exponents of modernism. On the southern

second-generation Puig i Cadafalch worked in both neo-Gothic and modernism, his mentor at the Escola Superior d'Arquitectura de la Llotja, Domènech i Montaner, was busy expressing the "theory of organic rationality" in which every element must be self explanatory. And Gaudí? Well, Gaudí was just being himself.

In reality, the best known of them all, Antoni Gaudí i Cornet, can't even be considered a modernist. According to Mendoza:

Left, La Pedrera by Gaudí. **Above left**, Casa Viçens, Gaudí's first work. **Above right**, inside Montaner's Casa Lleó Morera.

corner is Lluís Domènech i Montaner's Casa Lleó Morera, two entrances further north is the Casa Amatller by Josep Puig i Cadafalch, and next door to that is one of Gaudí's best-known buildings, Casa Batlló.

Style samples: The most original of the three is Gaudí's. Since he "ignored that which didn't pertain to his own work", his work is unique and quite free from previous and contemporary influences. It is marked by his distinctive sinuous expressionist shapes and judicious use of ceramics. It is obvious from its shape, both inside and out, that the author never had to think of mundane practicalities such as "where the desk was going to fit". The lack of attention to practicalities explains why some modernist buildings are not easily rented out or sold.

Next door the colourful geometric facade of the much younger Puig i Cadafalch competes very well for the attention of the passer-by. First planned when the architect was only 21, Casa Amatller was finally completed 10 years later, in 1900. Both the facade and the interior demonstrate the architect's combination of neo-Gothic and modernist influences. The majestic entranceway is heavily Gothic while passageways within are evidently neo-*mudéjar*. The

first-floor library is impressive for its stained glass and the enormous fireplace covered with mythical figures.

The final building is Montaner's Casa Lleó Morera. The facade, which shows definite similarities to its big brother the Palau de la Música in its overpowering attention to detail, has been partially disfigured by the shop at street level. The interior, housing the Patronat de Turisme (visits can be arranged), also has many similarities to the Palau in its stained glass and use of mosaics and tiling.

Career credits: Gaudí, whose bizarre creations inspired the none-too-complimentary

word "gaudy", is the creator of the best-known of Barcelona's long list of modernist buildings. Headed by the Temple of the Sagrada Família, the list runs through such landmarks as the Parc Güell and La Pedrera (both of which have been declared of world interest by UNESCO), Palau Güell, the pavilions of Finca Güell, Torre Bellesguard and the Col.legi de les Teresianes.

The list of modernist buildings attributed to Domènech i Montaner is just as long, if not as familiar to the visitor, as that of Gaudí. Following William Morris's lead, the architect, who became director of the Escola Superior d'Arquitectura de la Llotja, often worked with teams, installing a group of architects, ceramicists, sculptors, and glass and iron makers in a community workshop. Beginning with the site of the Museu Zoològic, a castle-shaped building within the confines of the Parc de la Ciutadella, his personal catalogue includes the Palau de la Música Catalana, Casa Fustes, Hotel España, La Rotonda and the monumental Hospital de la Santa Creu i de Sant Pau, an obligatory stop not far from the Sagrada Família (*see next chapter*).

The works of Josep Puig i Cadafalch are less impressive only because modernism had come and almost gone before he reached the height of his productivity as an architect. As well as Casa Amatller, he created such important buildings as the Casa Terrades (or Casa de les Punxes) which occupies a pie-shaped city block on the Diagonal.

Smaller successes: Other talented architects failed to achieve big-name status. Casa Comalat, for example, by Salvador Valeri i Pupurull, is two buildings in one. The floral building on the Diagonal (number 442) is difficult to reconcile with the tiled facade facing Carrer de Corsega (number 316), but these are two sides of the same building.

Other important names include Josep Jujol, who, as well as being the architect of Casa Planells, also on the Diagonal (number 332), created the serpentine ceramic bench in Gaudí's Parc Güell, a feature often mistakenly attributed to Gaudí.

Left, chimney detail in Casa Ametller. **Right**, the disturbing nocturnal face of Casa Batlló.

MAKING THE SAGRADA FAMILIA

Antoni Gaudí's fame has spread rapidly beyond Catalonia and books dedicated to his life and works have been translated into every major language. To the Japanese, for example, Gaudí is much more than a Catalan architect; he is a reason for visiting Spain. He is also responsible for introducing a new word – gaudy – to the English language.

Antoni Gaudí i Cornet was born in the Catalonian town of Reus on 25 June 1852, the son of a coppersmith. Two years after graduating from the Escola Superior d'Arquitectura de la Llotja in 1878, he finished his first architectural work: a house built for Manuel Viçens on Carrer de Carolinas. But it wasn't until he met Eusebi Güell, a wealthy industrialist who wanted to use his money to establish a unique identity for Catalonia, that his talents as a creator were to be realised.

The Sagrada Família, Gaudí's most famous work, was actually begun in 1882 as a neo-Gothic structure under the direction of the architect Francesc P. Villar. Gaudí took over the project nine years later, changing the temple's very style.

Well before Gaudí's death in 1926, he realised that the work which had filled the last years of his life, the Temple of the Sagrada Família, would not be finished in his lifetime. Because of his obsession with the "temple", Gaudí had become a virtual recluse. He died unrecognised in a hospital bed, two days after being crushed by the wheels of a tram. At the time of his death, at 74, only one of the planned towers had been finished; another three stood shrouded in scaffolding. Fittingly, his body is entombed in the crypt of his most famous work.

Piecemeal progress: During the Civil War the anti-Church sentiment which resulted in the pillaging of nearly all of the major churches in Barcelona left only two religious structures untouched – the Cathedral of Barcelona and the Sagrada Família. Except

for those years, the construction work has continued – at times sporadically, at times with great urgency – under the auspices of members of Gaudí's original team.

The project has never been without its detractors. George Orwell, for example, is quoted as describing the Sagrada as "one of the most hideous buildings in the world," and its four towers as "four crenellated spires exactly the shape of hock bottles." Many believe the temple should be left as an unfin-

ished monument to its famous creator. Why, they ask, is the work of one of the greatest 20th-century architects being finished in a style which often has little to do with his life, his time and his ideas? The debate has kept Gaudí's name alive all over the world.

Yet Gaudí was far from being rigid in his ideas; he bequeathed to his disciples complete liberty to carry on in whatever manner they deemed suitable for their time. Today the work progresses under the control of coordinating architect Jordi Bonet Armengol, son of one of the maestro's long-standing aides. Although the younger Bonet hadn't

Left, the Sagrada Família as it stands today. **Right**, a model of what it should finally look like.

been born when Gaudí met his untimely death, he recalls growing up playing among the piles of rocks that have always dotted the construction site.

From the earliest days, Gaudí steered away from the common solutions of academic architecture. He chose instead the complex geometry of nature. "Originality is to return to the origins," he is quoted as saying. While others were busy hiding chimneys, he would put them in the centre of the facade. While others were looking for the "non-colour" of classical archaeology, the young maestro used what he called *el revestimiento cerámico* (ceramic decoration).

each piece using the models designed and built by Gaudí, many of which were smashed in the Civil War and have had to be pieced together from mountains of fragments. As much as 15 percent of the work has had to be designed anew on the drawing boards of the five resident architects on the project.

Extrapolating shapes and concepts from the rough ideas left by their creator, models are built under the auspices of Jordi Cusso, who began working on the facades as an apprentice in 1967. If the shapes are geometric, the prototypes are normally built from plaster; if they are sculptures, they are modelled in plasticine. Jordi Cusso admits that at

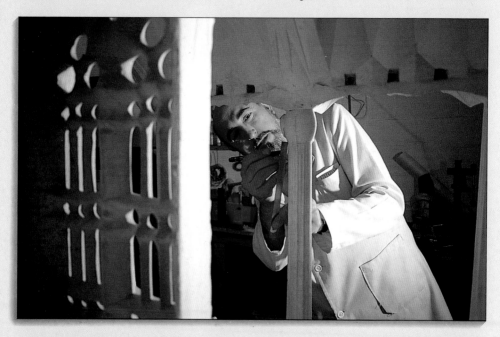

Team work: Although he was a "genius out of context", Gaudí was content to share with others some of the responsibilities in the building of the Sagrada Família. His collaborators included Francesc Berenguer, Josep Maria Jujol and Joan Rubio i Bellver, who was both his disciple and his student.

Because of the complexity of Gaudí's work – architecturally, symbolically and philosophically – every stage of the temple's construction is preceded by involved conceptual and engineering investigation by the team of architects. Once each step has been approved, draughtsmen draw up plans of

times he has nightmares about the gigantic jigsaw puzzle upon which he is working.

The Sagrada Família has three facades: the Pasión (Passion) on Carrer de Sardenya, the Nacimiento (Nativity) on Carrer de Marina and the Gloria (Glory) on Carrer de Mallorca. The first two, with their soaring tiled towers, have been instrumental in spreading the temple's fame throughout the world. The third, which was originally planned as the principal entranceway and is oriented towards the midday sun, is slowly beginning to take form, and with time will become as eye-catching as the others.

Price of liberty: Apart from the continuing debate about the temple's completion, a recent focus of controversy has been the work of local artist Josep M. Subirachs. Given "total liberty" by Bonet, he has designed a series of *avant-garde* sculptures for the Pasión facade (also known as the *Fachada del Dolor* or pain) which to most casual onlookers seem strongly out of character. The project, which is a series of sculpted scenes from the life of Christ, begins at the bottom left of the facade with the Last Supper, follows an S-shaped path towards the Crucifixion at the apex and finishes at the upper right with Christ's burial.

all of the work on the temple, is financed primarily though donations and bequests. Another small but significant source is ticket sales to visitors. Money was not a problem in the late 1980s and work progressed well; the chief architect has said he expects the roof to be on the nave in the mid-1990s, after which the work will proceed to the roof of the presbytery.

New tower: Work is also being considered on the almost forgotten central tower, planned to soar 200 ft (60 metres) above the existing towers, which themselves reach 450 ft (120 metres). Although a final decision on its viability will take years to be reached,

On the other hand the restoration and continuation of the sculptures on the opposite side of the temple – the Nacimiento facade – are being undertaken by a Japanese sculptor, Etsuro Sotoo. The statues, newer than the surrounding background of the three porticos of the eastern facade, are a joy to behold in themselves and in their fidelity to Gaudí's original work.

The work of Sotoo and of Subirachs, like

<u>Left</u>, Jordi Cusso working on a new model. <u>Above</u>, Jordi Bonet Armengol, co-ordinating architect on the project.

early experimentation with the plan has already required 50 workmen to pour up to 1,000 tonnes of cement a day into subfloor pylons which need to reach a weight of 8,000 metric tonnes in order to sustain the central tower in earthquakes and 100-mph winds.

With the aid of modern material such as reinforced concrete, subcontracting to outside workshops and using computers to design and to solve problems, some of Gaudí's original ideas, once discarded on the grounds of impossibility, are being re-examined. But the eventual shape of this overpowering project still remains uncertain.

MORE THAN JUST FOOTBALL

The Barcelona Football Club, known throughout the sporting world as the Barça, was founded in 1899 by Hans Gamper, a Swiss living in Barcelona. It is one of the oldest clubs in Europe. In a long and chequered history it has played a surprising political role, championing Catalan nationalism and liberty; it is the city's army, opera and ballet all in one and all Barcelona celebrates with its victories and weeps with its defeats.

The team lost no time in becoming well established. By 1922 it already had its own stadium, recognised at the time as one of the best in Spain and abroad, and it signed up two of the most sought-after and mythical players of the time: forward Samitier and goalkeeper Zamora.

Even at this stage matches between the Barça and rival teams, such as the club Español (founded in 1903, also in Barcelona), and the Madrid team, were studded with incidents. At times the rivalry was so heated that the public was not permitted to attend.

Suppression: In 1925 a band from a British warship played the Royal march *Himno de la España Monárquica* just before the game. Even before the band had completed the opening bars the public started jeering and whistling – a spontaneous reaction against the Spanish monarchy that had accommodated the dictatorship of General Primo de Rivera. Rivera's policy had been to suppress not only personal freedom but cultural events and, more important still for the fans of the Barça, the Catalan national spirit. After the incident the government ordered the Barcelona football ground to be closed.

Needless to say, popular dissatisfaction reached even higher levels during the long dictatorship of General Francisco Franco. The year 1939 saw a Franco loyalist nominated as the club's president and up until the 1950s the board of directors was kept under

control by the obligatory presence at meetings of a Falangist and a member of the armed forces. However, even though the vast majority of the club's presidents and governors were no less than government vigilantes, they all became ardent followers of the Barça's fortunes in football.

In 1941 a serious incident occurred during the cup match between Barcelona and Madrid. It had been ordained, before the match, that Madrid should win. As a gesture

of the absurdity of the fixture, Barcelona allowed them to win by 11 goals to one. The Barça goal-keeper was suspended for life for waving his cap on high each time he allowed the Madrid team to score.

Star sharing: The Barça's fortunes really improved with the signing of the player Kubala in 1951. So powerful was the team becoming that the government ordered the removal of the equally skilful Di Stefano, also a new signing. The club's president Martí Carreto was threatened to such an extent that he eventually had to agree to share Kubala (known as the *Saeta Rubia* –

Preceding pages: even monks can't resist a game. **Left**, Barça captain with the 1989 European Cup-Winners cup. **Right**, Kubala, the "blond arrow" of the 1950s.

the "blond arrow") with the Madrid team. The pact had the player alternating between the two teams – an absurd situation almost unparalleled in world football.

Martí Carreto came under intense pressure at the time. He was ordered to Madrid by the president of the Spanish Football Federation, Muñoz Calero, and told that the financial operation carried out to pay for Di Stefano's transfer was in fact illegal. The Federation's president – with the National Sports Delegate General Moscardó phoning every few minutes to increase the pressure – also threatened Carreto with reprisals against his textile industry. In the end the

ball stadium, which itself is the largest in Europe with a total capacity of 120,000.

Club power: The Barça has always been "more than just a club" (a slogan which became popular during the last years of the Franco regime). It has played a key role in Catalanising the enormous numbers of immigrants who have flooded into the city over the years. It is also, literally, more than just a football club, maintaining nine other sports sections, of which the most noteworthy are the basketball, hockey (on roller skates) and handball teams who compete in major European league competitions.

But the Barça has always been more than

entire board of directors of the Barça resigned in protest at the forcible removal of the great Di Stefano.

Since Kubala, many major football stars have been signed up to play for the Barça, including Cruyf, Schuster and Maradona.

The unusually high number of Barça members – 108,000 – is proof enough of the club's popularity. It is the world's largest organisation where memberships pass from father to son and where new-born babies are made members only hours after birth. No fewer than 80,000 of the members have permanent seats within the Camp Nou foot-

just a club in the way it has extended its activities beyond purely sporting events. During the last years of the dictator the club came to symbolise freedom. For decades thousands of members and fans frantically waved the blue and garnet flag of the Barça as a substitute for the Catalan flag, which in those days was forbidden by Franco. A victory over the Madrid team was equivalent to a victory over the oppressive central government which had tyrannised the capital of Catalonia since 1939. As long as General Franco lived, "no other major political victory of any importance was possible".

In this spontaneous fashion the Barça became the focal point for Catalan nationalism, and the nationalists could use the matches to maintain the fervour of their nation with much less risk than if they'd organised a rally or demonstration.

The Barça in its role as a political statement is not unique. The members of the Welsh rugby team regularly put their small country – and its champions of nationalism – on the European map; East Germany overcame its political stigma by winning Olympic medals, and more than one Third World country has made its mark through the achievements and triumphs of its athletes.

Cup Final match played in Seville. To its great shame, Barcelona lost. Yes, shamefully, because the public felt humiliated, and with every right: the Barça lost on penalties despite the fact that the goal-keeper performed the superb feat of blocking two of them. Since then the team has been unable to recover the mesmeric power that it once had over the souls of its legion of fans.

After the Seville debacle, the number of spectators slumped and some matches have been played to the unbelievably small number of only 10,000 or 12,000 supporters. Even though club membership remains high, it is not a propitious time to insist on enlarg-

But the re-establishment of democracy in Spain has not lessened the strength of support for the Barça. The club has continued to exert its power to the extent that Nuñez, the current club president, who himself owns a construction company, is obsessively determined to extend the Camp Nou stadium to a seating capacity of 135,000.

Humbling moment: The club's sporting fortunes have suffered in recent years. The worst moment was in the 1986 European

Left, fan club paraphernalia. **Above**, fan taxi with Catalan and Barça flags.

ing the stadium. Perhaps attendance has also slumped because the team has lost its political piquancy, now that Catalonia is an autonomous province.

Except for the odd major match for which it is impossible to obtain tickets, such as the fixture against Real Madrid, visitors should easily get in to enjoy the spectacle – if the match is good – of a fan-packed stadium. Such is the club's fame outside Catalonia that many travel agencies include a visit to the club's museum in their city itinerary. It has become Barcelona's second most visited museum, after Picasso's.

Barcelona is delighted to be hosting the 25th Olympic Games in July 1992 – it's a city which loves to show off and be looked at – but it's happier still to take stock of how much the ancient city stands to gain from such a prestigious event. "We're preparing the Barcelona of 1993," say the hoardings. And they are.

Had the Olympics not existed, Barcelona may well have invented some other pretext to attract international attention. "The games provide a deadline for a hundred and one things which have been on the cards to be done in the city for years but for which there was neither a time schedule nor the necessary budget," says Ada Llorens, who works for the Barcelona Olympic Committee (COOB) as an architect and town planner.

The city has a history of propping itself up with international events. "Barcelona is rather a fake city," says writer Eduardo Mendoza, whose novel *La Ciudad de los Prodigios* (City of Prodigies) opens with the Universal Exhibition of 1888 and ends with that of 1929. "It has to keep inventing itself because it really has no reason to be there. It grew up no-one quite knows how and so is constantly re-inventing itself by creating great prospects."

The 1888 Exhibition was just such a pretext for frenzied activity and for modernising the city, and so was 1929. "A city that doesn't grow organically decides from time to time that things can't go on as they are and that something must be done," says Mendoza. "So a pretext is thought up, a time limit set and the great bustle begins."

Barcelona, which has a complex about not being a capital city, is constantly trying to prove its importance both to Madrid, which holds Spain's purse strings, and to the rest of Europe. Without a great occasion to cling on to, the city tends to slip into a decline. The last such collective depression was in the late 1970s and early 1980s as Madrid woke up

from Francoism and became a vibrant and exciting place to be. The international airlines withdrew their flights to Barcelona and the Barcelonans moped.

Fourth time lucky: On 17 October 1986 the cloud lifted with the announcement that the city had been chosen for the 1992 Games, and the people took to the streets to celebrate. It was Barcelona's fourth attempt to attract the Games. It had tried for the 1924 and 1972 Olympics without success. In 1936 the city

tried to stage a "popular Olympics" as an anti-fascist gesture, but history played a nasty trick, delivering a civil war in the place of a sports meeting symbolising peace and fraternity.

The planners got to work in the autumn of 1986, once the initial elation had subsided. These were Barcelona's Games, Catalonia's Games and Spain's Games, in that order, and they were going to show the world what they could do. The stadium in Montjuïc, built at the time of the 1929 Universal Exhibition but with the clear intention of using it for the 1936 Olympics, had always been a strong

Left, Alfonso Mila (left) and Frederico Correa, architects of the Olympic stadium (above right).

point in Barcelona's candidacy and the diggers were soon in there, gouging out tonnes of earth so that the original facade of the stadium could be preserved but enough space could be created by digging downwards to reach the minimum required seating capacity of 70,000.

Montjuïc is one of the four nerve centres of the 1992 Olympics which cleverly occupy the four corners of the city – cleverly, that is, in terms of Barcelona's overriding plan to come out of the Olympics with as much done to improve the city as possible. The plan might not seem so clever to the innocent eye of the athlete or sports commentator, for which, in an unobtrusive, pragmatic way, stands to gain most from the 1992 Games as further sports facilities are added; and finally Barcelona's showpiece, the Olympic Village, sited across the port from Montjuïc and effectively opening up Barcelona's waterfront after centuries with its back turned to the Mediterranean.

The Olympic Village, which has been poetically named the New Icarius after the Avinguda d'Icaria which runs through it, is an ambitious project drawn up by Barcelona architect Oriol Bohigas and his partners David Mackay and Josep Martorell. Of all Olympic ventures, the Village – which will

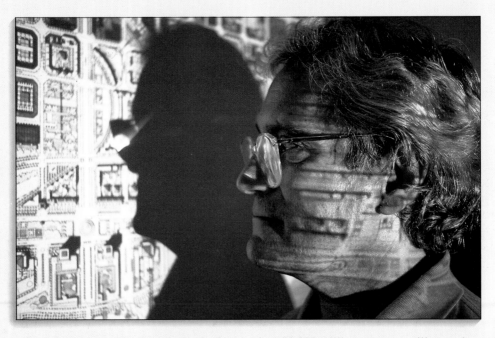

whom Barcelona will exist only for the fortnight the Games last and whose interest will not go beyond the simple logistics of getting from one venue to another.

Venues: The other three centres, working clockwise round the compass, are the Pedralbes–Diagonal area, an up-town, up-market residential zone where luxury sports like horse-riding and tennis already have their space, and the location of the 120,000-seater Barcelona Football Club stadium; the Vall d'Hebron, a working-class area north of the city which already houses an Olympic-class velodrome (indoor cycle-track) and

cost 70,000 million pesetas – will most dramatically change the shape of Barcelona.

Bohigas' name is already firmly linked to the evolution of the city, since he worked with the city council between 1980 and 1984, producing bold plans to undo some of the urban horrors committed during the Franco period when profitability came before the people's wellbeing. The plan for the Olympic Village has involved rerouting the railways and reconstructing the drainage system, as well as building a complex device placed offshore to tame the waves and prevent the sea from interfering with the man-made installations. A whole new dimension to Barcelona has been opened up without in effect expanding to new ground. In the expropriation of 320 acres (130 hectares) of land within the city confines, only 300 residents have had to be moved.

The waterfront: Nearly three miles of coastline have been "recovered" in an area which was a busy industrial zone in the 19th century but which has progressively fallen into disuse. Some of the old warehouses and workshops have been renovated and bought by artists, photographers and designers, but 250 acres (100 hectares) have been cleared for the Olympic Village.

tect Ricardo Bofill. Insalubrious *pensions* have been obliged to close and selective demolition work has been undertaken to allow more air and light into the dark labyrinth of many parts of the old city. Social workers are being trained to work with drug addicts and deprived young people in an attempt to control and improve a critical situation involving drug abuse and street crime. Shopkeepers and people working in liberal professions are being encouraged to move into the old quarters in order to prevent the formation of "no-go" areas.

Failures: It won't all be a success story. It couldn't be. Barcelona has been guilty of

The Village, which will house the 15,000 athletes and judges, should by 1993 become a young, dynamic, middle-class suburb with parks and services. Many of the 2,000 flats being built have already been sold.

But the improvements and innovations in the city go far beyond purely sports-related projects. The airport is being expanded under the guidance of the Barcelona archi-

Left, Oriol Bohigas, one of the brains behind Barcelona's urban plans. **Above left**, outside the stadium. **Above right**, the Camp Nou football ground, which will host Olympic events.

excessive pride and this has led to a couple of proverbial falls. Because of its desire to keep the Olympics as Barcelona's Games, the town did not ask for help from any other agencies (regional or national government) until too late.

This pride has caused some damaging delays. Some important plans are unlikely to be realised in time for 1992: the extension of the underground to the Olympic stadium; the completion of vital ring roads and a plan to build 10 big new hotels. But then the city has had half an eye on 1993 anyway, and everything should be ready by then.

Barcelona divides neatly and conveniently into chunks of city from different periods. The old city is "old" only in the sense that it predates the city's expansion at the end of the 19th century. The old city is clearly identifiable from any map as the area where the streets are not regimented and symmetrical, and down its spine runs the Ramblas, the nerve centre of Barcelona.

Encapsulated within the old city is an even older one, known today as the Gothic Quarter, surrounded by Roman walls and comprising most of Barcelona's best-known historical landmarks. Within this narrow-streeted quarter are the Cathedral, the town hall, the mansions of medieval merchants (now museums and galleries) and the bishop's palaces.

The new city that burst out of the old walls is called the Eixample, and even Barcelonans will admit that its grid-like streets are monotonous. But the overall monotony of layout is broken by the best restaurants, art galleries, parks and above all the best examples of modernism, that eclectic style of architecture which isn't really a style at all, but a collection of a wide range of styles amalgamated into one. Be prepared, though, to travel some distance, as the Eixample is huge and the best modernist buildings are widely scattered.

Barcelona is squeezed between a semi-circle of hills and the sea. The hills are significant landmarks in themselves. Montjuïc is the site of the 1992 Olympic Games and the place to retreat to when the city dust and heat becomes unbearable; it offers the best views of the city and of the harbour, which is crossed by a cable car from the hill to Barceloneta, the fisherman's quarter. The harbourside has received a great deal of attention in recent years. From having been an insalubrious area beyond the foot of the Ramblas where only the more daring visitors ventured, the waterfront has been cleaned up and remodelled. The modern promenade now rivals the Ramblas as a venue for evening strollers.

Street and place names throughout the city have been changed to Catalan in recent years, as have most maps. However, the Castilian equivalents are still fresh in the minds of taxi drivers and shop assistants, so beware seemingly misleading directions. Place and street names in this book are all in Catalan.

Preceding pages: magic fountains below the Palau Nacional; detail from Güell park; fairground attraction on Montjuïc. **Left**, the city from Tibidabo.

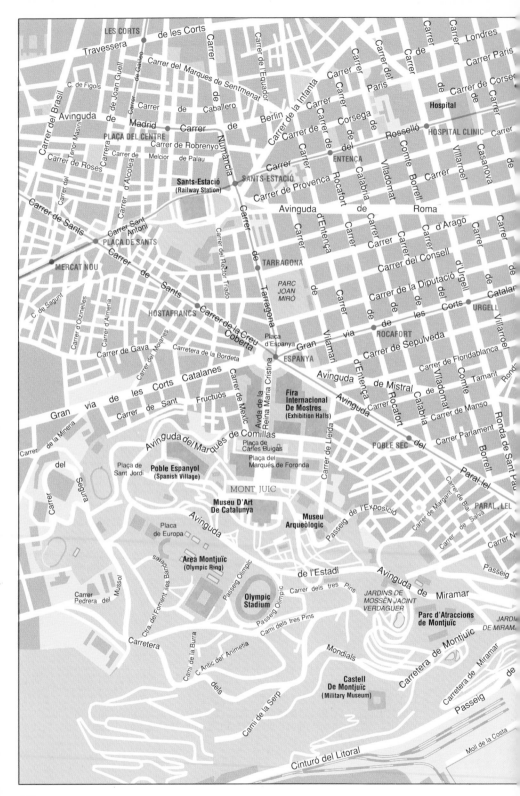

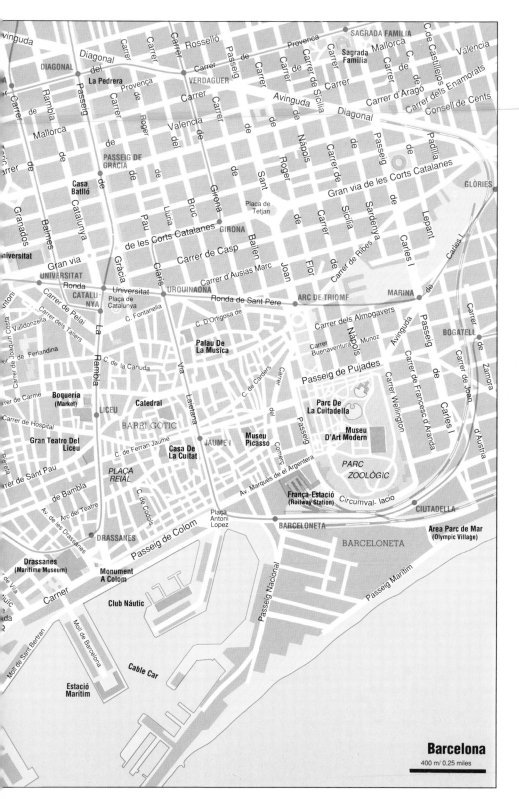

Barcelona

400 m/ 0.25 miles

1 Diagonal-Sarria
2 Carrer Tarragona
3 Meridiana
4 Plaça Cerdà
5 Nova Icaria (Olympic village)
6 Port
7 Plaça de les Glòries
8 La Vall D'Efaron
9 Sagrera
10 Diagonal-Prim
11 University
12 Olympic installations

THE PLAÇA DE CATALUNYA

The Plaça de Catalunya is the hub of Barcelona in terms of transport and city communications. But it is also the centre of the city in a much wider sense: in the middle of the square itself paving stones are arranged into the shape of a star which, they say, is also the centre of the capital of Catalonia.

To be in Barcelona and not find oneself returning again and again to this wide open, bustling plaza is almost an impossibility. One may return to participate in some cultural event, to rendezvous with an *amigo*, or simply to go shopping.

Catalunya is the pivotal point of the old and new cities. To the north and west of the square is the regimented Eixample, with broad avenues, business quarters, elegant shopping and modernist architecture.

To the east is the Gothic Quarter, a maze of dark, ancient streets walled by ancient history. The Ramblas, the spinal chord of the city, leads its flood of humanity down from the Plaça to the southeast, changing character several times before it reaches the recently revived port area. Further south still, the Olympic hill of Montjuïc dominates both port and town.

The Plaça de Catalunya was originally an outlying esplanade, traversed by a mountain stream (the stream bed was later to form the foundations of the Ramblas) and connected to the inner city by means of an entrance called the Portal dels Orbs. The entrance was later renamed the Portal de l'Angel because, so the story goes, when Sant Ferrer crossed through this doorway with his followers, he was greeted by an angel.

The Plaça as it stands today had a difficult birth. The 19th-century Plan Cerdà, a project for the redevelopment of Barcelona, called for the creation of a square a little further inland, at the junction of the Passeig de Gràcia, the

Gran Via de les Corts Catalanes and Carrer de Consell de Cent. Another rival project presented by Antoni Rovira i Trías proposed an enormous plaza 2,600 by 1,300 ft (800 by 400 metres) to be called the "Forum Isabel II". Yet another plan for a plaza similar to that which we know today was designed in 1868 by Miquel Garriga.

While the authorities were endeavouring to reach an agreement – planning permission was hard to get even then – the owners of the corresponding plots of land got fed up with waiting and began to build. In 1902, Lord Mayor Ledesma ordered the demolition of all these buildings but it was another quarter of a century before the Plaça took on its current manifestation. Based on a design by Francesc Nebot, the square was opened by King Alfonso XII in 1927. Three years later, the elaborate lighting of the square was duly initiated and much admired.

A series of statues was added to the furniture of the square: of particular note are two in front of the dominant buildings to the west: *La Diosa* by the great Catalan sculptor Josep Clará (there is a museum with a permanent exhibition of his works towards Tidibabo) and *El Pastor Tocando el Caramillo* (shepherd playing the flute) by Pau Gargallo. Unfortunately, pollution from the traffic which screams around the city's circuit of roads has eaten into their finer details.

Tea and politics: The buildings which surround the square combine nostalgia with business. The corner of **Carrer de Rivadeneyra** (next to the Ramblas), for example, was the site of the almost mythical Maison Dorée café. Such was the inherent character of this establishment that, when it finally closed its doors in 1918, another café of the same name opened at number 6. "It was never the same," wrote Lluís Permanyer, enthusiastic city historian, who relates that it was in this establishment that a tradition of "five o'clock tea" was introduced to Barcelona.

Preceding pages: Plaça de Catalunya, the heart of Catalonia. Below, goddess in the square.

Another meeting point of intellectuals was the old Hotel Colón, which has since become the headquarters of the Banco Español de Crédito (*Banesto*). Older generations of Republicans remember when the facade of the hotel was covered in portraits during the Civil War. With giant posters of Marx, Lenin and Stalin, there was no mistaking the fact that this was the headquarters of the Unified Socialist Party of Catalonia (PSUC), then the region's leading socialist group.

In the late 1960s, a student demonstration gave new meaning to that generation's slogan "Imagination is Power". A rebel with a sense of humour placed several boxes of washing powder in one of the fountains. A few hours later the cardboard boxes disintegrated and both the fountain and the police force attending the demonstration were awash in soapsuds.

Sooner or later all those who have something to say, be it in protest, acclamation or celebration, find their way to the Plaça de Catalunya. Among such demonstrations and just causes, one in particular will remain a memorable event: the Diada de Catalunya, which celebrates regional nationalism (actually the defeat of Catalan forces after the siege of 1714). The Diada held on 11 September 1978 was possibly one of the most massive popular demonstrations to be seen in the Plaça de Catalunya or, indeed, in Spain in recent years.

Demonstrations aside, the square is a splendid area, a place of contemplation full of sunlight, where the young and the not-so-young feed the pigeons or soak up the sun in a *cadira de lloguer* (rented chair).

But, because everything in Barcelona is constantly changing, a facelift is always an imminent possibility: more underground parking, an impressive shopping mall, a new stretch of promenade to establish the final link between the Ramblas and the Rambla de Catalunya, and a new facade for that monumental department store El Corte

Inglés, which is architecturally the poorest relation in the square.

Four corners: From the northern corner the **Ronda de Sant Pere** is a wide avenue of manorial residences, where once the great textile families were located. From the same corner the **Passeig de Gràcia**, a handsome avenue lined with the city's most elegant boutiques, heads west, through select bookshops and famous art galleries, into the **Eixample**, a region of rigid avenues with glimpses of Barcelona's best modernist buildings in the distance.

The plaza is a starting point for either version of **Las Ramblas**, the lower part of which starts with the **Rambla de Canaletas**, or the upper section, the **Rambla de Catalunya,** which runs parallel with Gràcia. The latter properly begins where a statue of a thoughtful bull (perhaps contemplating his breed's banishment from the city – no bullfighting here except at the height of the tourist season) marks the beginning of a traffic-free avenue; art galleries, bookshops, and cinemas adjoin bars specialising in hot chocolate and pastries.

Just southeast of the square, the **Cine Vergara** – in the street of the same name – is one of the city's most recommended cinemas, showing mainly original-language versions (i.e. not dubbed) of foreign films. Next door are two noteworthy terrace-cafés, **Eivissa** and **Leman's**. Either one is a good base from which to watch while two executives, probably both on their way to the airport, fight over the last taxi on the roadside rank. The Eivissa's specialities are breakfasts and salads while Leman's main attraction lies in its enormous range of beers, bar snacks and a daily menu for tourists.

Beyond, the square gets tacky. On the corner of **Carrer Pelai** subways lead down to the immense Metro station, which houses both the red and the green lines, and the Catalunya railway. Above ground is the **Café Zurich**, a favourite meeting place frequented by people with no pretensions to anything but philosophy and pennilessness, looking down the Ramblas.

Moving further around the plaza, the **Avinguda del Portal de l'Angel** is at its finest at Christmas time when the glittering shop windows vie with one another to create the greatest impact. Along the way are vendors with popcorn, sweetmeats and, throughout the festive season, roasted chestnuts. This avenue leads eventually into the heart of the *barri* **Gòtic** (Gothic Quarter).

Just before the Quarter begins is the **Plaça Nova**, the venue for gruesome public hangings and executions in the Middle Ages. In 1989–90 it was again the scene of controversy, when workmen making an underground car park stumbled upon Roman remains. There were calls for the work to be halted, but the city pressed ahead, removing the most significant of the discoveries to the city's museums. For a while, watching the workmen digging in such antique surroundings became quite a spectator sport for the Barcelonans.

Meeting place for excursions into the city (left) or just for talking (right).

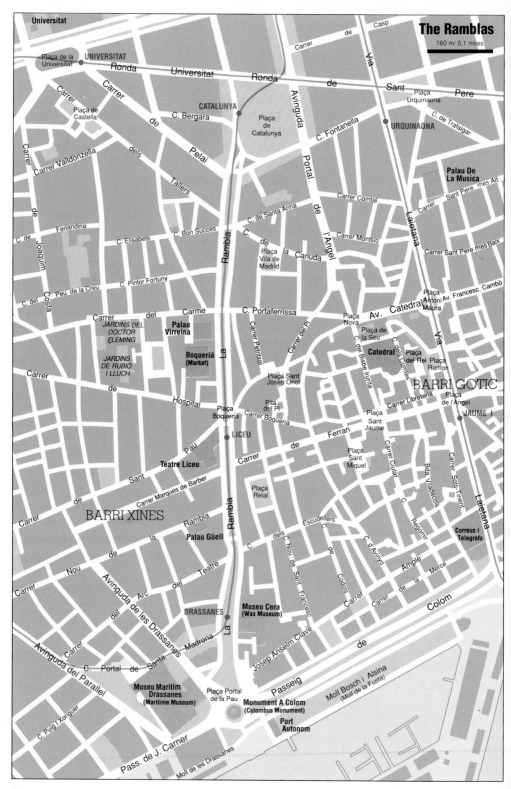

The Ramblas

160 m/ 0,1 miles

Universitat

Plaça de la Universitat
UNIVERSITAT

Ronda
Universitat
Ronda

Carrer
de
Casp

Carrer
Via
de
Sant
Pere

Plaça
Urquinaona

C. de Trafalgar

URQUINAONA

Carrer
Carrer
de
dels
Tallers

Plaça de
Castella

CATALUNYA
C. Bergara

Plaça
de
Catalunya

Avinguda
Portal
de
l'Angel

C. Fontanella

Palau De
La Musica

Carrer
Pelai

Carrer
Sant Pere mes Alt

Carrer Valldonzella

Carrer Comtal

Carrer
Carrer Sant Pere mes Baix

C. de
Joaquim
Costa

Ferlandina

C. Elisabets

C. Bon Succes

C. de Santa Anna

C. de
la
Canuda

Plaça
Vila de
Madrid

Carrer Montsio

Plaça
Antoni Av. Francesc. Cambó
Maura

C. del
Costa

Peu de la Creu

C. Pintor Fortuny

C. Portaferrissa

Plaça
Nova

Av. Catedral

Carrer
del
Carme

Carrer
Petritxol

Carrer del Pi

Plaça de
C. de la Seu

C. dels Comtes

Plaça
del Rei Plaça
Ramon

JARDINS DEL
DOCTOR
FLEMING

Palau
Virreina

Boqueriá
(Market)

La

Catedral

Plaça Sant
Josep Oriol

C. del Bisbe Irurita

BARRI GOTIC

JARDINS
DE RUBIO
I LLUCH

Plta.
del Pi

Carrer Llibreteria

Plaça
de l'Angel

Carrer
de

Hospital

Plaça
Boqueria

Carrer Boqueria

Plaça
Sant
Jaume

JAUME I

LICEU

Ferran

Plaça
Sant
Miquel

Carrer Ciutat

Bda. Viladecols

Carrer Sots-Tinent

Teatre Liceu

Pau

Carrer

de

Plaça
Ciutat

C.

Correus i
Telegrafs

BARRI XINES

Sant

Carrer Marques de Barber

Plaça
Reial

Escudellers

C. d'Avinyo

Regomir

Rambla

la

Palau Güell

Rambla

dels

C.

C. Nou de Sant Francesc

de

C. de Codols

Ample

de la

Merce

Nou

de

Teatre

del

Arc

Avinguda de les Drassanes

Carrer

DRASSANES

Museu Cera
(Wax Museum)

Carrer

Carrer

Colom

Avinguda del Parallel

Carrer
del

C. Portal de
Santa
Madrona

La

Josep Anselm Clavé

de

C. Puig i Xoriguer

Museu Maritim
Drassanes
(Maritime Museum)

Plaça Portal
de la Pau

Monument A Colom
(Colombus Monument)

Passeig

Moll Bosch i Alsina
(Moll de la Fusta)

Port
Autonom

Pass. de J. Carner

Moll de les Drassanes

Lalelana

THE RAMBLAS:
HEART OF THE CITY

It has often been said that nowhere else in the world does 5,000 ft (1,500 metres) of asphalt reflect so well both the lifestyle and the pulse of a city as does the **Ramblas** in Barcelona.

This avenue, or collection of avenues head-to-head, is a perennial attraction for visitors and locals, year in, year out. Yet the Ramblas is constantly changing, not only with the seasons but with every passing hour, by day and by night, in the afternoon and the small hours of dawn. It even changes in relation to its own configuration, since it is in no way homogeneous. Maps and Barcelonans are divided on whether the Ramblas is one or many; perhaps the best answer is that there are five individual components of this street, each different from the other, but the whole is greater than the sum of its parts.

The Ramblas is the thoroughfare of Barcelona *par excellence*, the spinal cord either side of which lie the city's main attractions. What used to be a river bed is now a river of vital movement – of people: a torrent of humanity comprising bankers, beggars, artists, intellectuals, workmen, vagabonds, clergy, tourists, anarchists and aristocrats. It is a concert of many languages blending with the noise of the traffic, the sounds of the birds and the scent of the flowers from the stalls, whatever the season. But it doesn't do to travel its length at too fast a pace; that way these 5,000 ft (1,500 metres) of tarmac become just a blur of colour.

The world on stage: The main promenade is a unique world of art and fantasy, tradition and deception, luxury and misery. It constitutes a free show for both onlookers and performers, and may even cause you to ask yourself which you are, spectator or spectacle. Rubbing elbows with musicians, mimics, artists, fakirs and faith-healers are men and women who read Tarot cards, fortune tellers and gypsies who will read your palm, a living statue, a man hitting ping-pong balls with a hammer, a trumpet player, a violinist. All along the promenade, groups of South American singers create the sounds of the Argentinian Pampa or the Peruvian Andes. And sometimes a couple of women will offer a free striptease show to passers-by.

Despite its dual personality – gay, flower-bedecked in the morning, sombre, disorderly but undeniably picturesque at night – the Ramblas continues to be the page upon which the throbbing history of this city is written. This is where rumours are generated, protests are raised and popular demonstrations take to the streets before marching to one of the squares.

This is the city's prime observation point, an immense gallery where every aspect of life is exhibited; to the extent where the city, in unconscious homage to the Ramblas, has invented two words: *Ramblejar*, a verb which means

to walk down the Ramblas, and *ram-blista*, an adjective which describes a person addicted to the act of the verb.

It is along this street that major football victories (which are like national battles to the Catalans) have been celebrated and where opera lovers have thrilled to the voices of Caruso, Pavarotti and Caballé. It is here that the best restaurants purchase their supplies, in the Boqueira market, and where the citizens of Barcelona enjoy one last refreshing drink after a long and heavy night of clubbing.

River to road: Originally, the Ramblas was the river bed (the Latin name *arenno* was replaced by the Arab word *ramla*) that marked the exterior limits of the city fortified by King Jaume I. But when the city expanded during the 15th century, the Ramblas became part of the inner city.

In due course a number of religious houses were built throughout the surrounding areas and the river bed came to be known as the "Convent Thorough-fare". It was not until the beginning of the 18th century that the Ramblas was to become a more clearly defined street, after permission was granted to build on the ancient walls in the Boqueria area. In 1775 a section of the city walls was torn down and a central walkway built, lined with poplar trees and higher than the roadway that ran along either side.

Within the small and densely populated area of the ancient fortified city, the Ramblas was the only street of any significance, and it became the city's focal point. Renovations were constantly under way during the 19th century, and the street settled down to become more exclusive and aristocratic; this change of status was aided by the disappearance of some of the surrounding buildings and convents, creating space for new plazas and mansions.

The Ramblas assumed its present shape between 1849 and 1856 when all the remaining fortifications were torn down. The first banana trees, brought from Devesa in Girona, were planted in

Discussing the latest match.

1851 and the street became "the fashionable promenade route, where the cream of Barcelona parades on foot, by carriage or on horseback," according to the 19th-century journalist Gaziel.

From the top: The course of this unique promenade (which runs from the Plaça de Catalunya to the Columbus Monument by the harbour) begins from the **Font de Canaletas**, one of the symbols of Barcelona. The uppermost section of the Ramblas is actually called the Rambla de Canaletas after the 19th-century cast-iron fountain on the right-hand side of the first pedestrian stretch. Here tramps wash themselves in the morning and executives drink in the evening; the flowing water is purported to have the power to convert all who drink there into true Barcelonans. To "drink the water of Canaletas" is synonymous with baptism for the true citizens of Barcelona.

For years the Fountain of Canaletas has been the favourite meeting place of casual visitors. In 1781, the "foremost and most distinguished" citizens of Barcelona gathered here (according to the chronicles of the time) in such numbers that rented chairs were placed on either side of the promenade – a practice which continues today. Thirty pesetas will procure a chair for the whole day and a bootblack will never be far away. Over the weekends, football generally takes precedence in conversations here.

This stretch of the Ramblas is like the hallway to the city's great salon. Solitary people gather around the fountain or at the entrance to the metro, clearly waiting the arrival of a partner who never seems to materialise. But if and when their partner does appear, the couple marches off arm in arm down into the throng.

At the junction with the Carrer Bonsuccés is the long-standing pharmacy of **Dr Masó i Arumí**, complete with ceramic pill-boxes and of notable modernist decorative elements both inside and out. Opposite, crossing the Carrer

Spectators or spectacle?

Santa Anna through a half-hidden doorway to the left, is the **Monastir de Santa Anna**, an oasis of peace amidst the roaring traffic. The Romanesque church and Gothic cloister are marvellous examples of the architecture of their time.

Returning to the Carrer de Canuda, at number 6, is the **Ateneu Barcelonès**, a traditional cultural enclave with walk-in exhibitions located in a building that dates back to 1796. Of the original structure, only the stairway to the inner courtyard, the romantic rear garden and the paintings on the ground-floor ceilings remain.

Back on the Ramblas, this is a good moment to buy a foreign newspaper in one of the numerous kiosks. The colourful equivalent of the flower stalls a little further down, the stands here boast a particularly lurid display of pornographic literature that proclaims post-Franco liberalism – no matter that you never see anyone buying it.

Hidden just down Carrer Tallers is the **Boadas Cocktail Bar**, the oldest in the city, and well known among the locals. Here, under the eagle eye of the first owner's portrait, or of his daughter who still runs the bar with some style, one can ask for the cocktail of the day or the strangest combination imaginable.

Beyond begins the Rambla dels Estudis, also called Rambla dels Ocells ("of the birds"). The name is due as much to the vast number of sparrows that nest in the trees as to the number of bird vendors, who also sell tortoises, fish and other small animals.

The name Rambla dels Estudis derives from the 16th century, when the Estudi General, or University, was located here. In 1714, as a result of the Catalan defeat at the hands of Castilian troops, the university was transferred to the township of Cervera in Lléida. The building ceased to exist in 1843.

Here, on the right-hand side, in the 18th century, was the Jesuit Col.legi de Nobles de Cordelles, the convent of the same order and the church. Today, part

Stall on the Rambla de les Flors.

of the plot is occupied by the Reil Acadèmia de Ciències i Arts and the Teatre Poliorama, with a ticket office looking like an massive ornamental wardrobe. On the exterior of the building is the clock which has been the official timekeeper of the city since 1891.

The **Vienna Café**, elegant and often with a pianist upstairs, is worth a stop. Parallel and one block south of the Rambla runs the Carrer de Sitjes, a narrow street of young bars and clubs.

Of all the vast conglomeration of the former university, only the **Church of Betlem** (beyond the Filipino tobacco company) remains, a long and rather depressing bulk. The baroque facade on the Carrer del Carme was built in 1690 but the main structure was not completed until 1729. On the exterior wall, the dressed stone that decorates the facade and the main front are both well preserved.

Detour down the Carrer del Carme for the **El Indio** corsetry shop (at number 24), founded in 1870, and little changed since. Its present aspect, with interesting carvings on the wooden facade and windows, is the result of renovations carried out in 1922. Inside there are long wooden trestle tables for proper display of the cloth, and wooden chairs for stout ladies to rest their legs and get into a good mood for buying.

Once it has passed the Ermita, the Rambla (here called Sant Josep) opens up again. On the left is the **Palau Moja**. This important neo-classical, 18th-century building houses a collection of beautiful murals by Francesc Pla. One, *El Vigatà*, in the main salon, was painted in 1790. Today, the palace has been converted into offices of the Department of Culture of the Generalitat (the Catalan government), with the main entrance in the Carrer de Portaferrisa at the side.

Opposite the entrance is the **Font de Portaferrisa**, one of the most ancient fountains of Barcelona, although its present location dates from only 1861. Earlier (from 1605) it was situated in the

Left, bookstall postcards. Right, the Boqueria market.

THE GRAN TEATRE DEL LICEU

The origins of Barcelona's Gran Teatre del Liceu are curious. Philanthropist Manuel Gibert i Sans, who was also a commander in the national militia, started the "Liceo Dramático de Aficionados" with the idea of organising soirées to raise funds for the survival of his own battalion. The theatre company was housed for a while in the former convent of Montsió, where the first opera staged was Bellini's *Norma,* on 3 February 1838.

Soon the old premises of Montsió became inadequate and in 1842 the decision was made to buy the land of the former convent of the Trinitarios, situated on the Ramblas. Around this time the militia was dissolved and the company became a wholly artistic and social foundation. Gibert recruited aristocrat Joaquim de Gispert i Anglí and banker Manuel Girona i Agrafel, one of the principal representatives of the new industrialist upper class, as backers for his project for the creation of the Gran Teatre del Liceu.

The construction work started in 1844 under the supervision of architect Miquel Garriga i Roca. This enormous project was second only to that of the Scala of Milan, with space for 4,000 spectators. Garriga's original design for the front of the building was rejected, and replaced by that of the French designer Viguié, who added an eclectic facade. The theatre boxes were sold for 15,000 pesetas each, in perpetuity, to the grand families who collaborated in the construction.

The Liceu was inaugurated in 1847, but, because of a fire which partially destroyed the theatre, it had to be refitted between 1861 and 1862. The directing architect, Josep Oriol i Mestres, although severely criticised, followed the style of Viguié. The interior decoration was the work of a team of respected painters, led by Josep Mirabent i Gatel.

In the same year the Círculo del Liceu was started. The Círculo was a club that functioned as a meeting place for the city's power brokers. The American social historian Gary Wray McDonogh said of the Círculo in his book *The Good Families of Barcelona*: "The club was isolated [from the Liceu] as a prerogative of the upper class... The boxes, an extension of the family dwelling, were the dominion of the women where they held their meetings and socialising. El Círculo itself, on the other hand, was converted into an extension of the men's offices. Both were central parts of the Liceu as an institution." Every imaginable type of performance, from musical galas, sophisticated operas and ballets to rowdy carnival dances, were held in the theatre, attended by every class of society, carefully segregated in their respective areas.

The golden age of the theatre, the early decades of the 20th century, lasted until the beginning of the Civil War. It was followed by the dark period of dictatorship. Surprisingly, when the decline of the theatre, which was linked to the crisis of opera all over the world, appeared to be inevitable, the Liceu experienced a remarkable comeback. Today the international renaissance of opera is particularly strong in the Liceu.

During its 150-year life, the theatre has hosted some of the most important figures in the arts, from composers such as Stravinsky, Albéniz, Falla and Pau Casals to singers such as Gayarre, Caruso, Callas and Pavarotti. Among the Catalan artists who have triumphed here are Raventós, Blanchart, Fleta, Monserrat Caballé and Josep Carreras.

A massive programme of restoration (including enlargement of the stage), with a budget of 5,200 million pesetas, means that the Liceu will open its doors again in 1992, once more among the world's greatest opera theatres.

Repeating past history, this renovation has whipped up a strong wind of controversy. The work affects a series of dwellings and shops, some of which (such as the Perfumería Ramblas) have significant historical value. During the closure, operas and plays will be performed elsewhere in the city, bestowing on the alternative venue the privilege of being the second opera centre in Barcelona. Open or closed, the Liceu, with its long history of social and artistic excellence, will always be number one.

Carrer del Carme, at the site upon which the Church of Betlem was built. In 1951 an impressive mural of Valencian tiles, representing the Ramblas of the 18th century, was added. The legend on the mural describes the origin of the name, which means "iron gate".

The Carrer Portaferrisa itself leads into a world of commerce and numerous fashion shops. A few metres in, on the right, is the picturesque and narrow **Carrer de Petritxol**, the street about which recent Nobel Prize winner, Camilo José Cela, wrote: "The Carrer de Petritxol can be compared to the drawing room of a well-run household, where everything is well cared for and in its right place, where every object has a specific function and a reason for being. In the Carrer de Petritxol one breathes a refined and peaceful air, commercial but serene, an air of trade unions and corporations, inherited not improvised. The Carrer de Petritxol was opened during the second half of the 15th century but its ambience – despite

its 17th and 18th-century buildings – is 19th-century; the houses specialising in drinking chocolate, the libraries, the opticians, the jewellers and, above all, the Sala Parés – doyen of the vibrant Barcelonan art galleries – all combine to enhance the decorative whole."

The street is indeed famous for its rich hot chocolate and from the middle of the afternoon it is impossible to find a free chair in any one of the so-called *granjes* (tea and chocolate rooms).

At this point back on the Rambla de Sant Josep (better known as the Rambla de les Flors, or "of the flowers"), the air smells sweet. During the 19th century this was the only place where flowers were sold and each vendor had his favourite clientele.

To the right is the **Palau de la Virreina**, a magnificent 18th-century rococo building set back from the road for greater effect. In 1771 Manuel Amat, Viceroy of Peru, sent a detailed plan from Lima for the construction of the house that he planned to build in the

Ramblas. The final building was not completed until 1778 and the Viceroy died only a few years after taking up residence. It was his young widow who was left to enjoy the palace, which became known as the palace of the "Virreina" or vicereine. Today it is an excellent exhibition venue; to one side is a good contemporary bookshop, and to the other is an ancient music store.

Further down the Rambla rises one of the most representative and best loved symbols of Barcelona, the **Mercat de la Boqueria**. Neither the market of Santa Caterina, inaugurated in 1842 as Catalonia's first covered market, nor any of the other 40 markets in Barcelona today has achieved the popularity of the "Boqueria", which was opened on 19 March 1836.

The market occupies a square surrounded by smooth Ionic columns that support the front terraces. The roofing, designed by Miquel de Bergue, was not in place until 1914; the whole structure stands on part of what used to be the convent of the Carmelites Descalças de Sant Josep.

Within, all the produce is presented in a careful and orderly fashion. The multi-coloured central avenue (a bit more expensive) is a particularly arresting sight, as much suited to an art critic as to a shopper with an empty stomach.

On the right of the market entrance from the Rambla is **El Pinocho**, probably the most popular and endearing establishment in the city at breakfast time. At the tiny bar it is wise to allow oneself to be led and advised.

Beyond the market the Rambla suddenly enters an execution yard, although it is hard to visualise now. The **Pla de la Boqueria** (marked only by a widening of the Rambla) was the site of executions in the 14th century, when it was paved with flagstones. The name dates from the previous century when tables selling fresh meat, *mesas de bocatería,* were erected here ("boc" was the Catalan for goat's meat). In the 15th century the tables of gamblers and

Left, inside the church of El Pi. **Right**, road to the Palau Güell.

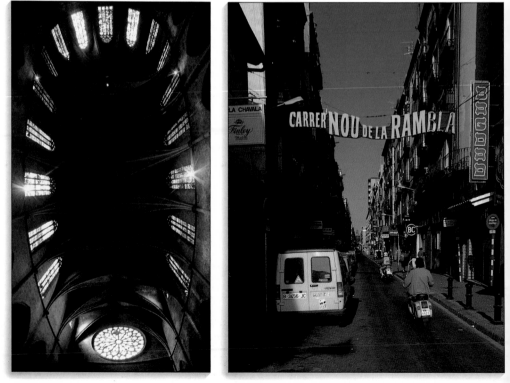

128

cardsharps replaced the meat stalls.

Today the flagstones have been replaced by a Joan Miró pavement created in the 1970s. The gamblers have been replaced yet again by musicians, poets and roving artists, and the gallows, symbol of death, by a neoclassical fountain, the symbol of life. At one corner is the **Casa Bruno Quadras**, built by Josep Vilaseca in 1891, in neo-Egyptian style. The decoration, complete with sunshades and fans forming a panoply and a great Chinese dragon supporting an umbrella and a lamp, demonstrates the oriental influence felt by the modernists.

The Carrer de Boqueria, which leads off the Rambla to the left, passes to the harbour side (dive up the tiny Carrer Alsina) of three hidden gems: the **Plaçeta del Pi**, the **Plaça de Sant Josep Oriol** and the **Plaça del Pi**. The last of these comes complete with a Gothic church of the same name (14th and 15th centuries), displaying one of the greatest rose windows in Europe (stand in the

square and look up after dark). During the weekend craft and artistic fairs are held throughout this rosary of small squares, which make up Barcelona's Montmartre. Look out too for the comic shop opposite the church, evidence of the quantity and quality of comic strip art coming out of this city.

Theatreland: Beyond the Miró paving, the Ramblas changes character again, giving way to the bar terraces, hotels and restaurants of the Rambla dels Caputxins. This is where people come to see and be seen. Here parade the most outrageously outfitted individuals, throwing down an unsubtle challenge to conventional notions of style. This particular stretch is most enjoyable at night and is best witnessed from one of the terraces or from inside the **Café de la Opera**, one of the few remaining old-fashioned cafés in Barcelona.

The Rambla dels Caputxins (so-called because, until 1775, the left side was the site of the Capuchin Convent and its adjacent vegetable garden) is

Caricaturist on the Ramblas.

known also as Rambla del Mig or the Rambla del Centre. It did not acquire its present aspect until the mid-19th century, when it was the first of the component parts of the Ramblas to become a promenade. All of this section is dominated by the **Gran Teatre del Liceu**, cathedral of the *bel canto* in Spain, across whose stage have trod the most important personalities of opera. Behind its discreet facade lies an architecture and decor worthy of the sumptuous taste of the musical world of 1861 when it was completed.

The **Hotel Oriente**, on the same side as the Liceu, is noteworthy; it's worth braving the reception desk for permission to look around. This establishment preserves the structures of the Col.legi de Sant Bonaventura, founded by Franciscan monks in 1652. The convent and cloister, built between 1652 and 1670, are preserved in their entirety. The cloister is now the hotel ballroom, surrounded by the monks' gallery. A wall plaque explains this and reminds read-ers that this was the first public place in Barcelona to use gas lighting.

A little further down is a rather surprising establishment: the *xarcuteria* (*charcutería*) **La Castellana**. Sample authentic gastronomic delights of smoked meats, cheeses and pâtés, either while standing at the bar (the chilled and unlabelled local red wine is ferociously strong) or seated at one of the four tables, surrounded by curious bottles from which the dust has not been removed in several decades. A cheap and authentic way of eating out.

Down the Carrer Nou de la Rambla on the right, numbers 3–5 are occupied by the **Palau Güell**, a notable residence built by Antoni Gaudí between 1885 and 1889. With this structure, which looks like a giant organ, the architect embarked on a period of fertile creativity. Both the severe facade of white stone and the interior reflect a dominating Gothic inspiration alternating with elements of Arabic influence. The layout of the building is structured around

The Plaça Reial.

an enormous salon, from which emerges a conical roof which is covered in bits of tiling and presides over an unusual landscape of capriciously placed battlements, balustrades and chimneys of differing shapes. The inside of the building houses the exhibits of the **Museu del Teatre** and the **Theatre Institute**.

Popular square: Back on the other side of the Ramblas, the diminutive Carrer Colom leads past bootblacks' stalls to one of the liveliest parts of the city, the **Plaça Reial**, an eddy at the side of the Ramblas in which representatives of all types of ramblers, from the richest to the poorest, local and foreign, come to rest for a while.

Inspired by the French urban designs of the Napoleonic period, it is the only one of the many squares planned in Barcelona during the past century that was built entirely according to its original plan. Francesc Daniel Molina built an architectural grouping of uniform, arcaded buildings on the plot of land where the Capuchin Convent of Barcelona once stood.

This square, which measures 184 ft by 275 ft (56 by 84 metres), contains a group of terrace-bars which are a permanent hive of activity. Stamp and coin collectors gather every Sunday around the Fuente de las Tres Gracias and the two *fanals* (street lamps) designed by Antoni Gaudí. During the rest of the week the plaza is a meeting point for the most diverse cross-section of people, and has a permanent police presence to discourage the seedier elements, who have traditionally adopted the square.

At the northern end of the Plaça Reial, by Carrer del Vidre, is a traditional herb shop known as **L'Herbolari del Rei**, one of the most fascinating places in Barcelona which still preserves all the character of the Romantic period. A visit is essential.

Close by, at number 8, is the **Museu Pedagogic de Ciències**, with its exhibition of strange desiccated animals. At number 18, between Pasatge Colom

Cosmopolitan bedmates.

and Bacardí, is the theatre housing the flamenco show of Maruja Garrido. However, what has really made the square famous are the beer houses on the north and east sides, the winos, the drugs, the cheap *pensions* and the atmosphere of suppressed excitement.

Tacky territory: Beyond the Carrer de Colom the Ramblas opens up again into the **Pla del Teatre** or **de les Comedies**, the second of the Ramblas' open areas. Here, during the 16th century, the city's first theatre was built. The present **Teatre Principal** has replaced the old wooden theatre building, which was for many years the only stage in Barcelona. Unfortunately, even the new structure has been seriously disfigured by various forms of mutilation and vulgar decorations. A 2,000-seater, it was built on the site of the historical "Corral de les Comédies", an early popular theatre, but it never appealed to the bourgeoisie and suffered a relentless process of decay which still continues.

On the other side of the promenade is a monument to Frederic Soler "Pitarra", founder of the modern Catalan theatre. Some of the few prostitutes that remain in this area choose the small square that surrounds the monument to offer their charms – almost as an epilogue of what once was, and a prologue of what still is throughout the adjoining streets that make up the *barri* **Xinès** (still better known as the *barrio* Chino). The women propping up the walls, together with the neon signs of the establishments that trade in sex, mark the beginning of the Rambla de Santa Mònica, the last stretch of the Ramblas before it reaches the sea.

This is a strange area, populated by fortune tellers, fakirs and gypsies. It is also the meeting place of artists, portrait painters and artisans, each setting up for his or her own particular market during the weekend. Along these few metres the threads of past history and future events cross over and meet each other. This is where, in 1895, films were first shown publicly in Spain by the Lumière brothers. Here, too, stands the **Centre d'Art Santa Mònica**. And, opposite, there is the **Palau March** (1780), today the head office of the Cultural Council of Catalonia. Along this same pavement, beyond the Pasatge de la Banca, is the **Wax Museum**.

The red light district is presently being gutted in honour of the Olympics; for many years it has been a distinctive area of Barcelona and many Barcelona-watchers will be sad to see it go.

The last building on the Ramblas (now occupied by the armed forces) has a curious history. In 1778 the foundry of the Royal Artillery, as well as its workshop, were transferred to this building, popularly known as El Refino. The foundry was one of the most renowned cannon factories of its time. From 1844 until 1920 it was occupied by the offices of the Banco de Barcelona (the first private Spanish bank) and, since the Spanish Civil War (1936–39), it has been converted into the offices of the military governor.

Left, **Superman at the Wax Museum. Right**, the **Columbus Monument at the foot of the Ramblas.**

THE GOTHIC QUARTER

The oldest part of the city of Barcelona is built around Taber Hill, a misnomer for that which is little more than a mound in an otherwise flat city. On the mound, the ***barri* Gòtic** (Gothic Quarter) is surrounded by the remains of Roman walls, within which very little has changed for centuries. The Gothic Quarter is an island within the urban metropolis, with its narrow, tortuous streets of ancient stone.

Around the walls: From the Plaça Nova, in front of the Bishop's Portal and before entering the heart of the Gothic Quarter, wander briefly around the remaining Roman walls. Built out of massive stone blocks 12 ft (3.5 metres) thick and 30 ft (9 metres) high and punctuated with defence towers, they circle the Quarter for more than a mile.

The cylindrical towers of the **Portal del Bisbe**, or Bishop's Portal (named in the Middle Ages because of its proximity to the Bishop's Palace), are, in fact, the northern entrance to the ancient Roman city. (The opposite axis of the city was Decumanus, located more or less where the Carrer de Ferran is today.) The towers were modified during the 12th century and windows were built into the facade two centuries later.

Looking port-wards from the **Plaça Nova**, the Roman wall opens momentarily to reveal the Cathedral square, full of photographers trying to get to grips with the heavily ornate facade of the Cathedral itself, which never seems to get much sun, and then curves along the Carrer de la Tapineria (*tapins* were a style of medieval footwear) to the **Plaça de Ramon Berenguer El Gran**. The equestrian statue of Berenguer, an 11th-century noble instrumental in the creation of the Catalan national identity, is the work of Josep Llimona.

The wall that fronts the square is the best preserved and restored of the Gothic Quarter. This section has nine towers, three of which were joined together during the 13th century to build the Royal Palace Chapel (the Capella de Santa Agueda). One of the towers was extended to house the chapel's belfry.

Beyond the Plaça de l'Angel, the street continues in the direction of Plaça d'Emili Vilanova to a point at which another stretch of Roman wall with seven towers still stands. All the structures built on Roman foundations date to the 12th century or later, when the city's limits were extended, allowing the original fortifications to be used as intermediary walls.

Inside the *barri*: If you enter the Gothic Quarter from the Plaça Nova, up the sloping Carrer del Bisbe Irurita, you are instantly among important historical landmarks. At number 5 (on the right) stands the **Palau del Bisbe** (Bishop's Palace). The entrance door opens on to a 12th-century medieval courtyard, the only remaining evidence for the original palace after centuries of modifications. The frescos on the facade (facing

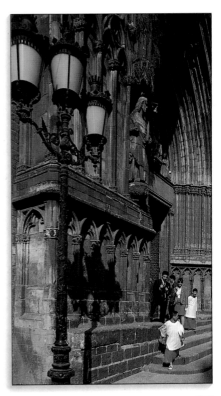

Preceding pages: aristocratic house in the Gothic Quarter. **Left**, in the old city. **Right**, Santa Maria del Mar.

the Carrer Montjuïc del Bisbe) date to the 8th century, while the triple recess windows and large *flamígero* window in the courtyard are 14th century.

Opposite the palace the Carrer de Santa Llúcia leads towards the cathedral. On the corner is a chapel dedicated to Santa Llúcia, the patron saint of the blind and, curiously, of seamstresses. The chapel, built in 1268, is a fine example of Romanesque architecture with images of the *Annunciation* and the *Visitation* decorating the facade capitals. The holy water font inside the chapel dates from the 14th century. A rear doorway leads into the cathedral cloister.

Opposite the chapel, on the other corner, is the Archdeacon's residence, presently the **Municipal History Institute**; it contains a valuable collection of historical chronicles and documents. The building as it stands today was reconstructed in the 15th century on 300-year-old foundations. A Gothic fountain is the centrepiece of the miniature oasis of the inner courtyard; the windows are Gothic *flamígero* although the sculptures have overtones of the Italian Renaissance.

The Dean's house, which forms part of the Archdeaconery, was first modified at the beginning of the 15th century, but continued to undergo successive modifications as the Cathedral esplanade was extended.

Magnetic point: The construction of the **Cathedral** itself began in 1298 under the patronage of Jaume II. The main area consists of three naves and an apse with ambulatory beneath an octagonal dome. Two 14th and 15th-century towers rise at each end of the transept. Beneath the main altar is the crypt of Santa Eulàlia and of particular note are the dome's multicoloured keystones. Some say that this is one of Catalonia's three "magnetic" points. The tomb of Santa Eulàlia, behind the altar, is an important work of art, executed in alabaster by a disciple of Giovanni Pisano (14th century) during the

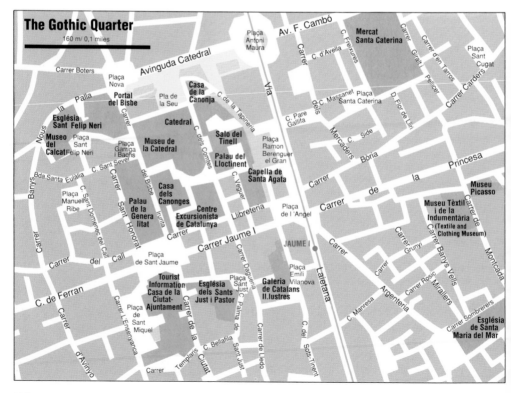

same period as the episcopal Cathedral.

The most outstanding of the aisle chapels behind the altar is that of the Transfiguration, designed by Bernat Martorell. Considered as a masterpiece by art critics, the chapel is dedicated to Sant Salvador and was built in 1447.

The high-backed choir pews are by Pere Sanglada (1399), and the lower-backed benches were carved by Maciá Bonafé towards the end of the same century. The retrochoir was built at the beginning of the 16th century by the artist Bartolomé Ordoñez. The Sala Capitular (Chapter House, beside the main entrance), and today known as the Capella del Santo Cristo de Lepanto (chapel of Christ Lepanto), was built in 1405 and 1454 and is considered to be the finest example of Gothic art in the Cathedral.

The Cathedral facade was finally finished during the 19th century by architects Mestres and Fontseré, modelled on a drawing by Mestre Carlí (15th century). The oldest part is that of the Porta de Sant Ivo (St Ives' Door) where some of the Romanesque windows and archways can still be seen. Although most of the Cathedral's more antique furnishings are now housed in the city museum, a small pavilion beside the Porta de la Pietat still shelters a 15th-century terracotta statue of St George by Antoni Claperós, and the door that leads to the western end of the transept is made from the marble taken from the earlier Romanesque Cathedral.

The Cathedral square, known as **Cristo Rei** or **Pla de la Seu**, was, until 1421, an open space, part of the plot of land on which the Deacon's house had been built, along with those of other canons, and part of the Roman wall.

On the far side is a singularly beautiful building, the 15th-century **Casa de la Canonja** (House of the Canonery). The oldest part is that which joins the corner of the Baixada de la Canonja (Canonery Hill). Later, in 1546, the building was extended and the wing that overlooks the Cathedral square was

Left, the Cathedral. Right, wishful candles.

built, becoming the headquarters of the Pia Almonia, a charitable organisation created at the beginning of the century and charged with the feeding of a hundred poor people daily.

Down the road: Back past the bishop's palace and on to the Carrer del Bisbe Irurita once again, the street opens into the diminutive Plaça Bachs (which commemorates those who died in battle during the Napoleonic wars). On one side is the Santa Eulàlia Portal which leads into the **Cathedral cloister,** a quiet, atmospheric place where pickpockets prowl. The sound of running water from the fountains can be drowned by the honking of the geese who sometimes occupy the centre of the cloister. Four splendid galleries with pointed archways surround a romantic garden of elegant palms, medlars and highly perfumed magnolia trees, all enclosed by the 15th-century wrought-iron railings which surround the garden.

On the other side of Plaça Bachs, the Carrer Montjuïc del Bisbe leads off to the **Plaça de Sant Felip Neri**, a charming square further enhanced if, by chance, a wandering musician happens to have made his way here for the day. Excellent concerts are held in the church of the same name, either in one of the aisles or in the adjoining convent, both of which were built towards the end of the 18th century. These concerts are normally advertised in local entertainment guides and are worth watching out for.

On its way to the Plaça de Sant Jaume, the Carrer del Bisbe passes under a neo-Gothic bridge. This joins the **Palau de la Generalitat** with the canons' residence. The Gothic doorway to the Generalitat, with its impressive St George medallion (wrought by Pere Johan), is the work of Marc Safont (1418) and opens first on to a typical Catalan-Gothic courtyard, complete with a loggia of pointed archways supported by slender columns of great beauty and supreme elegance.

The Generalitat's **Capella de Sant**

Gothic Quarter shopping.

Jordi is also the work of Safont and is a magnificent example of Catalan *flamígero*. Inside is a small 15th-century statue of the saint. The chapel was enlarged in 1620 and an interesting architectural feature is the dome with its hanging capitals.

The second courtyard, called **Los Naranjos**, is the work of Pau Mateu (16th century) and was completed by Tomàs Barsa. The original floors were of blue and white tiling but these were later substituted by marble from Carrara; the belfry is the work of Pere Ferrer (1568) and the bells toll a unique sequence of ancient melodies which imparts a singular and very special atmosphere throughout the surrounding district. The **Gold Salon** has magnificent examples of *artesanía*, delicate workmanship. Through a Renaissance doorway is the **Saló de Sant Jordi**, designed by Pere Blai; it is a room of classical simplicity.

The main facade of the Generalitat, overlooking the Plaça de Sant Jaume,

Left, *casteller* in the Plaça de Sant Jaume. Right, in the courtyard of the Archdeacon's house.

was begun towards the end of the 16th century and is of Italian style. The marble balcony is of a later date (1860) and includes a niche containing an equestrian statue of Sant Jordi (St George) by Aleu.

Civic heart: The area that today forms the **Plaça de Sant Jaume** was inaugurated in 1823, at the same time as the streets Carrer de Ferran and Jaume I. The square, with its restored Casa de la Ciutat (town hall) on the seaward side, is considered to be the civic heart of the city, not only because it is the scene of political meetings and has witnessed great historical events, but because the Barcelonans gather here to hold public and political demonstrations. This is where President Tarradellas was given a warm and clamorous reception when he returned from exile to attend the birth of the new democracy. Here the carnival bigheads are greeted with great excitement during the city's festival.

But perhaps the key confrontation across the square these days is the oppo-

THE JEWS IN BARCELONA

Throughout Catalonia the Jewish quarters are known as *call*, from the Hebrew word *qahqal* which means "meeting". The most important *call* was that of Barcelona. Situated west of the Roman metropolis on Mons Taber (now the Gothic Quarter), it reached the peak of its importance during the Middle Ages.

In the Barcelonan *call,* which enjoyed a remarkable cultural reputation, lived many famous philosophers, writers, astronomers and intellectuals during the period between the 9th and 12th centuries. Among them were poet Ben Ruben Izahac, astronomer Abraham Xija, philosophers Abraham Ben Samuel Hasdai, Rabi Salomon Arisba and Bonet Abraham Margarit and the Biblical scholar Joseph Ben Caspí.

The thriving commercial activity of the Jewish community was the envy of the rest of Barcelona. Such was the importance of this group of merchants that for several centuries the only university institution throughout all of Catalonia was the "Universidad Judía" or "Escuela Mayor".

Such was the wealth of these people, with their special talent for finance, that reigning monarchs were not above applying to them for loans. Their knowledge and customs were so advanced that certain monarchs, such as Jaume II, nominated them as ambassadors to his Court. But what really caused feelings of great envy towards the Jews was their unfettered display of wealth and their superior lifestyle.

The fortunes of the Jews began a slow decline in 1243 when the reigning king, Jaume I, ordered not only the separation of the Jewish quarters from the rest of the city but that the Jews should wear long hooded capes with distinguishing red or yellow circles. From then on small fights began to break out, and became worse when the Castilians spread a rumour that the Jews were responsible for bringing the Black Death to Spain. Full-scale rioting broke out in several cities throughout the province in the summer of 1391, provoked mainly by a group of people from Seville who encouraged the population to storm the houses of the Jewish quarter and murder their occupants.

These riots began in Valencia on 9 July 1391 and spread to Mallorca, Barcelona, Gerona, Lléida and Perpignan. But those in Barcelona were by far the most violent; the *qahqal* was virtually destroyed and about 1,000 Jews died. The survivors were forced either to convert to Christianity or flee, despite the efforts of the national guard who defended the lives and properties of the persecuted as best they could.

King Joan I of Catalonia and Aragón eventually ordered the arrest and execution of 15 Castilians responsible for the uprising; however, the monarch's good intentions could not prevent the fact that the *call* was never rebuilt. By 1395 the flow of anti-semitism had reached such proportions that the synagogue on the street then called "Sanahuja" was converted into the church of the Trinity (today Església de Sant Juame, in the Carrer de Ferran). In 1396, the principal synagogue was rented to a pottery maker.

The *call* of Barcelona finally disappeared completely in 1401 when the synagogues were abolished and all the Jewish cemeteries were destroyed. And it was not until 1931 that the first Spanish synagogue since 1492 was established, at the corner of Balmes and Provença streets.

The Barcelona synagogue was shut down at the beginning of the Spanish Civil War, but reopened again in 1948. Initially located in the Avinguda de Roma, it was moved eventually to Carrer d'Avenir number 24, where it still stands.

Today the only noteworthy evidence of the prosperous era of Jewish dominance are certain stretches of streets in the Carrer de Banys Nous and in the Carrer del Call, the historic main street of the Jewish quarter. To a lesser extent, Carrer de Sant Domènec del Call, once the Carrer de la Sinagoga Major, preserves some interesting historic buildings.

The Carrer de Marlet, by the Arc de Sant Ramon, has the most tangible evidence of the Jewish city. Here, a memorial stone which dates back to 1314 reads: "Holy foundation of Rabi Samuel Hassardi for whom life never ends. Year 62."

sition of the two main buildings, the Casa de la Ciutat and the Generalitat, whose occupants often have different views on matters where co-operation is necessary, and both of whom are at work in the city.

The oldest part of the **Casa de la Ciutat** is the **Saló de Cent**, created by Pere Llobet in 1373; its baroque style was introduced during the 17th century. It was partly destroyed during World War II but its appearance today is essentially similar to that of 1925. Another room, the **Saló de Festes**, or Saló de Cròniques, was designed and decorated by the world-renowned muralist Josep Maria Sert. His paintings tell the tale of the Catalan *corps d'élite's* heroic feats, based on the chronicles of Muntaner and Declós.

The building's Gothic facade (finished in 1402) on the Carrer de la Ciutat is by Arnau Bargés and Francesc Marenya. The portal that we can see today is somewhat smaller than its original size as a result of 19th-century modifica-

tions; the door is crowned by the figure of an angel attributed to Jordi Johan and the richly fluted windows on the upper storey correspond to those of the Sala d'Eleccions.

Quiet corner: Down the Carrer de Hercules (opposite the facade of the Casa de la Ciutat) is the **Plaça de Sant Just**, once the site of the cemetery of the same name. The fountain at the top of the incline is dated 1367 and is in the Gothic style, albeit with certain details of later neoclassical influence, such as the balustraded enclosure which surrounds the overhanging terrace.

At the top end of the square is the **Church of Sant Just and Sant Pastor**, an ancient Royal chapel until the 15th century. The actual building, by Bernat Roca, was begun midway through the 4th century. According to legend, it is built on the site of Barcelona's first Christian temple. Pere Blay's belltower was the last phase to be completed, in 1567. The interior has several interesting features: the polychrome reliefs of

Left, the Jewish quarter of the old city. Below, preparing for wedding photos in the *barri*.

the vault's keystones and, close to the apse of the chapel dedicated to Sant Fèlix, the altarpiece and holy water fonts which are Byzantine.

The **Carrer de Lledó** leads past a number of 14th and 16th-century merchants' houses, not in particularly good repair. At number 4 is the Palau de Filliver, while the inner courtyards at numbers 3 and 5 are beautiful examples of the architecture of 400 or 500 years ago. Next door, at number 7, is a building dating to the 15th century. At number 11, there is another of later date (18th century).

At the end of the Carrer del Bisbe Cassador is Barcelona's most important medieval palace – that of the Comtessa de Palamós, headquarters of the **Acadèmia de las Bones Lletres & Galeria de Catalans Illustres** (Academy of Literature and Illustrious Catalans), with a fine gallery of paintings.

Return tour: Facing once again towards the Plaça Nova, the Carrer de Dagueria, Carrer Llibreteria and Carrer

Veguer lead to the **Museu d'Història de la Ciutat** (Museum of the City's History), located in what was once the house of Clariana-Padellás, built in the 17th century for a family of rich traders. This museum is worth visiting for its contents and architecture and to view the **Plaça del Rei** from its terrace.

This medieval square, living testimony to the nobility of the ancient city of Barcelona, was a cattle fodder market for three centuries. It was here that all the flour brought into the city in payment of taxes was collected. Today a modern sculpture by the Basque artist Chillida guards the entrance to the square, but it is the only evidence that anything has changed since the days of the markets.

At one end of the Plaça del Rei is the **Palau Real Major** with its huge archways, 13th-century triple-recess windows and 14th-century rose windows. The silhouette of the Renaissance tower of Rei Martí is an outstanding feature of the palace. Inside, the great **Saló del**

Left, the Palau del Lloctinent. **Right**, shop dummy.

144

Tinell, whose construction began with Pedro "El Cerimoniós" in 1359, was later converted to a baroque church, only to recover its original appearance after restoration works were carried out during and after the Spanish Civil War. During the 15th century this was where the Inquisition held court. Legend has it that the walls of the tribunal cannot bear a lie to be told and that, when this occurred, the ceiling stones would move, to the further terror of the unfortunate victims. These days it functions as an exhibition area.

On the north side of the Plaça del Rei is the **Palatine Chapel**, that of Santa Agueda, apparently thus named because it houses the stone on which the saint's breasts were mutilated. Construction began at the beginning of the 14th century and in its interior can be found the *Condestable* altarpiece by Jaume Huguet.

The centre depicts the Adoration of the Three Kings and, above, the Crucifixion. On both sides are scenes from the lives of Christ and the Virgin Mary.

Opposite the chapel is one of the sides of the **Palau del Lloctinent**. When the kingdoms of Catalonia and Aragón were joined with that of Castile, Carlos V created the office of Deputy (*Lugarteniente*) for the court's representative, and this palace, the official residence, was built in 1549 by Antoni Carbonell. The facade is Catalan-Gothic; however, the inner courtyard is one of the few extant examples of Renaissance architecture left in the city. Today the palace is the headquarters of the **Arxiu de la Corona d'Aragó** (Archive of the Kingdom of Aragón).

The Baixada de Santa Clara leads up behind the Cathedral's transept. To the left, down the Carrer de Paradís, is the **Centre d'Excursionistes de Catalunya** (a sort of Outward Bound headquarters) whose interior houses some of the Roman columns that belonged to the 1st/2nd-century Temple of Augustus.

The **Casas dels Canonges** (Canons' Houses) stand opposite the cathedral.

Religious icons a speciality.

This is where the canons were transferred when they abandoned the life of the cloister, hence the name. Once a typical 14th-century Catalan-Gothic building, the block was somewhat unorthodoxically restored in 1929. The house on the corner of the Carrer de Bisbe displays a series of serigraphs (silk-screen prints) carried out at the beginning of this century. Opposite, the **Porta de la Pietat** leads into the Cathedral cloister.

During the Christmas period (8–24 December), the Fira de Santa Llúcia (Festival of Santa Lucia) is held in the area surrounding the Cathedral. The narrow streets and alleyways are filled with crowds of festively dressed citizens and small handicraft gift stalls.

Museum district: A second itinerary through the Gothic Quarter of Barcelona leads through the Santa Maria district, starting at the Plaça de l'Angel and following Carrer de Princesa up to **Carrer de Montcada**.

This latter street, named after the fallen during the conquest of Mallorca, was the city's most elegant district between the 12th and the 18th centuries. The street linked the waterfront with the commercial areas, such as that of Bòria whose enormous maritime and commercial industry reached its zenith between the 13th and 16th centuries, coinciding with the growth of Mediterranean trade. In 1947 the entire area was declared a national artistic monument and, in 1957, the town hall of Barcelona began to restore the most notable palaces, converting them into museums. These days the street is lined both with original art and poster art.

At number 12 Carrer de Montcada is the **Palau de los Marqueses de Llió** whose inner courtyard is the best preserved section of the original 14th-century building. The doors and windows of the palace are from the Renaissance period and a result of the renovations carried out during the 16th century. Today the **Textile and Clothing Museum** is housed in the noble building.

Gardening in the city.

The **Picasso Museum**, which no visitor should miss, is located in the old **Palau Berenguer d'Aguilar**, presumed to be yet another of the works of Marc Safont in the 15th century. An outstanding feature is the courtyard with its surrounding first-floor gallery whose pointed archways rest on slender columns. In one of the rooms a huge 13th-century mural depicting scenes from the conquest of Mallorca was discovered. The adjoining Palau Castellet also forms part of the museum.

At number 25 on the same street is the 16th-century **Casa Cervelló-Giudice** whose facade is among the least decayed and where genuine Gothic elements blend with an essentially Renaissance ambience. The inner courtyard has suffered several drastic changes but still preserves a large *flamígero* Gothic window. The house belonged to the Cervelló family, aristocratic Catalans, and was later sold to the Giudices, a family of Italian merchants from Génova. The family aroused the anger

of the local populace and during a popular revolt the house was destroyed by fire. Today it is the Barcelona branch of the **Maeght Gallery** which organises key exhibitions at regular intervals.

The **Palau Dalmases**, at number 20, was completely renovated during the 17th century with only a few features surviving from the original 15th-century building. The magnificent courtyard stairway is unanimously considered to be a baroque masterpiece. During the 18th century it housed the "Acadèmia dels Desconfiats" (a name given to a group founded to defend the Catalan culture) and later it became the Acadèmia de las Bones Lletres; today it is the premises of the gallery "Omnium Cultural".

Amongst all this exhausting art are several venues for rest and refreshment. Experts recommend an aperitif in a tavern: sherry or cider, icy cold, accompanied by anchovies or other specialities of the house.

Markets: Carrer de Montcada leads

Street festival.

eventually into the **Born**, the site of fairs, tournaments and jousts from the 13th to the 17th centuries. Here, too, were held the glass and tin fairs, and some of the surrounding shops continue to specialise in these articles.

At the far end of the Passeig del Born is the **Mercat del Born**, a massive green building that looks like a cross between a railway station and a conservatory, built by Fontseré and Mestres between 1873 and 1876 and a fine example of wrought-iron architecture. A few years ago the building was renovated and became the venue for popular fiestas, political meetings and fairs, such as the Antique Trade Fair.

The transept entrance of the **Church of Santa Maria del Mar** closes off the other end of the Born. It may not look much from the outside – grass grows on the frontage, and you'd have to be a pigeon to get a good view of the whole – but Santa Maria del Mar is probably one of Barcelona's most beautiful Gothic churches; some call it the River-

side Cathedral. It was built between 1329 and 1384, a comparatively short time for churches of that size and that era, and a contributory factor to its great purity of style.

All the local corporations collaborated in the building of the church, and it became a symbol of the economic and political power of Catalonia in this period. The interior – best viewed from the main portal in the Plaça Santa Maria, which has glass doors expressly for that purpose – is built in what is known as a "salon" design. Three extraordinarily lofty and almost identical naves give it a feeling of great spaciousness and airiness. The octagonal columns are absolutely without ornamentation and are separated from each other by a distance of 43 ft (13 metres) – a distance that no other medieval structure was able to achieve.

The church's magnificent glass windows allow the sunlight to filter through and bathe the interior in a captivating light. The central rose window is a product of the 15th century, as is the sculpture of the *Virgin and Child* on a pedestal near a side door. The church also houses some extremely valuable treasures such as a 16th-century silver cross, an equally old washbasin and an 18th-century jewelled chalice.

The facade (never mind the grass growing out from between the stones) exhibits all the characteristics of the Catalan-Gothic style: "prevalence of horizontal lines; flat terraced roofing; wide open spaces; strong buttresses and octagonal towers ending in terraces," which is how Cirici defines the style of the Gothic period in one of the best books on Barcelona.

Try to co-ordinate your visit to Santa Maria del Mar with one of the many events held in the church, particularly a concert. If you do, the performance will remain with you for a long time both for the quality of the music itself and for the manner in which the haunting notes seem to belong to another age – perhaps to the *barri* Gòtic itself.

<u>Left</u>, the Maeght Gallery. <u>Right</u>, Santa Maria del Mar, the Riverside Cathedral.

148

MONTJUIC

Montjuïc was once known as the "Exposition Mountain", referring to the Universal Exposition of 1929; today it is called the "Olympic Mountain". During the six decades which separate the two major events in the hill's history, one attempt after another has been made to convert it into Barcelona's greatest park.

From the first attempted urbanisation in 1890, Montjuïc has been used for a variety of purposes, ranging from a stone quarry to the orchard of Sant Bertran, from a military installation to its present status as a recreation park, with 540 acres (218 hectares) of landscaped gardens that have become a cultural, commercial and panoramic focal point.

All this has happened on the flanks of a rocky hill just 570 ft (173 metres) high that rises from the estuaries of the Rivers Llobregat and Besós which was once the site of a primitive pre-Roman settlement and was later known as Mons Jovis (Mount Jupiter).

The beauty of this mountain was discovered by the Romanticists towards the end of the 18th century and in 1908 the town hall purchased the Laribal Garden with its 9th-century Arab pavilion. But the real transformation of Montjuïc began with the celebration of the Universal Exposition of 1929. The sides of the mountain were landscaped in accordance with a plan drawn up by the Frenchmen Forestier and Nicolau Maria Rubió i Tudurí. Fifteen palaces were built (most of them still standing), together with national and commercial pavilions, a stadium, a swimming pool, the Spanish Village, ornamental fountains, the Greek Theatre, several towers and the access avenue.

The Exposition itself, opened by King Alfonso XIII, was a political *tour de force* of the Primo de Rivera dictatorship and was built around the themes of industry, art and sport. Much of Montjuïc's features and buildings today still date from that era.

Front door: Montjuïc's main entrance – its most imposing aspect – is from the **Plaça d'Espanya**, which architect Ramon Reventós planned in the form of a circle, part of which was surrounded by a colonnade similar to that of the church of St Peter in Rome – even though the square and rather modern-looking towers at the beginning of the Avinguda de la Reina Maria Cristina were of Venetian inspiration. Up the Avinguda there are impressive views of the fountains and the grand flights of steps that lead to the National Palace (today an art museum).

The central fountain of the Plaça d'Espanya is the work of Josep Jujol, a disciple of Gaudí. Although slightly disfigured, the fountain and statue represents Spain's main rivers with marble and bronze sculptures by Miquel Blay. Another unmistakable feature of the surroundings is the **Las Arenas** bull

Preceding pages: rest and recreation on Montjuïc. **Left**, cable car to the top. **Right**, gateway to Montjuïc on Plaça d'Espanya.

ring, designed by August Font. Boasting a diameter of 170 ft (52 metres) and with a capacity for 15,000 spectators, it was opened on 29 June 1900 with a bullfight featuring the unusual number of eight bulls. These days, however, no bulls pass through its doors, Catalans not being great bullfight fans. The ring has fallen into disuse and now hosts visiting circus troupes and open-air concerts. It seems likely that it will be permanently converted into either an outdoor theatre or a trade fair centre.

Another singular building in the same area (on Carrer de Llansa, 2–12) is the **Pabellón** dog track which dates to the early 1950s. Although the structure was designed as a race track, throughout the 1950s the greyhounds were obliged at times to share the facilities with prize fighters and hockey players. Local journalist Jaume Cleries is enthusiastic about the track's ambience: "To enter the Pabellón dog track is like entering a time warp which leads to an anachronistic redoubt closed in upon itself, a rusty

depot of hopes and hunches and bets of 10, 20 or 40 *duros* [a *duro* is a five peseta coin] on the outcome of the races… The bets are in direct ratio to the poverty that pervades the ambience… so it is that the world of the dog tracks belongs to a bygone era which, miraculously, still gives signs of life."

On to the hill: From the twin Venetian towers the Avinguda de la Reina Maria Cristina passes between exhibition halls from the 1929 Exposition, up to the **Plaça del Univers**, an ideal place from which to see the magnificent **Fuente Mágica** or magic fountain, a spectacular interplay of moving water, coloured lights and music which comes to life on Saturday and Sunday evenings from 9 to 11 p.m. Carlos Buigas engineered this work of art and he was also responsible for the lighting along the Avinguda, where glass lamps also constantly change colour during the show.

From the fountains, access to the **Palau Nacional**, a neoclassical building topped by a central dome, is by

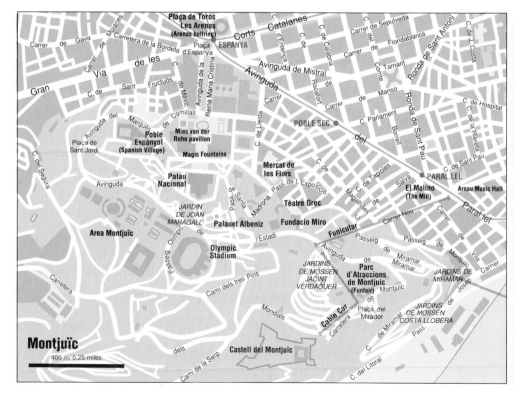

climbing twin flights of steps, from the top of which there is a magnificent view of Barcelona. The building, designed by the architects Enric Català, Pere Cendoya and Pere Domènech, was conceived as a synthesis of different Spanish architectural styles; it works from a distance, but somehow loses its appeal close up. Inside, it's a bit like a mausoleum.

Since 1934 this massive building has housed the **Museu d'Art de Catalunya,** the most important Romanesque art collection in the world. It includes murals peeled off the walls of tiny churches in the Pyrenees in the province of Lléida. The building is currently undergoing extensive alterations to accommodate the Museum of Modern Art, presently in Ciutadella Park. The author of the project, Gae Aulenti, also converted the Quai d'Orsay station in Paris into one of the French capital's most important museums, so the future looks good.

Before its time: Back down the steps, hidden behind the Olympic offices to the left of the "magic fountain", there is an authentic architectural jewel: the **Mies Van Der Rohe Pavilion**, named after its German architect and built originally for the 1929 Exposition. It is a spare, plain, and surprisingly haunting building. Peter Berhens, the architect's professor, wrote: "This building will one day be remembered as the most beautiful of those built throughout the 20th century", and the Deacon of the College of Architects of Barcelona said that it "has become an inevitable reference point in the history of art and architecture of the 20th century".

Despite all this donnish enthusiasm, there were those who couldn't comprehend the beauty of the pavilion, and it was dismantled. In 1985, architects Cristià Cirici, Ferran Ramos and Ignasi de Solà-Morales, after overcoming numerous technical difficulties, rebuilt it in its original location. The pavilion doesn't seem dated, even now.

Unreal village: Behind the pavilion the road winds up the hill to a convincing

The Palau Nacional and magic fountains.

pastiche: one suddenly finds oneself confronted by a rampart and a doorway, through which lies the **Poble Espanyol** (Spanish Village).

After passing through a reproduction of the San Vicente de Avila Portal, you find a group of buildings representing various styles of architecture from all over Spain (an explanatory plan is provided with your entrance ticket). This village was created, again for the Universal Exposition of 1929, as a stimulating architectural exercise, albeit only a temporary one. But the architects, Miquel Utrillo, Xavier Nogués and Ramon Reventós, did such a convincing job that the Village escaped the bulldozer and has since established itself as one of the city's most important recreational centres.

The basic concept of the Village (which has a distinctly commercial bias) is the preservation of architectural styles, the development of handicrafts, the promotion of cultural events and the development of an active recreational centre, with an emphasis on regional gastronomy. At present the village incorporates 34 artisan workshops, an exhibition gallery, an apprentices' school, nine art studios, nine handicraft shops and a small cinema.

The gastronomic section is built around 14 restaurants (three of which include a cabaret), a cafeteria and six bars, supplemented by four night clubs and four music bars. There are also areas dedicated to museums and other cultural themes such as the **Museum of Popular Arts and Industries** in which, each weekend, a show is presented based on the traditions and lifestyle of Catalonia. The central square is a venue for artistic and musical events.

Further uphill: Beyond, Montjuïc has more museums, gardens and sports facilities. On 25 December 1921 the 25,000-seater **La Fuxarda Stadium** was inaugurated. Six years later, architects Domènech i Montaner and Vega i March designed a new stadium with a capacity of 2½ times its predecessor.

Left and right, giants and spectators in a fiesta in the Poble Espanyol.

The new stadium was the largest in Europe and was to have hosted the "Popular Olympics" of 1936, but the outbreak of the Spanish Civil War forced the Games to be cancelled – one reason why the city is so pleased to be hosting the first Olympics of the 1990s. Most of the facilities for the 1992 Olympics are in the vicinity.

On the Carrer de Lléida side of the mountain is the **Agricultural Palace** which has been converted into a flower market. Since 1983, a municipal theatre has retained the name of Mercat de las Flors in remembrance of the original market. A short distance away is the Greek Theatre which, like almost everything in Montjuïc, was also built for the 1929 Exposition. Inspired by a model of Epidaurus, the theatre's backdrop is a solid wall of rock which was part of an old abandoned quarry. During the summer it is an important venue for outdoor events.

The accompanying gardens are part of a landscape project drawn up in 1914 which was to include the whole of the Montjuïc area. Landscape architects Forestier and Rubió i Tudurí designed various aspects of the mountain based on the ideal of a Mediterranean garden. The gardens of Miramar, Font del Gat, Plaza del Polvorí, Laribal Park and the Rosaleda are outstanding examples.

The peaceful and elegant gardens of **Joan Maragall** surround the **Palacete Albéniz**. This Palacete or "little palace" is now the official residence of visiting dignitaries to Barcelona, after having undergone extensive restoration works in 1970. It was built as a Royal Pavilion for the 1929 Exposition and during the years of self-government in Catalonia – from 1931 until the end of the Civil War – was used as a music museum.

Beyond, the **Miró Foundation** – a cool, smart building in the heat of the day – holds a wealth of that artist's work, as well as being a mecca for students of Miró's contemporaries.

Transport choice: The next corner offers a choice of routes: *up* to the castle,

In the Maragall Gardens.

over the funfair with the cable car, or *down* to city-level with the funicular.

Upward travellers who resist the attractions of the fair reach **Montjuïc Castle,** built in the 17th century during the battle between Catalonia and Felipe IV, known as the "War of the Harvesters". At the beginning of the 18th century Bourbon troops ransacked the castle; it was rebuilt between 1751 and 1779. The new fortress was in the form of a starred pentagon, with enormous moats, bastions and buttresses. For many years it was used as a military prison, and hosted many executions, including that of Lluís Companys, the last president of the Generalitat before the Franco regime; he was shot here in 1940. Today the castle is a military museum, and keen climbers spend their weekends abseiling down its walls.

Downward travellers who opt for the **funicular** are using yet another product of the 1929 exhibition, although the track was renewed in August 1984. The rail descends a distance of 2,500 ft (760 metres) with a gradient of 280 ft (85 metres) and disembarks at one of Barcelona's most typical avenues, the **Avinguda Paral.lel.**

Back on *terra firma*, the funicular exit emerges into Barcelona's can-can district, under the shadow of three enormous 235-ft (72-metre) chimneys. The three are the remains of the "Grupo Mata", an electricity-producing plant dating from the turn of the century.

Strange name: The Avinguda Paral.lel was originally the Calle Marqués del Duero, in honour of the man himself. Then, during 1794, a Frenchman called Pierre François André Méchain discovered that the Avenue's pathway coincided exactly with the navigational parallel 44°44'N. In honour of this discovery a local cook (influenced no doubt by Pierre, her astronomer husband) opened a tavern catering to travellers to and from Barcelona. She called it "El Paralelo". The popularity of the place did the rest.

The Paral.lel has been called the

Still shaking on the Paral.lel.

"Montmartre" or "El Pigalle" of Barcelona and during the first quarter of the 20th century this was not very far from the truth. This is the quarter of Barcelona that lives between innocence and sin. It is a neighbourhood full of life with slums, cabaret starlets, night clubs, theatres and dirty bars; here work lottery vendors and vendors of sex – or anything else, for that matter. Lluís Cabañas in his *Biography of the Paralelo* describes it as that "truculent, orgiastic and funfair world; the world of fleas and Apache dances, of semi-nudity and shameless flesh, of lustful songs and disdainful gestures".

The Paral.lel looks like taking on a new lease of life. It is showing a tendency to return to the "bad old days", to the music halls and a dish of rice at El Elche, a glass of wine at El Recó del Arnau – a favourite meeting place of actors and cabaret stars – or a visit to El Rosal for *tapas*. The cinemas and many of the theatres have disappeared. But **Arnau's Music Hall** remains, as does

Atracciones Apolo where, among other things, one may see the Lagarto Orchestra, which is made up entirely of robot dolls. Here also is the **Baghdad**, which offers some of the hardest porn shows to be seen in Europe, and the Apolo, Condal and Victoria theatres.

And **El Molino** (Carrer de Vila i Vila, 39) must rate as a top attraction. This is one of the most characteristic locales and spectacles in the city. Built on the site of a barracks towards the end of the 19th century, it was first known as the Petit Palais and later renamed Le Petit Moulin Rouge. Between 1916 and 1939, it became known only as the Moulin Rouge and ever since it has been simply "El Molino". In the same way as anyone who has not drunk from the waters of Canaletas (the fountain at the top of the Ramblas) cannot be regarded as a true Barcelonan, neither can anyone who hasn't stepped inside the smoky, alcohol and fume-laden premises – where silence is a forbidden commodity – say that he truly knows Barcelona.

Barcelona's bit of Paris.

THE WATERFRONT

The rediscovery of Barcelona's waterfront began in earnest in the late 1980s, prompted by the 1992 Olympics. The development is one of the most pleasing transformations in the city, and is part of a drive to put Barcelona among the Mediterranean's most important commercial and recreational ports. For years city planners have been reproached for having turned their backs to the sea. The port areas have been progressively abandoned in preference for the foothills of what is today the smart residential district of Pedralbes.

But now several miles of beaches have been renovated and provided with first-rate facilities, including centres for water sports. Along the coast Nova Icària, the site of the Olympic Village, is the work of intelligent architectural design with an eye for future as well as present needs. The development has laid bare some of the city's more run-down areas, particularly the *barri* Xinès (*barrio* Chino or red-light district), with patches that have emerged, blinking, into the sun.

Starting point: Today it is possible to stroll along the waterfront from the Columbus Monument to the Plaça Palau before entering the port and Barceloneta districts; once this was an unpleasant and hazardous journey.

Any waterside strolling begins in the **Portal de la Pau**, at the foot of the Ramblas and right beneath the feet of the rather over-enthusiastic monument to the intrepid mariner, adventurer and discoverer Christopher Columbus, here pointing in the wrong direction for the sake of simplicity. (Pointing southwest would mean pointing inland).

To the right, opposite the entrance to the Trasmediterranea ferry terminal, are the **Drassanes**. Although the buildings do not look exceptional from the outside, this is the world's greatest extant medieval shipyard. The enormous

sheds were begun in 1378, but the extensions were not completed until the 18th century. Even for the more modern additions, the original design and layout of the construction was adhered to – simply because it was considered impossible to improve upon.

The shield above the doorway on the facade is a fine example of Gothic sculpture. To the right are three 17th-century halls and to the left of the entrance are the eight huge sheds, covered by a continuous peaked roof, which gives them an elongated appearance even though they are subdivided by semicircular arches.

Access is through a doorway in one of the four towers. The interior area is such that it allowed the simultaneous construction of 30 galleons. Today it is the location of the **Maritime Museum**, which occupies a large area of the dockside. The museum's most noteworthy display is an in-house reproduction of Juan of Austria's flag-ship as well as extensive documentation on Catalan

Preceding pages: the port. **Left**, view from the Columbus Monument. **Right**, inside the Drassanes.

navigation and naval prowess during the halcyon years (1377–88) when trade and commerce were the normal business between Greece, the Byzantine world and Alexandria.

Fragments of the medieval wall can be seen opposite the main entrance. Extensions carried out during the 16th century include the Sea Tower and the Tower of Sta Madrona.

Between the Drassanes and the sea is the **Duana Nova** (customs house), which was built between the years of 1895 and 1902 from a project drawn up by Enric Sagnier and Pere García. Crowned by a massive winged sphinx and various other mythical flying beasts (Barcelona's port buildings seem to specialise in fine roof-top silhouettes), the Duana Nova is designed in the form of the letter "H", the most practical design for processing cargoes.

Another monumental building within Portal de la Pau, to the left of the Columbus Monument, is the **Junta d'Obres del Port** (Port Authority Building), designed by the engineer Julio Valdés and built in 1907. The original use to which this building was put – and it shows in the high style of its decor – was as the reception for passengers arriving in the city from the sea. The interior is in a variegated, eclectic style reminiscent of the great French casinos, rather ornamental for its now mundane function.

Modern Moll: The finest illustration of Barcelona's recent harbour improvements is the **Moll de la Fusta**, a recently finished promenade on the site of the old wooden cargo sheds that once led north from the Junta d'Obres building. This important project was designed by the architect Manuel de Solà-Morales i Rubio, who made laudable efforts to minimise the noise of an increasingly traffic-saturated highway (the Passeig de Colom) with surrounding recreational zones. The run-down buildings on the inland side of the Passeig are indicative of the state to which the harbour had declined.

Visitors find refuge from the heat of

Café on the Moll de la Fusta.

the city beneath the sunshades that surround the beach bars. **Distrito Marítimo** specialises in cocktails and croissants; **Trafic** offers succulent sandwiches and ice creams; **Cervesería del Moll** serves bar snacks, canapes and almost every brand of beer available on the international market. In **Blau Marí** the speciality is Catalan cuisine and seafood, and in **Gambrinus** the forte is obvious from the massive plastic lobster on the roof.

The Moll is the cruising place for Navy boys off the boats, keen to pick up Barcelona's girls – or even visiting Americans attracted by the uniform. Out in the port the **Moll d'Espanya** is home for the Reial Club Nàutic and the Reial Club Marítim, two of the city's most élite sports clubs.

On the other side of the Passeig de Colom is the **Plaça del Duque de Medinaceli**, a popular bus stop for coach parties and a moment of peace from the traffic. The central cast-iron fountain and statue was erected in 1849 to commemorate the naval skill of Galcerà Marquet who, in 1331, led the Catalan fleet against the Genoese.

A little further down the Passeig is the 17th-century convent of La Mercè which has been used since 1846 as the **Capitania General** (army headquarters). The facade built by Adolf Floresa on the occasion of the Universal Exposition of 1929 and the restored cloister columns and the facings of blue Valencian tiles within the convent are an architectural delight. Ask before taking pictures, however, as the military is liable to confiscate cameras.

Ample architecture: On the corner of Via Laietana is the headquarters of the **Correus** (Post Office), a rather pompous and grand building completed in 1927. The architects charged with the design of the building, Josep Goday and Jaume Torres, were obliged to bow to the wishes of the General Post Office Ministry who required "suitable" offices, hence its somewhat monumental appearance. The enormous vestibule

The Reial Club Marítim with Barceloneta behind.

COLUMBUS ON THE QUAY

Once upon a time passengers arriving in the port of Barcelona disembarked across a wooden footbridge at the Portal de la Pau and through an open doorway that led on to the Ramblas. Today only travellers who have booked a passage aboard the *golondrinas* (sightseeing boats) arrive by sea in this way.

Tradition has it that the name *golondrinas* was given to these vessels because, like the swallows they are named after, they always returned to port after each passage.

When the traveller boards the *Paloma, Lolita, Encarnación, Anita, Maria del Carmen* or *Mercedes*, he embarks on a 30-minute adventure at a speed of four knots, through the litter of ships, yachts and fishing boats that crowd the port, to the end of the breakwater. The journey starts and ends under the eye of someone whose adventure involved going considerably further: Christopher Columbus.

The monument to the tireless explorer – a rather florid and over-elaborate thing – which stands at the foot of the Ramblas was built to celebrate the Universal Exposition of 1888, nearly 400 years after the event it celebrates. Columbus himself, the Italian-born navigator for whom Spain was his adopted homeland and

sponsor, arrived in the port of Barcelona from the newly discovered Indies in the middle of April 1493 with his wife, three sons (Diego, Cristóbal and Fernando) and a small escort including seven Indians, the sole survivors of the many who had embarked from the island Columbus christened "Española" (Cuba) .

The monument, designed by Gaietà Buïgas and weighing 233 tons, was created to celebrate that first voyage. It is divided into three parts. The first part is a circular podium reached by four stairways and supporting eight wrought-iron heraldic lions, cast by Josep Carcassó. The eight bronze bas-reliefs on the pedestal illustrate the feats of Columbus. The originals, cast by Josep Llimona and Antoni Vialnova, were destroyed and replaced by the existing ones during the restoration of 1929.

The second part is the column's base in the form of an eight-sided polygon, four sides of which act as a counterbalance, each displaying four stone sculptures representing the kingdoms of Catalonia, Aragón, Castilla and León.

Backing the four sides are four more sculptured groups depicting the Montserrat monk, Fra Bernat Boil, a missionary in the Indies, representing civilisation; Captain Pere Margarit, symbol of the conquest and Spanish might in America; Jaime Ferrer de Blanes, a famous astronomer representing the link between the sciences and the discovery; and Luis de Santángel, who provided the financial means with which Columbus was able to equip his fleet. On the side walls are eight medallions, each carrying the likenesses of other personalities connected with the voyage.

The third part of the monument is the column itself, which is Corinthian in style and reaches 170 ft (51 metres). In the lower part a bronze sculpture depicts a caravel, two griffins and the four winged figures representing "Fame".

On the top of the column Europe, Asia, Africa and America are represented. Finally, upon a prince's crown and a semicircle that evokes the newest discovery on the globe, stands the bronze statue of Columbus, 25 ft (7.6 metres) high, the work of Rafael Atché. The figure's outstretched arm flung out over the sea is, of course, pointing in entirely the wrong direction for the Americas, but to have had Columbus pointing in the true direction of his destination would have been to have had him pointing inland.

The interior of the iron column has a lift which reaches a viewing platform dominating the port and city of Barcelona, open to the public for a small entrance fee from 10 a.m. until 7 p.m. The view is excellent both for the city and the port.

Berthed near the foot of the monument is a reproduction of the *Santa María*, the flagship of Columbus's first voyage to the New World, also open to the public from 10 a.m. until 7 p.m. The visit can be combined with a tour of the nearby Maritime Museum.

was decorated by the prestigious *noucentistes* (from the 1900s) artists Canyellas, Obiols, Galí and Labarta.

On the other side of the Via Laietana, behind the monument to Antonio Lopez, rises the **Llotja** (Market Exchange), a rather subdued building which houses the stock exchange and is also the headquarters of the Acadèmia de Belles Arts. The entrance is in the Carrer de Consolat de Mar.

Within the Llotja, the Saló de Contració is the work of Pere Arberí and was built between 1380 and 1392. Four hundred years later a series of extensions and modifications were carried out and the courtyard and vast hall have both been preserved in excellent condition. A remarkable feature (go up the stairway) is the timber roofing which rests on archways and not on columns, as would be usual at this period. During Barcelona's occupation by Felipe V, this building was temporarily converted into a military barracks.

The building stands out as a structure of ample proportions which is based on a balanced, neoclassical concept. On several occasions the enormous 14th-century salon has been the scene of masquerade balls.

The Llotja's main facade (not used as an entrance) overlooks the **Pla del Palau** (Palace Square) where, as the name indicates, a royal palace once stood. During the 18th and 19th centuries the square became the city's political centre – previously this honour was held by the Plaça de Sant Jaume. The reason behind the change was the loss of Catalan power, as represented by the Generalitat (which occupies Sant Jaume), under the dominant Viceroy.

Opposite the Llotja, on the other side of the Passeig d'Isabel II, is a neoclassic arcade known as the **Porxos d'en Xifré**, built by "Indiano" (a name given to anyone who left Spain to make their fortune in the Americas) Josep Xifré, between 1836 and 1840. The main facade, which appears as one whole block, is actually divided into three

Sailors onshore.

sections: a ground floor composed of shop premises and three lofty storeys of living accommodation.

The archways and pilasters are adorned with terracotta medallions by Damià Campeny depicting commercial and industrial events. Also there is a series of busts of personalities connected with the conquest of America such as Juan Sebastián Elcano, Cortés, Ercilla, Colón, Magellan and Pizarro.

One of these apartments was the first home of the Picasso family in 1895 when they arrived in Barcelona from Málaga. The artist, then 13 years old, was enrolled in the Belles Arts de la Llotja school, where his father was a professor. Five years later the local *Vanguardia* newspaper was to write: "almost a child, Picasso has organised an exhibition [in the 4 Gats café]".

On the ground floors of both this building and its neighbour, a unique, densely populated area of port bazaars has developed, with a strong oriental atmosphere. Traditionally, the goods sold – mainly watches and clocks, electrical goods and naval artefacts – were cheaper here than in other parts of the city. Sadly, the prices have gone up as they have everywhere.

Masonic doors: The arcade is also the site of one of Barcelona's most historic and exclusive restaurants, the **Set Portes,** first established in 1838 by Josep Cuyás. According to the journalist Josep Carandell, who wrote the history of the restaurant, the name Set Portes (Seven Doors) comes from the original owner's desire to suggest the Masonic Doors of Knowledge.

According to Carandell, there is plenty of evidence to support this theory: the iron columns, the tiled floor laid out to resemble a chess board, or the branches of the acacia tree painted on the blue tiles of the walls. It is also true that the cafés surrounding the Pla de Palau were popular meeting places of the Barcelona Freemasons and that Cuyás owned two more establishments in the area: the Café Aurora and the Café **Tour boat.**

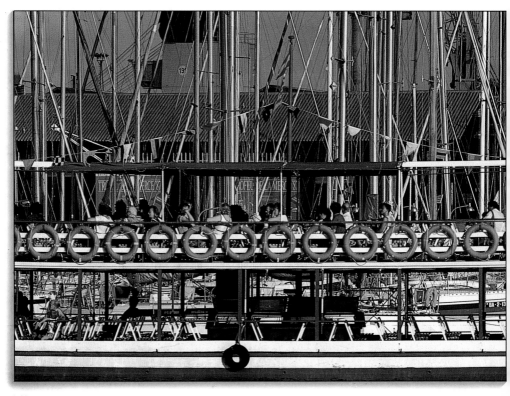

Constitución, both names with Masonic connotations. Set Portes was the very first bar to have an outdoor terrace set with tables and chairs and was among the city's leading café-theatres. Now it offers elegant, old-fashioned dining, but at a fair old price.

Opposite the restaurant on the other side of the square is the **Civil Governor's Palace**, the original "Antiga Duana" designed by Count de Roncali, who personally directed the construction works between 1790 and 1792, replacing the first "Antiga Duana" which was destroyed by fire in 1772. Count de Roncali's desire to pretend to a greater nobility than was actually the case has detracted from the architectural value of the building. But its well-preserved state, despite alterations carried out in 1902 when it was converted into the Civil Governor's headquarters, make it noteworthy.

On the port side of the square, where the historic Portal del Mar crossed the Roman walls, is the **Escola Nàutica** (Naval Academy), which once faced the palace that gave its name to the Pla de Palau. Since 1714 this has been the official residence of the Chief of Naval Operations, and it was also a court house until the fire of 1875.

Lonely genius: Today the **Font del Geni Català** (literally the fountain of the Catalan genius), built in 1855, is isolated by traffic in the middle of the square. The fountain is in memory of the Marquis de Campo Sagrado and commemorates the installation of the first fresh water conduits to the city. The "Geni Català" is in the form of a winged figure, symbolising Catalonia, with four mouths allegorising the Rivers Llobregat, Ter, Ebre and Segura which, in turn, correspond to the four provinces of Catalonia represented by four statues, one at each corner of the fountain.

The **Avinguda del Marquès de L'Argentera** was once the "Jardí del General" (General's Garden), created in 1815 only to be demolished again in 1877. In 1848, Spain's first railway line

Montaner's Castle (Zoology Museum) in Ciutadella Park.

was inaugurated here with a route that ran from Barcelona to Mataró. The railway station was little more than a shack, close to the modern-day **Estació de França** (on the right-hand side halfway down the avenue) which at the time of its opening, in September 1929, was the largest station in Europe. In 1988 the station closed for extensive redevelopment, a phase of which will convert the basements into a cultural centre.

Parklands: At the end of the avenue is one of the main gates to the **Parc de la Ciutadella**. The name (citadel) has its origins in the use to which Felipe V put this land when, after the fall of Barcelona in 1714 following the siege by Franco-Spanish troops, he ordered a fortress to be built capable of housing 8,000 soldiers, thus ensuring control of the city. To achieve this it was necessary to demolish most of the district of Ribera; 40 streets and 1,262 buildings disappeared completely.

In 1869 General Prim ceded the land to the city for conversion into a public park; the Town Hall issued a public tender for the landscaping and construction of the gardens which went to Josep Fonseré, whose plan was approved in 1873. The project also included model arcade buildings which were to surround the park; however, it was not until 1888, the year of the Universal Exposition, that the park began to be a reality, emerging in a shape later to be damaged by bombing in the Civil War.

Of the original idea, only the Governor's Palace, the chapel and the arsenal (today the site of the Catalonian Parliament, inaugurated in 1932) remain. When Francisco Franco became dictator of Spain in 1939 the Parliament House was once more relegated to its original function of military barracks and the Salón de Sesiones (which had, even earlier, been the throne room of a royal palace), became a warehouse. In 1945 the building was converted once again, this time becoming the **Museum of Modern Art**.

The French landscape architect, J.C.N. Forestier, created the oval plaza (Plaça d'Armes) facing the main facade, of which the great beauty of the "El Desconsol" statue – the work of Josep Llimona – is an important feature as it emerges from the central pond. The Plaça is well stocked with benches and chatting Catalan old-timers.

Other elements of note in the park are the grotesque modernist cascade and the artificial lake, both designed by Josep Fonseré. In fact both the cascade and the lake were intended to camouflage a huge water deposit; in the central section of the waterfall, which can be reached by two flanking, symmetrical stairways, a statue of Venus predominates, sculpted by Venanci Vallmitjana; he was assisted in his labours by a young student of architecture working with Fonseré: Antoni Gaudí.

There are further important architectural buildings, such as the very noticeable pseudo-castle **Castell dels Tres Dragons** (Castle of the Three Dragons), built by Lluís Domènech i Montaner as

Who's walking who?

a café-restaurant for the 1888 Exposition; however, the works were not finished in time and the café never opened. Today it is the **Zoological Museum** but it was one of the first modernist projects and home for years to the architect. Close by is the **Hivernacle**, built of iron and glass by Josep Amargós; it has been restored to become a cultural centre. The same is true of the **Umbracle** next door, a wood-and-brick structure designed by Josep Fonseré.

Bohemian quarter: The Passeig Picasso separates the Ciutadella Park from the old quarter of Ribera, and features the **Porxos d'en Fonseré**, the arcade that was designed by Fonseré as part of the park environs; Antoni Tàpies' statue *Homenatge a Picasso*, a bizarre and not particularly attractive work on the *paseo*, is worth a moment's contemplation; the old gents playing *petanca* (a game normally associated with France) are worth a few more.

The **Ribera** district, behind the massive Mercat del Born, which was opened as Barcelona's central market place in 1876 but is now a social and cultural centre, has enjoyed a renewed lease of life thanks to the proliferation of bars, restaurants, night clubs and art galleries. The district, with its spattering of graffiti, crazy paving and iron features, is attractive for its bohemian appeal. It is, according to designers Juli Capella and Quim Riera, "the ugliest and the most beautiful place in Barcelona".

There is no doubting the historic value of the area and the fact that this is one of the city's oldest suburbs, or its magnetic appeal to artists such as Gargallo, Nonell and Picasso, all of whom, successively, set up their studios on the top floor of Carrer de Comerç number 28. This was Picasso's last studio in Barcelona. On the corner of the same street, where it joins the Carrer Marques de l'Argentera, Spain's only **Mineral and Precious Stone Museum** contains the world's third most important collection of gems.

From under the shadow of the church

Snowflake poses prettily.

of Santa Maria del Mar (one of the finest interiors in Catalonia), narrow streets lead back to the Carrer Consolat de Mar.

The street has existed since the 14th century, and its name alludes to the book, also titled *Consolat de Mar*, the first-ever treatise on maritime laws. Two special features of the street are the groups of arches, the **Voltes dels Encants** and the **Voltes dels Pintors,** now rickety constructions which existed even before the port itself was built. Despite the fact that the buildings appear to be from the 18th century, it is probable that the prismatic stone columns of the Voltes dels Pintors date back to the 1400s.

Fishermen's wharves: A dusty walk from the Pla de Palau leads out on to the lengthy Passeig Nacional, in the district known as **Barceloneta**, or small Barcelona. On the waterfront to the right lies the Magatzem General de Comerç (1878), a group of brick warehouses built by Elías Rogent and a fine example of maritime architecture.

Further along are the crumbling *tinglados* (sheds) that have provoked a certain amount of controversy between those who wish to preserve them as cultural, recreational or commercial centres, and those who advocate their total disappearance in order to provide an uninterrupted view of the sea.

The northern side of the Passeig Nacional is lined with seafood restaurants offering plate upon plate of delicious scampi, mussels and crayfish. These establishments change so fast that it is hard to make any recommendations of where to eat; follow the crowds and your nose, and don't expect to eat particularly cheaply.

Behind are the arrow-straight roads of La Barceloneta, misleadingly called the fishermen's quarter. The rigidity of the street plan gives a clue to the origin of the district, which does not stem from the needs of a port; Barceloneta was born of a political, military decision. It was to this area that the inhabitants of La Ribera were reallocated when their

Shanty restaurant in Barceloneta.

homes were demolished to give way to the building of a fortress after the siege and conquest of Barcelona by Felipe V.

The military engineer/architect Juan Martín Cermeño was the author of the project; his plans were based on the construction of 15 short, identical, streets crossed at a perpendicular angle by other, longer streets, thus giving rise to a series of narrow, rectangular blocks all facing in the same direction (towards Ciutadella), facilitating the easy military control of the population. During the second half of the 19th century the lack of living accommodation in the city and pressure from the proprietors resulted in the buildings being raised to three storeys.

The first inhabitants of Barceloneta were therefore refugees under careful military control, but from this inauspicious beginning, the suburb has gradually emerged as one of the most appealing areas of the city as well as an area of important urban experiment.

At the end of the Passeig Nacional is a roundabout with the **Institut d'Investigacions Pesqueras** (Fisheries Research Institute) on the seaward side, with an aquarium of local specimens (currently closed). Beside the Institute are the *Banys* (baths), one of the first to combine swimming pools and sea bathing.

The road that leads off the other side of the roundabout leads to the **Moll de Pescadors** – the "fishermen's wharf", unfortunately closed to tourists. On the wharf's tip is the clock tower or Torre del Rellotge. An historical symbol of the port, the clock tower's original role was that of a lighthouse. Close by is the Market Exchange (first opened in 1924) where auctions are held twice a day on weekdays: one at six o'clock in the morning to auction the blue fish caught during the previous night, and the other at five o'clock in the afternoon selling the same day's trawler catches.

Beyond the roundabout the Passeig Nacional passes the base of the **Torre de Sant Sebastià** whose 257-ft (78.4-

The beach, Barceloneta.

metre) height marks the end, or the beginning, of the cable car's route which completes its 3,876-ft (1,292-metre) journey at Miramar, on Montjuïc. The tower does not look in the best repair and it is not immediately obvious from ground level that it is possible to take the lift to the cable-car platform. If you can, do, because the cable-car offers spectacular aerial views over the city and the port, and the view from the tower spreads out the fishermen's wharf and Barceloneta at your feet.

The "Aeri del Port" as the cable car is known, is the result of an idea conceived in 1926 by Carles Buigas. It began operating four years later. The 390-ft (119-metre) Torre de Jaume I, on the ferry port, is a popular half-way stop-over.

On the beach: The very nature of the maritime district of Barceloneta has generated a tradition of good seafood. Proof of this lies with the restaurants, known as *chiringuitos,* that have sprung

up on the beach side of the suburb (to the left off the roundabout). It has been said that nothing is comparable to the bustling street that runs parallel to the **beach of Sant Miguel**, where the restaurateurs cry their wares to passers-by in the hope of enticing them inside their establishments.

"There is," wrote journalist Llorenç Torrado, "[an] undeniable charm in the *chiringuitos* lining the beach like dominoes at the sea's edge, and in the 10 bars every few metres and the crowds on seemingly perpetual vacation strolling to and fro.

"There is an air similar to that of a health spa, or of an overpopulated, promiscuous one-way street, or even a low-class district, scene of Sunday outings. Theoretically, a place such as this, packed with eating and drinking houses, full of people, should produce a high proportion of special dishes, good entertainment for moments of relaxation and an air of festivity. But, in reality, this is not the case.

"In La Barceloneta one eats with a monotonous uniformity, as if only one restaurant owner has planned every menu, and only one chef stirred every pot. Finally, one reaches the conclusion that one goes, and will continue to go, to La Barceloneta for the ambience more than for the food. But, specially, because here one may eat with one's fingers, top trouser button undone – familiarities that are not permitted in the hallowed halls of the top-class establishments; to share one's space with other patrons, without having to take heed of the niceties that are expected in those places where one eats out of social duty."

Once you've tried this experience – as everyone does – take your digestive walk along the newly built **Passeig Marítim**, yet another example of the regeneration of Barcelona's maritime facade that links this old, venerable, quarter with the city's most modern, progressive project: **Nova Icària**, site of the 1992 Olympic Village.

Left, beach lunch, Barceloneta. **Right**, cable-car tower on the ferry terminal.

THE EIXAMPLE, MODERNIST QUARTER

It is safe to say that virtually every city can be identified by one particular monument. In Paris it is the Eiffel Tower, in New York the Statue of Liberty; Rome wouldn't be the same without the Coliseum, or London without Big Ben.

Barcelona's most identifiable monument has to be Antoni Gaudí's modernist skyscraper, the Sagrada Família, the city's as yet unfinished cathedral. But all around the Sagrada is another important distinctive entity which, although it is less showy, is at least as important to the city as Gaudí's creation. This entity is the grid-like expansion outside the old walled city which is known as the **Eixample**, loved and hated by locals and visitors alike.

At the end of the 19th century, while the rest of Spain was fighting against a growing decadence brought about by the loss of the American colonies, Barcelona's flourishing industrial middle class aspired to create a new city from the foundations of one that had become too small. They wanted to break out of the medieval walls which until then had imprisoned the city, so they created the Eixample. Within its confines they sponsored the creation of some of the most ludicrous and imaginative buildings in the world – examples of modernist architecture that today symbolise the city.

Expansion areas: The original design of the Eixample was the work of a liberal-minded civil engineer who was permanently preoccupied with redesigning the 19th-century city, Ildefons Cerdà i Sunyer. The actual work began in 1859 when a Royal Decree finally gave the green light to Cerdà's project. The Eixample (Catalan for "expansion") was to cover the areas between the old city centre and the equally historic municipalities of Sants, Sarrià, Sant Gervasi de Cassoles and Gracia.

The plan's principal characteristic, and one which broke completely with the tradition of urban planning in Spain, was its absolute adherence to geometric forms. The concept was of a grid of streets running parallel to the seafront, crossed perpendicularly by others running southeast to northwest, rather in the style of an American city.

The concept has not been well received. Carles Soldevila writes in *Barcelona*: "We are not going to try and hide the fact that we Barcelonans tend to speak very badly of our Eixample. We deride it (above all) as being monotonous. The rigorous parallel streets, the unvarying width of 20 metres, the inexorably perpendicular crossroads, the total absence of squares and gardens, the impossibility of separating an outstanding building and providing it with four facades…"

Cerdà is not responsible for this state of affairs, since what he designed was not merely what we know today as the Eixample. He planned a garden city in

Preceding pages: office buildings on the Diagonal. **Left,** at Gaudí's La Pedrera. **Right,** arresting shop window.

which only two of the four sides of each block would be built on. The other sides, together with the central open space, were to have been attractive, shady squares and the *chaflanes* (angled street corners) were meant to be open spaces, not packed with double-parked vehicles as they are today.

Cerdà's plan was not adopted in its entirety for various reasons. He came from a liberal background, and was at the time strongly influenced by the doctrines of so-called "Utopian socialism" – which did not necessarily appeal to the more conservative elements in the city, who had their own vested interests. His original concept immediately caused a flurry of controversy. Those places where the project did, in fact, become a reality are the sites of some genuine architectural marvels.

Dividing line: The Eixample is broken down principally into two halves, La Dreta (right) de L'Eixample and L'Esquerra (left) de L'Eixample, which are defined as the areas on both sides of

Carrer de Balmes as one looks inland towards Tibidabo. Within the two halves are well-defined neighbourhoods such as those of the Sagrada Família and Fort Pius (on the right) and Sant Antoni and a *barri* near the old municipal slaughterhouse called L'Escorxador (on the left). Most of Barcelona's greatest landmarks can be found in the Dreta.

Since the 1960s, the right-hand sector of the Eixample, **La Dreta**, has undergone a profound transformation. With the earlier inhabitants moving to other districts such as Bonanova, Pedralbes and the upper reaches of Carrer de Balmes and Carrer de Muntaner, the larger houses have been converted into offices and multi-family dwellings. Old-time residents of the district have had to mix with newcomers such as bank employees, hotel staff, office personnel and shop assistants.

Starting point: At the point where the Carrer d'Ali Bei leaves the Ronda de Sant Pere is a monument to **Rafael de**

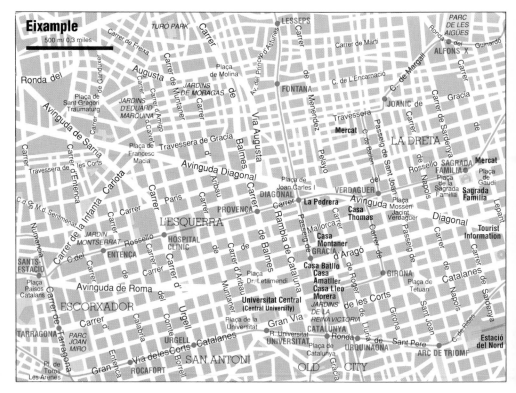

Casanova, a politician who was injured in this place on 11 September 1714, during the siege in which the city was sacked and its special privileges abolished by Felipe V. The defeat is remembered every year in the Diada de Catalunya – the Catalan national day. The statue and monument are by Rossend Nobas and Josep Llimona respectively.

Directly opposite – and a taste of what is to come – is a modernist building by Telm Fernández i Janot, with another in the same style on the corner of Carrer de Girona, the work of the architect Enric Sagnier. A group of pre-modernist "eclectic" buildings is further up the street. Also close by, at Carrer d'Ausias Marc, 42–46 bis, is still another block in the modernist style, this one noted for its asymmetric tribunals (enclosed balconies or window boxes) and iron railings.

In front are two examples of Sagnier's mix of the eclectic and medieval in houses built for Tomàs Roger and Antoni Ricard. Toward the Plaça Urquinaona is the **Farmàcia Izard**, which dates to 1903, and **Casa Puget**, with exceptional wrought-iron balconies.

Stiff-neck streets: Admirers of modernism will also get a stiff neck from walking up Carrer de Casp. The eclectic facade of number 46 – **Casa Salvado** – shows the clear influence of the Renaissance on architect Juli Batllevell i Arus. A good stopping place here is the patisserie **Tívoli** – "good pastries each morning" – or the **Bracafé**, which is considered to be among the best in Barcelona. Its terrace is a good vantage point from which to view the local population in all its variety: journalists from the nearby radio stations of Cadena SER, Radio Nacional and Radio Miramar, all of which are within a few hundred feet of your coffee cup.

A little further along Carrer de Casp, at number 48, is the first of the works by Antoni Gaudí encountered in the Eixample. **Casa Calvet** was built at the beginning of the 20th century and clearly reflects the fashion for borrowing from other periods of architecture.

The Rambla de Catalunya.

One street further into the Eixample, along the La Gran Via de les Corts Catalanes towards the **Plaça Tetuán**, is another monument by Josep Llimona, dedicated to Doctor Robert, who was both a politician and a doctor of medicine. The bronze represents the *pàtria* with a great Catalan flag, and the monument's base has so much in common with La Pedrera (one of Gaudí's best-known works) that experts speculate that the master must have had a hand in its design.

Further down the Gran Via is Barcelona's second *plaça de braus* (bull-ring), the **Monumental**, which is situated at the intersection of the Gran Via and the Passeig de Carles I. It was built just after Les Arenas, the bull-ring in Plaça d'Espanya, and the two show considerable similarities – although this one has more strongly Islamic influences in its architecture.

From the Plaça de Tetuán, the Passeig de Sant Joan leads back down to the Arc del Triomf, a rather overlooked imitation of the arch of the same name in Paris. To the northeast is the **Estació del Nord**, renovated for the Olympics as a community area and a sports complex. Originally built in 1861 for the Lléida railway line, the neoclassical facade of this depot is actually its side. It was enlarged in 1910 with the addition of an enormous iron roof and a principal entrance, by Demetri Ribes. The building gives character to a neighbourhood situated between the old train tracks and the Gran Via, once the site of the old Roman thoroughfare out of the city.

Kerb crawling: The city block bordered by the streets Consell de Cent, Pau Clarís, Diputació and Roger de Llúria was built in 1866 with a small walking street in the middle. The architecture along this **Passatge de Permanyer**, which was built towards the end of the 19th century, has echoes of British influence and is a worthwhile detour. At the corner of Carrer Roger de Llúria and Consell de Cent is the first of the thousands of angled corner junctions

The Manzana de la Discòrdia with buildings by Cadafalch (left) and Gaudí (right).

(*chaflanes*) to be constructed in the Eixample. Originally planned to reduce walking distances and increase space and light, the *chaflanes* have reduced roadside kerbs and provided something of a parking problem.

Southwesterly from this point along **Carrer Consell de Cent** is the traditional location for the most important art galleries in the city (although the Carrer de Montcada area is challenging that title). Here also is **El Golfiño,** a pleasant bar with a selection of excellent *tapas*, or an equally excellent although expensive restaurant, the **Orotava**, which specialises in seasonal game. **El Gran Colmado** (number 318) is a shop in New York style for international grocery.

At 299 Carrer d'Aragó is the *claustre* (cloister) and the **Church of the Conception**, one of the very few really old buildings in the Eixample, dating back to the 14th and 15th centuries. Nearby (at number 317) is a **market** of the same name, with a fine array of fresh produce and groceries. Towards the Passeig de Gràcia is a well-known eating place, the **Madrid-Barcelona**. Although it seems somewhat run down, it is well known for good food at a good price.

Elegant avenue: The monotonous uniformity of the Eixample has always been a sore point amongst the Barcelonans. Yet they complain, maybe with tongue in cheek, that even this very dullness is inconsistent, broken by the beauty, diversity and enchantment of the **Passeig de Gràcia**.

This wide, tree-lined avenue was designed to link the old city and the outlying neighbourhood of Gràcia even before the ancient walls of the city were torn down. The broad promenade is still in a state of excellent preservation due to the prosperity of the period in which it was built, which ensured the use of prime quality materials only in its construction. In his plan Cerdà increased its width to 180 ft (60 metres), which gives it an air of exclusivity among the more uniform streets of the rest of the Eixample. The eye-catching iron street lamps were designed by Pere Falqués.

The most famous block on this street, between the streets Consell de Cent and d'Aragó, is popularly called the **Manzana de la Discòrdia** (the Block of Discord). The name stems from the close juxtaposition of four buildings, each of which is in a conflicting style, although they are all categorised as modernist. **Casa Lleó Morera**, by Lluís Domènech i Montaner and decorated with the sculptures of Eusebi Arnau, is the first. On the first floor it houses the headquarters of the town hall's tourist office. Next to it is the less spectacular **Casa Mulleras**, by Sagnier; slightly further along stands the outstanding **Casa Amatller** by Josep Puig i Cadafalch, next door to which is Gaudí's **Casa Batlló,** remodelled in 1906.

In the same block, but around the corner on Carrer d'Aragó, sits yet another building by Domènech i Montaner, **Casa Montaner i Simón**. Originally built for the editorial house of

Gràcia street lamps.

Montaner i Simón, it has become, in its new designation as the **Fundació Tàpies**, a much discussed structure due to the "sculpture" called *Núvol I Cadira* (cloud and chair) which Tàpies designed for the roof. Observers' opinions vary from "Genius!" to "If I had done that, they would have put me in jail".

This architectural richness continues at number 74 with **Casa Coma**, another modernist building by Enric Sagnier, while at the next corner is **Casa Enric Batlló**, a building displaying pre-modernist Gothic elements by Josep Vilaseca. Very close by, on Carrer de Mallorca (253–257), is the **Casa Angel Batlló**, built in the same prolific years (1893–96) by the same architect.

World favourite: Perhaps the best-known building on the Passeig de Gràcia is Antoni Gaudí's **Casa Milà,** more popularly known as **La Pedrera** (the quarry), at number 92 on the corner of Carrer de Provença. At the time of its construction in 1910 it was the subject of passionate debate between enthusi-asts and denigrators. For many years it was left to fall apart but UNESCO recently declared it a monument of world interest and it is now cared for by a Catalan bank.

The best area for refreshment after visiting the Pedrera is the nearby Rambla de Catalunya, a quieter extension of the more famous Ramblas. Here the pedestrian area is lined with *granjes, xocolateries* and ice-cream shops, such as the **Jijonenca**, **El Turia** and maybe the city's best venue for breakfasts and sandwiches, the **Confiteria Mauri**.

Back on the other side of Gràcia is the **Palau Montaner**, built in 1893 at the corner of Carrer Roger de Llúria and Carrer de Mallorca. Decorated with multi-coloured ceramic murals and a bas-relief facade, it was the work of one of the principal architects of the time, Domènech i Montaner.

The palace, owned by the Marquis de Júlia, was one of the great buildings of the new architectural style. The same architect then built **Casa Tomàs**, also

In the neighbourhood of the Sagrada Família.

on Carrer de Mallorca (number 293).

Not far away, Josep Puig i Cadafalch's **Casa Quadras** was unveiled in 1897 on the Avinguda Diagonal (number 373). The house, erected for the Barón de Quadras, has since been acquired by the Town Hall and converted into the Conservatory of Music. The following year, Puig completed the **Casa de les Punxes**, a little further up the road.

Both of these, together with the **Casa Serra** on the last block of the Rambla de Catalunya, show definite influences of Nordic neo-Gothic. But, while Casa de les Punxes has also recently been declared of world interest by UNESCO, Casa Serra, which was originally a monastery, needed a massive campaign in the press and among local residents and architects in order to save it from being torn down.

The **Diagonal** (so called because it runs perversely across the rigid grid of the Eixample) is the city's main business thoroughfare, lined with buildings in the latest architectural style and office blocks for much of its length.

Temple quarter: The Carrer de Mallorca leads into the heart of the *barri* of the **Sagrada Família**, the neighbourhood at the northern extreme of the Eixample. The area, as its name suggests, has Gaudí's unfinished temple at its centre, but this is not the only monument of interest. At the end of the Avinguda de Gaudí is the **Hospital de Sant Pau**. The complex, made up of over 20 buildings, is another of the many buildings designed by the modernist architect Lluís Domènech i Montaner between 1902 and 1912.

If you can drag yourself away from the staggering architecture of the Sagrada Família itself, which still has an estimated 50 years to go before completion, and spend half an hour walking through the public areas of the hospital, you are in for a treat which serves as a reminder that, although Gaudí is the best known of the modernists, there were others just as creative as he was.

Not all eyes are on the architecture.

On the left: Although the Dreta (right side) of the Eixample attracts most of the visitor's attention, the **L'Esquerra** (the left side) is not unimportant. It was built later, and houses a mixture of residents comprising the newly emerging lower middle classes and those from small artisan industries.

In the two neighbourhoods of L'Escorxador and Sant Antoni, the dominant architectural structures were built by *mestros d'obres* (master builders). For example, there is a modernist building by Jeroni Granell at number 260, Carrer de Corsega, although it is not considered one of his best works. Nearby, at number 271, there is another house with its vestibule decorated in the modernist style. The building on the corner with Carrer d'Enric Granados is the work of Ruíz i Casamitjana. The outstanding feature of this house, which dates to 1910, are the railings on the upper balconies.

The Carrer d'Aribau is known for several restaurants which have made a

name for themselves in the past few years. At the corner where Aribau and Carrer d'Aragó meet, the **Gargantua I Pantagruel** offers the best in cooking in the style of Lléida. Not far away, at number 73, the **Chicoa** serves one of the best cod dishes in the city as well as *calots* (roasted spring onions) when they are in season. Also on Aribau, between Aragó and València streets, the **Sibarit** serves its speciality of *lubina al hinojo*, a fisherman's dish from the Costa Brava. Here also is the **Yamadori,** one of the first Japanese restaurants to be opened in Barcelona and still arguably the best.

The **Sant Antoni** region, delineated by the Gran Via de les Corts Catalanes, the Avinguda del Paral.lel, the Ronda de Sant Pau and the Ronda de Sant Antoni, has in its centre a highly recommended artery for a stroll – the Avinguda de Mistral. In the spring and summer there are many restaurants and café-terraces worth sampling here.

Nearby Carrer de Tamarit leads to the **Mercat de Sant Antoni**, a bigger and more diverse market than its more famous colleague on the Ramblas. Within its eye-catching columns and beams, among other things, are inexpensive clothes, plus paintings, comics, pirated computer programs and, on Sundays, a market for collectors of old books. On the northwest corner of the market is a bar which specialises in *tapas* of mussels, crayfish and clams.

Situated at the southwest corner of the Eixample is the neighbourhood which takes its name from the ancient slaughterhouse which once stood here, the **Escorxador**. This region, bordered by Hostafrancs to the south, is a relatively recent development. Perhaps the most interesting landmark in the neighbourhood is that of the **Parc de L'Escorxador** itself. The park (sometimes known as the **Parc de Joan Miró**, because of the artist's sculpture) is on the site of the municipal slaughterhouse. It was built 100 years after the Plan Cerdà which had provided for it.

Left, modern imitates modernism. Right, Eixample shopping.

186

GREEN OR CONCRETE URBAN SPACES

The *avant-garde* thinking which transformed Barcelona's architecture and design has also permeated what the town planners call the *espais urbans* (urban spaces), both green and concrete. Architects have been commissioned to create new spaces and upgrade existing ones. This is not to say, of course, that "traditional" parks have been transformed into space-age cement factories; they have been left essentially untouched.

Barcelona's public parks date from as far back as 1869 (in the case of the Parc de la Ciutadella) up to the most recent transformations of city centre plazas and demolished buildings in the late 1980s. Some are little more than a rearrangement of the benches and flowerpots at the convergence of two or three streets and consequently of far more benefit to the locals than to visitors.

Preceding pages: in the Maragall Gardens. **Left**, the industrial park.

Others, such as the Parc del Clot, which today occupies the ruins of a Renfe (Spain's national railway) shunting shed and roundhouse, are large, complex and interesting for everyone.

The **Parc del Clot** (Metro line I to Clot station) is an excellent example of the latest thinking in urban planning by the architects Dani Freixes and Vicenç Miranda. The word *clot* means "hole" in Catalan, and, like the modern urban parks, this one was partially created within a large depression in the ground. In this case, the basin is a natural amphitheatre housing a sizeable playing field which even on the gloomiest winter day sees its fair share of children playing football. A long bridged walkway passing overhead links the sunken portion of the park with a grass park of equal size sporting a long geometric pergola, trellises and sculptures by Bryant Hunt.

But the one element which makes this park worth a visit is the remains of the old train roundhouse; its walls and arched windows enclose and criss-cross the site, creating an area where people can walk or play among the remnants of the not-too-distant past.

Slaughter quarter: Originally, the **Parc de Joan Miró** was the site of a slaughterhouse and consequently is sometimes nicknamed the Parc de l'Escorxador. The cement square, which covers an entire city block, has undeservedly become something of a mecca for tourists because of the enormous phallic sculpture by the genial Catalan artist Joan Miró called *Dona i Ocell* (woman with bird) which towers 70 ft (22 metres) above the concrete.

But, apart from the sculpture and its surrounding pool, the park shows none of the imagination which has pushed Barcelona into the forefront of Europe's urban renewal schemes and the visitor is better off buying a postcard and skipping the trip. If you insist, Metro line III, station Tarragona, or line I, station Plaça d'Espanya, or a variety of bus routes will get you there.

Other spaces which are catalogued as

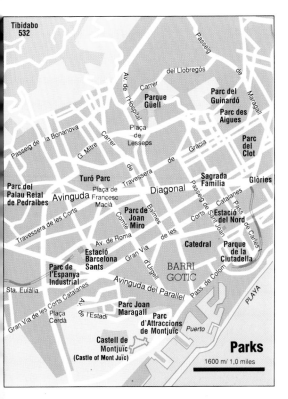

Tibidabo 532

del Llobregós

Passeig de la Bonanova

Av. de l'Hospital

Carrer

Parque Güell

Parc del Guinardó

Parc des Aigues

Plaça de Lesseps

G. Mitre

Carrer

Gracia

Parc del Clot

Turó Parc

Travessera

Sagrada Familia

Glòries

Parc del Palau Reial de Pedralbes

Plaça de Francesc Macià

Diagonal

Avinguda

Balmes

Comte d'Urgell

Parc de Joan Miró

Corts Catalanes

Estació del Nord

Travessera de les Corts

Av. de Roma

de les

Catedral

Parc de la Ciutadella

Estació Barcelona Sants

Gran Via

BARRI GOTIC

Sta. Eulàlia

Parc de l'Espanya Industrial

Avinguda del Paral·lel

Pass. de Colom

PLAYA

Gran Via de les Corts Catalanes

Plaça Cerdà

l'Estadi

Parc Joan Maragall

Parc d'Attraccions de Montjuïc

Puerto

Castell de Montjuïc
(Castle of Mont Juïc)

Parks

1600 m/ 1,0 miles

parks, such as La Plaça de la Palmera, El Parc de la Creueta del Coll, El Fossar de la Pedrera, Moll de la Fusta and the Jardins d'Emili Vendrell, are notable for the combination of the natural with the man-made.

A good example of this innovation is the park of the **Estació Nord** (Metro line I, Arc de Triomf station). The park is being built around the abandoned train station, a part of which houses the Eixample headquarters of the Guardia Urbana police. In keeping with the policy of preserving existing structures, the station's covered platform area is to be converted into a multi-sport centre and the abandoned shunting yards will become the site of an auditorium and a national theatre. It is visually enlivened by Beverly Pepper's enormous multi-toned blue-and-white ceramic sculpture (either a wave or a hill, according to your point of view) and an avenue-wide walking path.

Meeting point: At the junction created by the convergence of three of the city's principal arteries, Gran Via de les Cortes Catalanes, the Meridiana and the Diagonal, a single pole tower spoked with suspension cables supports a series of elevated curving ramps which unite three sections of the small but interesting park called the **Glòries** (Metro line I to the station of the same name). From various vantage points on the overhead walkways can be seen alternating areas of grass, flower beds, a man-made river and a children's playground. The park is also an interesting indication of where Barcelona, and perhaps Europe, is going in terms of urban leisure spaces.

The most remarkable modern urban space has to be the **Parc de l'Espanya Industrial**, situated on the west side of the Sants railway station. It can be reached on Metro line V, station Roma-Renfe-Sants, or by bus. The park, built between 1982 and 1985 by architects Luis Peña Ganchegui and Francesc Rius i Camps on a parcel of land which once supported a textile factory, has both a romantic and an industrial face.

Beverly Pepper's sculpture in the Estació Nord.

192

The lower and more romantic part comprises a large lake, usually complete with teenagers splashing one another from rented rowing boats, and an expansive lawn area with paths, willow trees and sculptures by such notable Catalan artists as Fuxa, Casanovas, Alsina, Anthony Caro and Palazuelo.

The upper esplanade is the industrial area and by far the most controversial section. It is dominated by 10 towers, each with megaphone-shaped spotlights and lookout platforms which would not be even slightly out of place in a German Stalag of World War II. Happily, Andrés Nagel's immense play-sculpture titled *Drac de Sant Jordi* and a series of water spouts and cascades help to contradict the concentration camp atmosphere of the upper levels. It is a park that few love at first sight, but it has a habit of growing on people.

Green zones: The concrete parks aside, a second group of *espais urbans*, including Parc Pegàs, Turó Parc, Aigües, Parc de Cervantes-Roserar and

Guinardó, demonstrates the broad spectrum of styles and ideas which make up the green zones of the city.

An interesting walk for adults and an adventure for children is **Parc Pegàs**, which can be reached on Metro line I, station Fabri i Puig. The park is principally made up of a long serpentine lagoon with rowing boats for rent. A path snakes along the edge of the waterway, crossing it from time to time on a variety of bridges, climbing uphill to lookout areas and descending again to the water level. Stands of heavy tree growth and flower gardens enclose the entire area and turn it into a labyrinth.

Turó Parc, which is also known as Parc del Poeta Eduard Marquina, is a short walk from Plaça de Francesc Macià, and any of the buses which run westward along the Diagonal stop at the roundabout. The park, a project of Rubió i Tudurí, has two distinct areas. One is made up of lawn, hedges and flower beds laid out in a classic geometric pattern. The other contains child-

The Parc del Clot.

ren's playgrounds, a small lake with lilies and an open-air theatre with the polyglot title Teatret del Turó Parc.

The entrance to the park is divided by a monument dedicated to Catalan cellist Pau (Pablo) Casals. The sculpture, by Valls, is aptly composed of a host of angels playing trumpets and violins and a poem by Catalan poet Salvador Espriu. Other sculptures by Clarà, Villadomat, Eloïsa Cerdan and Borrell i Nicolau dot the interior of the park.

The **Parc des Aigües** or water park is named after the massive reservoir upon which it sits. On top of the underground cistern, part of Barcelona's water distribution system, is a small well-trimmed classical garden. Because it is owned by the city water company, this garden is closed to the public, though parts of it may be seen through the fence. The surrounding public park, whose entrance lies very close to the Alfons X station on Metro line IV, is an ideal place for a picnic or just to watch the local *petanca* (boules) matches.

The **Parc de Cervantes-Roserar** is, as its name suggests, a rose garden. Located near the Zona Universitaria station (on Metro line III), the 20-acre (8-hectare) park is a little boring for those who have no particular penchant for roses. But, with 11,000 rose bushes comprising 245 different varieties, the park is an essential visit for devotees of the plant.

One of the last of the Barcelona parks which refuses to fall easily into any category is **Guinardó** (Metro line IV to Guinardó). Although the greatest part of this park is hill-side forest, the most southerly tip holds the most interest. This is a *torrent ajardinat*, or "cultivated water course". In Guinardó, a section of a shallow gorge has been made into a garden by the French gardener with the appropriate name, Jean Forestier. The water, when there is any, spills from a small reservoir and passes through a series of tiny dykes and canals between trimmed shrubs and over a series of terraces and flower beds.

Parc Pedralbes.

Fort park: The great-grandfather of all green spaces is **El Parc de la Ciutadella** (citadel). Ciutadella is today the site of Barcelona's zoo, various museums and the city's parliament, and has a well-documented history dating back more than 250 years. At one time a fortress stood on this site. In order to accommodate it a whole neighbourhood was razed to the ground and the evicted population moved to the newly created Barceloneta district by the port.

Beginning in 1869, a Catalan botanist and gardener named Oliva was put in charge of the project to transform the whole area into a park, but it wasn't ready until the opening of the 1888 Universal Exposition. The remains of its pre-park military past are still present in the names of its buildings, such as the **Arsenal de la Ciutadella** (Parliament) and the ancient **Plaça de les Armes** which is now the central ornamental garden.

Besides the Arsenal, which houses the **Museu d'Art Modern de Cata-** lunya and the **Parliament**, notable landmarks are the **Museu de Zoologia** in the pseudo-castle café-restaurant of modernist architect Lluís Domènech i Montaner, the **Museu de Geologia,** the **Hivernacle**, a tropical greenhouse, and a similar structure for shade-loving plants called the **Umbracle**. The paths which zig-zag through the park and around the lake and the cascade are decorated with statues of various Catalan writers, artists and politicians.

The park is permanently changing as the neighbouring zoo bites into it in an attempt to simulate the natural habitats of the species it houses; some observers believe that the zoo is disfiguring the park, but it is a popular disfigurement – particularly its superstar "Snowflake" (*Copo de Nieve*), an albino gorilla. Zoo and park are reached by Metro line I, station Arc de Triomf, or line IV, at stations Barceloneta or Ciutadella.

Forgotten classics: At the city's opposite extreme, along the Diagonal, is one of the few parks which has been passed

over by the *avant-garde* regime in the present-day Town Hall. Next to the Palau station on Metro line III is the **Parc del Palau Reial de Pedralbes,** the result of a 1919 conversion of the antique Can Feliu into a residence for the Spanish Royal family.

Today the elegant palace hosts a large classical garden built to a "geometric decorative outline". It was designed and built in the 1920s by landscape architect Nicolau Maria Rubió i Tuduri and integrated the existing palace garden with land ceded by the Count Güell. After various uses by kings and heads of state, the garden and the palace were opened to the public in 1960. Today the palace is closed once again, although the park around it remains open to lovers of classical gardens.

As "traditional" as the Parc Pedralbes may be, it is almost modern when compared to the **Parc del Laberint**. The garden dates back to the 18th century and is the work of Joan A. Desvalls – the Marques of Alfarràs – and Domenic Bagutti. Entered through the grounds of the Velòdrom in the Barri Verge del Cami, the garden is Barcelona's best example of Romantic-neoclassicism, with strong Italian influence in its layout.

As well as a labyrinth of trimmed hedges, Laberint is composed of a system of visual axes, reservoirs, bowers, niches, temples, water channels and a series of icons depicting love in various aspects. The nucleus of the estate was a medieval tower around which the Marques built his fortress-like house in the eclectic style of the 19th century, with more than a touch of Arabic fantasy.

Twin hills: Everywhere in the world parks have a playground section for the children, and Barcelona is no exception. But as well as the "in park" play areas the city boasts two outstanding parks of year-round attraction: Montjuïc and Tibidabo.

Montjuïc hill, the site of the 1992 Olympics and Barcelona's best-known natural landmark, is a mecca for Sunday hikers, playing children and courting couples. As well as its parks, its museums, its ferris wheels and its roller-coaster rides, it has two outstanding gardens. The largest, **Mossen Costa i Llobera**, specialises in exotic tropical plants and cactus. **Joan Maragall**, the garden of the king's residence in Barcelona, the *palacete* (small palace) of Albéniz, is in classical style with illuminated fountains and a large area for concerts and theatre.

This is the most inviting garden in the city, and it is unfortunate that it is open to the public only on Sunday and holidays, from 10 a.m. to 2 p.m., due to its official role as a venue for diplomatic meetings and conferences. Montjuïc's immense size is best managed with the help of bus number 101 (from Plaça d'Espanya) or number 13 (from El Polvori), both of which travel around a large part of the park's interior.

For an adult, getting to **Tibidabo Park** is almost more fun than being there. First, take the urban train from

Church on Tibidabo.

Plaça d'Espanya to Tibidabo station, then the semi-open tram to the end of its line. From there the Funicular climbs the steep hill to the park. Two interesting sidelights are the climb to the top of the church steeple for the highest lookout you're going to get without an airplane (ride the latter in the fairground below), and the **Museu d'Autòmats**, inside the amusements area.

Modernism rampant: Without a doubt Barcelona's best-known park is **Parc Güell**, designed by Antoni Gaudí i Cornet. The present-day park was originally planned to be a garden city encompassing 60 building plots on the estate of Eusebi Güell. Happily, the development was a flop. The only buildings which were completed were two pavilions flanking the entrance and two houses, one of which is today the **Casa-Museu Gaudí**.

In creating Güell, Gaudí used shapes which harmonised with the landscape. Always aware of the struggle between man and nature, he built a complex garden of staircases, zoomorphic sculptures, sinuous ramps and viaducts. The most important single element of the park is a two-tiered plaza 280 by 130 ft (86 by 40 metres). The lower part, made up of a series of columns in the form of a *sala hipóstila*, was designed to be the development's market-place. The upper portion is surrounded by an undulating bench of mosaics, whose detailing is largely the work of Josep Jujol. The park, built between 1900 and 1914, has recently been declared a monument of world interest by UNESCO.

Parc Güell has become one of the symbols of the city, along with the monument to Columbus and the Sagrada Família. But that isn't to say that there aren't *espais urbans* of equal interest within the capital. Barcelona has a spectrum of parks broad enough to satisfy everyone from the traditionalist to the *avant garde*, from the backpacking hitchhiker to the most demanding of upmarket tourists who arrive in Barcelona in the airport limousine.

Tibidabo's "airport".

MUSEUMS

With almost 40 collections, Barcelona is a city of museums *par excellence*. As far as possible we have tried to group venues by areas, and it should be possible comfortably to visit several during one excursion. Remember that most remain closed to the public on Mondays.

Montjuïc: One of the most attractive places in Barcelona is the hill of Montjuïc (Metro lines I and III to Plaça d'Espanya). The **Museu Arqueològic** (Archaeological Museum) is on Carrer de Lléida. It has recently been rearranged and in a new part of the building a section has been dedicated to the *Mundo Ibérico* (the Iberian world). These rooms contain important discoveries from Catalonia, the Balearic Islands, the rest of the Iberian peninsula and parts of Europe. The museum has collected evidence of the different phases of man's evolution from the Palaeolithic to the Visigothic ages. (Visiting hours are from 9.30 a.m. to 1 p.m. and from 4 p.m. to 7 p.m., mornings only on Sunday and Feast Days.)

Further up Montjuïc is the **Museu Etnològic** (Ethnological Museum) on Passeig de Santa Madrona, open from 9 a.m. to 8.30 p.m., except on Monday when visiting hours are from 3 p.m. to 8.30 p.m., and Sunday and holidays when the museum opens in the morning only. This is a modern structure (built in 1973) and is the only building in the city, with the exception of the Joan Miró Foundation, that was constructed specifically as a museum. For all of the others, former palaces and historic buildings have been converted into museums by private foundations; no Barcelona museum is state-funded.

The Ethnological Museum houses a collection of more than 25,000 pieces, which can be visited by specialists with prior authorisation from the management. Open to the general public are ex-

hibitions on two floors. Every exhibit is clearly marked with explanatory texts in both Catalan and Castilian. A new exhibition dedicated to Latin America is being prepared for 1992.

On the Mirador de Palau, the imposing Palacio Nacional houses the **Museu d'Art de Catalunya** (entrance fee 400 pesetas, open during the morning only, except Monday, when it opens during the afternoon) and, provisionally, the **Museu de Ceràmica** (Ceramics Museum). It is a pity that such a large museum with a potential exhibition area of around 345,000 sq. ft (32,000 sq. metres) is limited to just 65,000 sq. ft (6,000 sq. metres), with many of the galleries closed to the public.

Although the museum's future is uncertain, it houses the most extensive and valuable collection of Catalonian Romanesque art in the world. There is also a display of Gothic art and a somewhat more fragmented collection of 16th and 17th-century art which includes works by Tintoretto, El Greco

Preceding pages: fresco from the Museu d'Art de Catalunya. **Left,** *salchichona* from the Picasso Museum. **Right,** the Museu Marítim.

and Zurbarán. References and explanatory texts are erratic and are exclusively in Catalan. The museum has created an extensive listing of all its works of art, published in the form of a catalogue.

The **Fundació Joan Miró**, which was founded by the artist himself in 1971, is also situated in the Montjuïc Park near to the Montjuïc Funicular Railway. The Foundation exhibits a large part of Miró's art and is also dedicated to the promotion of contemporary art in general. Every year it organises the "Premi Internacional de difuix Joan Miró" or "Premio Internacional de Dibujo Joan Miró" (International Joan Miró Drawing Prize) and a constant round of conferences, debates and round-table talks focusing on different cultural and artistic subjects.

The museum's library of contemporary art is undoubtedly one of the most extensive in the city. From October to May, the Foundation also produces a monthly programme of children's theatre. The centre is open to the public from Tuesday to Saturday between 11 a.m. and 8 p.m. and on Sunday between 11 a.m. and 2.30 p.m.

On top of the hill is the **Museu Militar** (Military Museum), in Montjuïc Castle (bus number 11 from the Plaça d'Espanya and the *teleferique* will take you to the castle gates). The museum houses collections of military artefacts and arms, and has an excellent library of the history of light and heavy armaments.

The Montjuïc venues are completed by those in the **Poble Espanyol** (Spanish Village). Here are the **Museu d'Arts**, **Indústrias i Tradicions Populars** (Museum of Art, Industry and Popular Traditions) and the **Museu de les Arts Gràfiques** (Museum of Graphic Arts). At present both are closed to the public, although for unclear reasons. It would appear that the former will continue to be closed at least until 1993, even though a resident conference hall has recently opened. Both museums offer facilities to specialists.

On the Ramblas: In the environs of the Cathedral between the Ramblas and Via Laietana is another area with a range of museums. In the Ramblas is the **Palau de la Virreina**, an 18th-century palace with occasional art exhibitions which is also home to the *Gabinet Numismàtic* and the *Gabinet Postal* (Coin and Postal Collections). Both exhibitions are for specialists only since they are not, strictly speaking, museums but research centres. Rumour has it that, in time, the Numismatic Collection will be integrated into the Archaeological Museum.

At the bottom of the Ramblas is the **Museu Marítim** (Naval Museum) in Drassanes Reials, the old covered shipyard. Thanks to recent intensive restoration, the museum is in impeccable condition. The entrance fee is 150 pesetas and visiting hours are from 9.30 a.m. to 1 p.m. and 4 p.m. to 7 p.m., except Sunday and holidays when it is only open in the morning. The collection of ships on display includes a massive

The Miró Foundation.

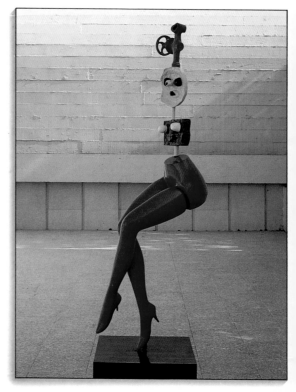

202

reproduction of the flagship of Juan of Austria. There are also extensive documentary and photographic libraries, a specialised reference section (open mornings only) and a workshop specialising in the preservation and restoration of models.

Also at the end of the Ramblas, in the Passatge de la Banca, is the **Museu de Cera** (Wax Museum – entrance fee 150 pesetas), a paler imitation of Madame Tussauds in London, and a popular venue for business presentations and events.

Cathedral quarter: There are three museums close to the Cathedral: the Museu d'Història de la Ciutat (Museum of the History of the City), the Museu Frederic Marés and the Museu de la Catedral (Museum of the Cathedral).

The **Museu d'Història de la Ciutat** is interesting because it conserves archaeological finds from the first Roman city, the Iulia Augusta Paterna Barcino colony. Excavations carried out in the subsoil beneath the building have been widened to investigate the Plaça del Rei, Tinell, Plaça Sant Iu, Carrer Comtes de Barcelona and the Cathedral. Unfortunately, as in most of the city's museums, the explanatory notes are only written in Catalan.

The impressive **Museu Frederic Marés** is located in the Plaça Sant Iu. Complete with its own library and a teaching-oriented facility, the museum was created by Frederic Marés and donated to the city in 1946. The museum has 48 galleries covering both mainstream and folk art. The sculpture section exhibits pieces from the classical period to the present day. The chronological method of presentation allows the visitor to obtain an overall idea of the development of Spanish sculpture from the Iberian to modern periods. The folk art area has magnificent collections of unusual and surprising objects, including fans, dolls, bicycles and toys.

The **Museu de la Catedral** is housed within the Cathedral itself. Located in the Sala Capitular, it is largely dedicated to Catalan Gothic paintings and sculptures from the 16th, 17th and 18th centuries. They can be viewed daily from 11 a.m. to 1 p.m.

Paintings and jeans: Not far from the Cathedral are the Museu Picasso and the Museu Tèxtil y de L'Indumentària (Textile and Clothing Museum), both on the Carrer de Montcada.

The **Museu Picasso** (entrance fee 400 pesetas) is open from Tuesday to Sunday from 10 a.m. to 7.30 p.m. An entire day can easily be spent in this well-designed museum, which presents the artistic evolution of the artist from his earliest works. The quality of the lighting reveals the magnificence of *Las Meninas* (a series of 58 works on a theme of Velázquez) as well as the mastery of his graphic art, bullfighting themes, etchings and lithographs. The museum, which possesses its own teaching facility, also contains a comprehensive library.

Just opposite is the **Museu Tèxtil y**

The Clothing and Textile Museum.

de L'Indumentària. The exhibits follow a strict chronological order right up to the blue-jeans era, even though explanations of the beautiful displays are scant. Worthy of mention is a hand-operated silk weaving machine from València, found on the first floor, as well as a collection of dolls on the entrance floor. This museum can be visited from Tuesday to Sunday, from 9 a.m. to 2 p.m. and 4.30 p.m. to 7 p.m., Sunday and holidays, morning only.

Park places: The third corner of Barcelona with various museums is the Parc de la Ciutadella (Metro line IV, Barceloneta station). At one end of the park the Palau de la Ciutadella houses the **Museu d'Art Modern**, open from 9 a.m. to 7.30 p.m., Tuesday to Sunday; visiting hours on Monday are from 3 p.m. to 7.30 p.m. and on Sunday and holidays from 9 a.m. to 2 p.m.

The collection includes paintings, sculpture, drawings, engravings and decorative arts from the 19th and 20th centuries, but particularly from the second half of the 19th century and first quarter of the 20th. These are the works of Catalan artists from the neoclassical period up to the present time. In order to follow a logical and chronological sequence, the visitor should start at the left of the entrance. All explanatory notes are, as usual, in Catalan.

At the opposite end of the Park, in the Passeig dels Tillers, are the museums of geology and zoology. Entrance to the **Museu de Geologia** costs 200 pesetas and visiting hours are from 9 a.m. to 2 p.m. The **Museu de Zoologia**, housed in the extravagant modernist castle built by Domènech i Montaner, has two halls: the ground floor is used for temporary exhibitions related to fauna and biology, including a section dedicated to zoological taxonomy, and the upper floor is entirely given over to exhibits of stuffed animals, birds and reptiles.

One of the most important functions of this museum is education. Staff attempt to bring an awareness of environmental problems to the whole of soci-

Roman Casas and Pere Romeu on a tandem, by Casas, in the Museu d'Art Modern.

ety, not just to visitors. The administration has organised mobile exhibitions and short lectures for schools on such topics as recycling.

The museum also has an active research function whose work is reflected in its two publications, *Miscel.lània Zoològica* (a multi-author periodical) and the monograph series *Treballs del Museu de Zoologia*, which are exchanged with publications of a similar nature from other countries.

Citywide exhibits: Numerous other museums are dispersed far and wide.

The eye-opening **Museu de la Ciència** (Science Museum, open 10 a.m. to 8 p.m.) is at 55 Carrer de Teodor Roviralta (accessible by bus numbers 17, 22, 58 or 73, or a train to Av. Tibidabo station). Exhibits cover such diverse subjects as optics, sound waves, perception, computer techniques and mechanics. There are also two further temporary exhibitions, a splendid planetarium, a computer section and a meteorological station.

Along the same railway line (Tres Torres station) is the **Museu Clará** at 27–29 Carrer de Calatrava. It houses the work of the great sculptor Clará along with items of the artist's personal memorabilia and the works of several friends. It is a pity that such a beautiful museum should be so poorly cared for.

Beyond the Tres Torres station the same line continues to Reina Elisenda; get off here for the **Museu-Monestir de Pedralbes**, 9 Carrer de Baixador del Monestir, 9. Built in the 14th century, the church consists of only one nave and the Gothic cloister is built on three floors. This museum has a small library specialising in the art and history of Catalonia.

The **Museu de la Música** is in a beautiful modernist building restored by Puig i Cadafalch at no. 373 Diagonal (Metro lines III or V, Diagonal station). The exhibits are grouped together into families of musical instruments. On the mezzanine floor are the keyboard instruments. The second floor exhibits percussion instruments and the string section is on the third floor.

On the road from Vallvidrera to Tibidabo, on Tibidabo itself, is the **Gabinet de Física Experimental Mentora Alsina** (the Mentora Alsina Experimental Physics Collection), reached by the funicular railway which stops very near to the museum.

Here are all kinds of apparatus and instruments related to classical physics (optics, electricity and magnetism). Entry is free and the museum is open every morning from Monday to Saturday, but visitors must call beforehand (tel: 2475734).

The association "Amics de Gaudí" founded the **Museu Gaudí** in the Güell Park located on Carrer d'Olot. And another admiration society founded still another museum to its mentor: the **Museu de Jacint Verdaguer** (open mornings only) in Villa Joana (Vallvidrera), where the great writer and poet, who played a key role in preserving the Catalan language, spent his last years.

Gallery on the Carrer de Montcada.

JAGGER

BRUCE

600 P

600 Pts.

SHOPS AND SHOPPING STREETS

Barcelona is a commercial city and a correspondingly excellent shopping centre. Not without reason, the Catalans are popularly known as a "nation of shopkeepers". Here, emporia from the last century coexist with *avant-garde* shops of the latest design. Most shops are open from 9.30 a.m. to 2 p.m. and from 5 p.m. to 8 p.m. on weekdays and Saturday mornings, and department stores dispense with the midday break. However, thanks to the Catalan instinct for commerce, many shops stay open late and on Saturday afternoons.

From its vantage point as Barcelona's centre, a large part of the city's commerce gravitates around the Plaça de Catalunya, on one side of which is **El Corte Inglés**, Barcelona's largest department store, where everything imaginable can be acquired on any one of the eight floors that it occupies, including the making of travel arrangements in the store's own travel agency. El Corte Inglés even has a supermarket selling baked beans and frankfurters for the homesick. Shopping here can be quite a scrum, though its air-conditioning is an attraction during the hot summer months. Not the place to seek the famed Barcelona style.

Diagonally across the square is the Carrer Pelai, which offers cheap fashion, shoes and hi-fi equipment.

Leading portwards towards the Gothic Quarter is the Avinguda del Portal de l'Angel, which has a personality all of its own: classic fashion shops rub shoulders with modern boutiques specialising in younger fashions. A sombre building houses a branch of the **Galerias Preciados** department store. Among the shops specialising in sweaters and woollen goods is **Las Tiendas de Lolín**. **Benetton** has a branch here and there are numerous shoe shops and leather goods stores as well as the haberdashery **Santa Anna** which has a

beautiful selection of embroidered and lace articles. On the side streets of Carrer Comtal, Carrer de Santa Anna or Carrer de la Canuda are many bookshops, ceramic and art shops as well as a few antique dealers.

From the Plaça de Catalunya you can opt for the elegant and expensive in the Eixample by going up Passeig de Gràcia or Rambla de Catalunya which runs parallel to it; or you can head down the Ramblas in the direction of the port.

The Ramblas: Barcelona's main promenade starts at the Plaça de Catalunya and ends almost at the sea's edge. The shops on the Ramblas, apart from a few exceptions, are mainly dedicated to the sale of souvenirs and leather goods. Far more colourful are the stalls on the Ramblas promenade itself, which sell flowers, birds, animals and books and magazines of all descriptions. At weekends the promenade becomes a hive of activity with a traditional flea market selling anything from clothes and ceramics to costume jewellery and silver.

Preceding pages: glittering prizes. Left, some shopping is universal. Right, but some is distinctive to Barcelona.

Opposite the La Boqueria market (open for fresh foods until 8 p.m.), **Carrer de la Boqueria** is lined with long-established family businesses offering gloves, fans, hats and Spanish shawls, together with numerous costume jewellery shops aimed particularly at tourists. At the end of the street, just before Plaça de Sant Jaume (where the Town Hall and Generalitat are situated), are several ceramic and toy shops and others selling typical artisan stoneware.

The old quarter: The main shopping area in the old city is bordered by the Plaça de Catalunya, the Ramblas, Carrer de Ferran and the cathedral.

The pleasure of shopping down the narrow streets of Barcelona's *barri* Gòtic is heightened by the street shows which spontaneously appear throughout the intimate little squares. One of the most popular is that of the **Plaça del Pi**, which can be reached from the Ramblas down the Carrer Cardenal Casañas. The surrounding buildings and church create an atmosphere not unlike Paris's Montmartre. On the square itself is an old knife shop as well as another tiny business dedicated to the sale of antique engravings and postcards.

Off the corner of the square behind the knife shop is the narrow **Carrer Petritxol**, typical of this quarter with its overhanging balconies adorned with ferns and hanging plants catching what little sunshine they can. Wall tiles depict various scenes from the history of the tiny street. Up here, the **Sala Parés** gallery (founded in 1887) is well worth a visit; each work of art is accompanied by a guarantee of authenticity. Perhaps you are looking for a wastepaper basket? There is a grand selection in every colour possible. Another feature is the number of shops serving home-made chocolate and pastries.

The Plaça del Pi joins with the charming **Plaça Sant Josep Oriol** where, every Saturday, an art fair is held. Artists fill the square with their easels – but they don't start early in the morning. Surrounding the square is a

Servicio Estación, eclectic hardware store.

number of small shops selling products typical of the region, particularly ceramics and papier mâché dolls. At one corner is the **Cosas de Casa**, a long-established shop that sells everything for the home and whose multi-coloured display windows add a gay note to the little square, as does the display in the **comic shop**, next door to a chair maker's alley. The enormous stock of the comic shop reflects the city's huge subculture of comic-strip art.

Antiques tradition: A tiny street, Carrer Ave Maria, leads from the Plaça Sant Josep Oriol and leads to the no less narrow **Carrer dels Banys Nous**, once the Jewish quarter, with antique shops at every step. Barcelona has a long tradition in the antique trade and this street is its most popular exponent. All purchases carry a guarantee of origin.

In the heart of the Gothic Quarter is the Carrer del Bisbe Irurita. An old candle shop and another selling typical odds and ends are the only two commercial enterprises along this ancient street which leads to Barcelona's cathedral. However, there are many other narrow alleys leading from the Plaça Sant Jaume, whose shops offer a wide variety of ceramics, souvenirs and even recycled paper transformed into original and colourful articles.

The Carrer de Ferran, which leads back to the Ramblas from Plaça Sant Jaume, is best known for its bookshops full of old books, as well as several textile and leather shops.

Eixample shopping: Inland from the Plaça de Catalunya up the **Rambla de Catalunya** is a wealth of sophisticated stores specialising in furs, a traditional Barcelona trade, such as the **Peletería Solsona** or **La Siberia**. Here, too, are some of the city's most renowned art galleries, for example, the **Galeria Joan Prats** with permanent exhibitions of both Spanish and international artists, and **Galeria Ignacio de Lassaletta**.

Among the haberdasheries, with their embroidered shirts and quality bed

linen, are famous-name boutiques such as **Massimo Dutti** (on the corner of Carrer d'Aragó), **Zara** and **Japan**, as well as several good shoe shops, including **Vogue** and **Tascòn**. Nearer the Diagonal is the mall **La Avenida**.

Another traditional trade of the area is that of interior design, examples of which can be found in the beautiful *objets d'art* on display in **Artespaña**. Here are entrances to the exclusive shopping malls Bulevard Rosa and Catalunya Center.

The traditional centre for art galleries in the city has always been Carrer de Consell de Cent, near its crossing with the Rambla de Catalunya. At number 333 is the **Dau Al Set** gallery and, almost next door, another well-known venue, **Sala Gaspar**. On the Carrer de Mallorca at number 291 is the **Barcelona Edicious de Disenny** which displays a wide range of furniture based upon designs by Gaudí, Thonet and Le Corbusier, among others.

For gastronomy, the **Colmado Quilez** on the Rambla and Carrer d'Aragó offers a wide selection of Spanish and international food products. A little further on is the sweet and cake shop **Mauri**, one of the most famous in Barcelona with an irresistible variety of chocolates and pastries. No less well stocked a window, although of a totally different flavour, is that of the **Servicio Estación**, a hardware shop and drugstore combined. Across the road is the new Fundacio Tàpies topped by the controversial "cloud and chair" sculpture by the artist himself.

On the avenue: The broad avenue of the **Passeig de Gràcia** was chosen by the Catalan bourgeoisie as the most select residential area in the city. The avenue continues to preserve its original elegance, particularly in the tasteful shops lining either side of the promenade – mainly art galleries, jewellers, lingerie shops and hand-tooled shoe and leather shops. New sophisticated shopping malls in no way detract from the original charm of this street.

Weird welcome to a designer mall.

One of the first shops at the beginning of Passeig de Gràcia is **Gonzalo Comella,** housed in a magnificent towered building at the corner with Carrer de Casp, offering its own line of men's and women's clothing. A little further on, at number 12, is **Casa Furest**, reputed to be one of Barcelona's finest men's shops. **Loewe**, at number 35, is a traditional fashion and accessory shop, whose classic designs are famous for their Italian influence; it also carries a broad range of leather goods which, although of Spanish design, follow marked Italian, French or English style. It is on the ground floor of one of the best-known modernist buildings, Casa Lleó Morera, and rather disfigures the frontage. By contrast, at number 41 in the same block, the **Bagués Joieria** derives some of its style from the Casa Ametller in which it is housed.

The **Roca** jewellery shop, founded in 1858, oozes elegance and distinction and occupies a place of honour at number 18; every article purchased here carries the company's own guarantee.

From the junction of Carrer d'Aragó, the Passeig de Gràcia changes its commercial look – dominated by banks and airline offices – to one that combines typical family businesses and modern boutiques. A classic example of the former is **Santa Eulàlia**, at number 60, traditional outfitters to the female Catalan bourgeoisie. By contrast, the shopping mall **Bulevard Rosa** (one of three) across the street is full of trendy fashion boutiques with Spanish and international labels. The shops seem to go in for unlikely names, such as **Spleen** (jewellery), **Plexiglass** (women's clothes), **Zambo** (women's shoes), **Humm** (confectionery), **Pepa Paper** (paper goods) and **Tu Tarzan yo Jane** (women's clothes).

Further towards the Diagonal, and next door to Gaudí's La Pedrera mansion, is **Vinçon**, at Passeig de Gràcia, number 96. This shop is regarded as the ultimate authority in design in a wide range of products, from tableware, bed

Barcelona has a strong tradition in textile shopping.

linen and bathroom products to garden articles and many other unusual items, all hallmarked with the elegance and modern lines of Vinçon's design team. The shop also has its own art gallery. Despite its elegant, up-market appearance, prices can be a pleasant surprise.

Designer Diagonal: The "designer" shops along the Avinguda Diagonal, in the direction of the Plaça de Francesc Maciá, are in the most exclusive area of Barcelona and reflect local spending power. **Conti**, at number 512, is a good example, displaying Lanvin, Valentino and Ermenegildo Zegna fashions. Almost on the corner of Via Augusta, at number 462, is the **Cinc d'Oros,** a small, unassuming bookshop specialising in art. Just over the road is **Pilma**, a leading store in home design, now facing up to competition from the newcomer **Habitat** (on the corner of Carrer Tuset) with its familiar graphically designed products in a magenta-coloured building that seems made for the company.

Along the length of the tree-lined Diagonal, an air of sumptuousness prevails over the noise of the traffic. At number 469 is **Jean Pierre Bua** with his sober but modern designs in women's fashions. Nearing the Plaça Francesc Maciá is the large department store **Galerias Preciados** (which plays host to a small Marks and Spencer's within), surrounded by elegant boutiques.

Beyond the Plaça the Diagonal continues through a modern architectural landscape of office blocks. About halfway to the university is a small shopping oasis with another comprehensive **El Corte Inglés** and the most recent of the **Bulevard Rosa** shopping malls.

Variety of markets: Other attractive features in Barcelona are the markets and flea markets. Barcelona also has its own very special flea market, **Encantes**, situated at the end of Carrer Dos de Maig and the Plaça de las Glòries (Metro line I from Plaça de Catalunya). This little market-place is redolent of a Moroccan *souq* and bartering is the order of the day. Everything imaginable is sold here, from genuine antiques to modern furniture. The market is open Monday, Wednesday and Saturday, from early morning.

On the **Pla de la Seu** (the Cathedral Square) another kind of open-air market is held every Thursday: the antiques market. The venue is ideal but the prices can be exorbitant.

Yet another open-air market is that of **Sant Antoni,** at the junction of Carrer Comte d'Urgell and Carrer de Tamarit (near the permanent market of the same name). It is held on Sunday morning and offers book collectors an opportunity to browse among old books, magazines and back copies of newspapers.

Finally, there is also a **Philatelic and Numismatics** market, held on Sunday morning in the Plaça Reial (close to the Ramblas), which draws a considerable number of collectors and admirers. The charm of the square itself lends a special ambience to those who come here to buy, sell, swop or browse.

Left, Ramblas cake shop. Right, bargain hunting at a Christmas market.

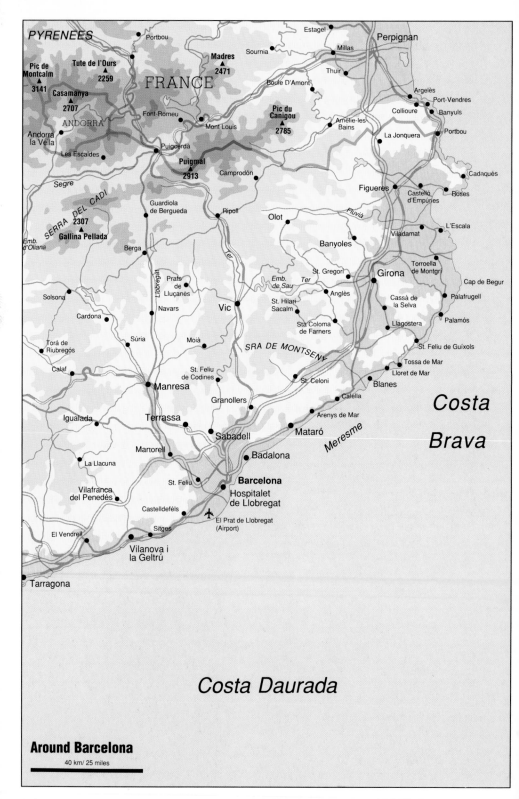

PYRENEES

Pic de Montcalm 3141

Tute de l'Ours 2259

Casamanya 2707

ANDORRA

Andorra la Vella

Les Escaldes

Portbou

FRANCE

Font-Romeu

Mont Louis

Puigcerdà

Segre

SERRA DEL CADI 2307

Gallina Pellada

Emb. d'Oliana

Berga

Llobregat

Guardiola de Bergueda

Prats de Lluçanès

Ripoll

Ter

Camprodón

Puigmal 2913

Estagel

Sournia

Millas

Perpignan

Thuir

Boule D'Amont

Madres 2471

Pic du Canigou 2785

Amélie-les-Bains

La Jonquera

Argelès

Port-Vendres

Collioure

Banyuls

Portbou

Cadaqués

Figueres

Castelló d'Empúries

Roses

L'Escala

Olot

Banyoles

Pluvià

Viladamat

Solsona

Cardona

Torà de Riubregós

Calaf

Súria

Navars

Moià

Vic

Emb. de Sau

Ter

St. Gregori

Anglès

St. Hilari Sacalm

Sta Coloma de Farners

SRA DE MONTSENY

Girona

Torroella de Montgri

Cap de Begur

Cassà de la Selva

Palafrugell

Palamós

Llagostera

St. Feliu de Guíxols

Manresa

St. Feliu de Codines

Granollers

Terrassa

Sabadell

Igualada

Martorell

La Llacuna

Vilafranca del Penedès

St. Feliu

Castelldeféls

El Vendrell

Sitges

Vilanova i la Geltrú

Tarragona

St. Celoni

Calella

Arenys de Mar

Mataró

Badalona

Barcelona

Hospitalet de Llobregat

El Prat de Llobregat (Airport)

Blanes

Tossa de Mar

Lloret de Mar

Meresme

Costa Brava

Costa Daurada

Around Barcelona

40 km/ 25 miles

AROUND BARCELONA

Trips out of Barcelona by car or train are an important part of city life. Beaches, mountains, wine country, religious retreats and provincial cities are all within reach for day trips or overnight visits. Travelling to and from these places can be a nightmare, particularly on Sunday evenings, and visitors should avoid coinciding with the so-called "operation return".

Ten trips: Of excursions, two are to the south (Sitges and Tarragona), two to the west (Sant Sadurní and Montserrat) and the remaining six are northward: Montseny, Vic, Santa Cristina, Figueres and Girona, Núria and Puigcerdà. This last, which is in the Pyrenees on the border with France 2½ hours away, is the only trip which may be too far for a one-day excursion.

Sitges and Santa Cristina are beaches; Montserrat and Montseny are natural and religious mountain-top retreats virtually overlooking Barcelona; Vic, Tarragona, Figueres and Girona are provincial cities; Sant Sadurní d'Anoia is wine country; Núria is a sanctuary high in the Pyrenees, and Puigcerdà is the central town of the Pyrenean Cerdanya valley.

Best beaches: Little more than an hour below Barcelona, **Sitges** is the closest clean and uncrowded bit of the Mediterranean coast. While sand and sun can be enjoyed in Castelldefels, 20 minutes from Barcelona, or even on Barceloneta beach itself, the gleaming, white-washed houses and flower-festooned balconies of Sitges are well worth the extra time on the train. This trip is especially suited for rail travel, even if you do have a car, because the road between Castelldefels and Sitges is one switchback curve after another. A tour through the vineyards and olive groves of the Penedès via the *Autovia* to Tarragona, however, would make a good drive.

A day on the beach at this convenient watering spot, with a *paella* for lunch at one of the many places available on or very near the beach itself, is a good idea at any time of the year. All you need is good weather. If it's raining, change plans and stay in Barcelona. A train leaving at 9 or 9.30 a.m. allows plenty of time to get installed on the beach before 11 o'clock. Paella can probably be organised as late as 3.30 or 4 p.m. or as early as 1.30 or 2 p.m., according to hunger and strategy.

Fringed by palms and populated by an intriguingly cosmopolitan range of bathers, the gently curving **Platja d'Or** (golden beach) runs from the rocky point, La Punta, at the northeast end of Sitges Bay; it starts from the simple white facade of the 17th-century Sant Bartomeu i Santa Tecla Church and extends 3 miles (5 km) south and west past the Hotel Terramar.

The **Cau Ferrat Museum**, **Maricel** and the **Museu Romantic** are the prime points of interest in the town of Sitges, although the tiny streets and bite-sized

houses are no less charming. Cau Ferrat, in a 16th-century house built over the rocks next to the sea, has two El Greco paintings, several Picasso drawings, and a unique collection of Catalan wrought iron. The work inside and the Mediterranean close by outside are a powerful combination of art and nature.

Maricel (*mar i cel* means sea and sky in Catalan), two buildings connected by a small bridge over the street, is most notable for the mural paintings by Josep Maria Sert, while the Museu Romantic at number 1, Sant Gaudenci allows a fascinating insight into well-conserved 18th-century living conditions.

A cosmopolitan and international party in summer, Sitges is quieter from October to May except during *Carnaval* when it becomes wilder and stranger than Rio de Janeiro itself.

Roman remains: Ninety minutes from Barcelona by train or car, **Tarragona** still has the feel of a provincial capital of the Roman Empire. Captured by Rome in 218 BC and later the capital of the Spanish province of Tarraconensis under Augustus, the town was the major commercial centre on this part of the Mediterranean coast until Barcelona and Valencia overshadowed it after the Christian Reconquest of Spain in the early 12th century.

Rich in Roman ruins and stunningly beautiful ancient buildings, Tarragona may be approached from top to bottom, beginning within the walled upper part of the city surrounding the cathedral, continuing on for a tour of the wall itself, the **Passeig Arqueologic** or Archaeological Promenade. One can then descend to the next level of the city, featuring the Rambla and the **Balco del Mediterrani**, and conclude with a stroll through the fishing port and lunch on the quay.

Tarragona's cathedral, the centrepiece of the top part of the city, has been described by Catalonia's own travel writer Josep Pla, who has something to say about every town, as "easily and serenely mighty, solid as granite,

On the beach at Sitges.

maternal – a cathedral redolent of Roman virtues projected on to carved stone – a lion in repose, drowsy, unabashedly powerful". The mass of the wall itself and the tiny perforations in and out of this ancient cloister are hauntingly archaic, as if leading to some secret older than time itself. The Passeig Arqueologic offers views south over the city itself, west out to the mountains, north to the hills and trees surrounding the city, and finally east to the coastline and the sea.

Below the walls is the middle section of Tarragona, with the wide and stately Rambla ending in the Balcó del Mediterrani (Mediterranean Balcony) suspended over the ocean below. The city's luminosity at this point has been much commented on and is indeed remarkable: a crisp elegance and clean air shimmer over the golden sandstone of Roman structures which are more than 1,000 years old.

The **Serrallo** section of the port is the main attraction in the lower part of the city, the multi-coloured fishing fleet unloading the Mediterranean's varied marine life every afternoon, the fish auctioned off within minutes. A late lunch at a dockside restaurant – featuring Tarragona wines, fundamental to the Roman Empire, and seafood just out of the nets – makes a delicious ending.

Wine routes: Sparkling wine made in Catalonia is not champagne; it is *cava*. And don't confuse **Sant Sadurní d'Anoia** with Vilafranca del Penedès. Both towns are fundamental to the wine industry, but Sant Sadurní is closer to the production end of the process and is the true founder and home of *cava*.

A 45-minute train ride from Sants station in Barcelona will drop you in Sant Sadurní d'Anoia next to Freixenet, the world's leading producer of sparkling wine, with vineyards in California and operations now starting up in the People's Republic of China. Freixenet is by no means the only sparkling wine producer in the Penedès, but it offers the most spectacular tour, including a

Tarragona's Roman remains.

screening of its famous series of Christmas greetings featuring stars like Liza Minelli, Gene Kelly, Raquel Welch, Plácido Domingo and Paul Newman.

Cava, produced in Sant Sadurní since 1872 by Jose Raventós, who carefully studied the wine-making techniques, the *méthode champenoise*, of Dom Perignon, is an important part of life in Catalonia: baptisms, weddings, even routine Sunday dinners are occasions for popping corks. On 20 November 1975, the day Franco died, *cava* was given away free in Barcelona.

In addition to tours of the Freixenet or Raventós Codorniu wine cellars, Sant Sadurní offers excellent gastronomical opportunities at local restaurants well-known for fine *cava* and seafood. Held between late January and mid-March, the *calçotada* is a traditional feast starring the long-stemmed white leeks, *calçots*, dipped in *romesco*, a sauce made of oil, peppers, garlic and other ingredients. *Cava*, of course, flows freely at these earthy banquets, accompanied by lamb or rabbit grilled, as are the *calçots*, over coals.

The Penedès region, one of the world's leading wine producers, is to landscape what Bach is to music: spare, pure, geometrically logical, moving. The Montserrat massif to the north rises above rows and rows of vines stretching down to the Mediterranean in the south, with moist sea breezes and 2,500 hours of sunshine a year. Around Sant Sadurní even children have opinions on *bruts*, *secs* and *brut natures*; in the Penedès, Bacchus reigns.

Mountain retreats: Catalonia's most important religious retreat is **Montserrat.** Here athletes pledge barefoot pilgrimages if prayers are answered and vital competitions won. Groups of young people from Barcelona and all over Catalonia make overnight hikes at least once in their lives to watch the sunrise from the heights of Montserrat. "La Moreneta" (the black virgin), Catalonia's patron saint, resides in the famous sanctuary of the Mare de Deu de

The monastery at Montserrat.

Montserrat, next to the Benedictine monastery nestled among the towers and crags of the mountain.

Montserrat (*mont*, mountain; *serrat*, sawed), 30 miles (48 km) west of Barcelona, can be reached easily and spectacularly by train and funicular, starting from Sants station. The advantage of going by car, on the other hand, is the opportunity of seeing this unique landmark from different angles, especially from the northern or southern sides. In the words of the Catalan poet Maragall, from varying perspectives Montserrat can look like "a bluish cloud with fantastic carvings, a giant's castle with a hundred towers, thrown toward the sky, its needles veiled by the fog hanging among them like incense: Montserrat, above all an altar, a temple".

Looming nearly 4,000 ft (1,200 metres) over the valley floor, Montserrat, the highest point of the Catalan lowlands, stands central to the most populated part of Catalonia. Visible from Barcelona, Sabadell, Terrassa, Manresa, Igualada, and Vilafranca, the massive conglomerate stone monolith is ideally located to play an important role in the cultural and spiritual life of Catalonia. During the 40-year Franco regime, when the Catalan language was officially forbidden, baptisms and weddings in Catalan were still held at Montserrat.

The basilica itself is packed with works of art by a long list of prominent painters and sculptors, including works by El Greco in the sanctuary's museum. Catalan poets have dedicated some of their most inspired verse to Montserrat while maestros such as Nicolau and Millet have composed some of their finest pieces in honour of this mystical Catalonian retreat. Goethe is said to have dreamed of Montserrat and Parsifal sought the Holy Grail here in Wagner's musical drama.

Montserrat's highest point, **Sant Jeroni**, can be reached by funicular from the Romanesque monastery of Santa Cecilia. From Sant Jeroni almost all of

<u>Left</u>, inside the monastery chapel. <u>Right</u>, wine making in the Penedès.

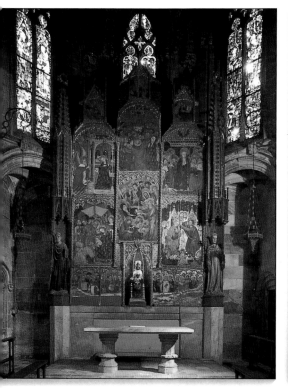

Catalonia can be seen; the Pyrenees, the Cañigó mountains in France and even, on a clear day, as far away as Mallorca in the Balearic Islands.

Rugged forest: The **Serra de Montseny** and Montserrat occupy, in some way, polar extremes in Catalonian spiritual life. Whereas Montserrat is dramatically vertical, acute and passionate, Montseny is smooth, horizontal, massive and placid. *Seny* in Catalan means sense, restraint, patience, serenity; and Montseny, well-named, seems to be a rich lode of this resource.

Best explored by car, this monumental mountain forest, considered one of Europe's most important sources of oxygen, is presided over by four peaks: Turó de l'Home, Agudes, Matagalls (all around 5,000 ft or 1,500 metres) and Calma i Puigdrau, a lower peak at 4,050 ft (1,215 metres). Lesser terrain features and water courses connect and define these four pieces of high ground, tracing out an autonomous geographical entity which always appears hulking and mist-shrouded on the horizon, often confused with cloud formations.

The village of **Montseny** itself, an irresistible nucleus of stone and vegetation attesting to sounder, saner times and places, can be reached via Palautordera and Sant Esteve de Palautordera. This road continues on to Brull, through the pass at Collformic and over to Tona, near Vic on route N 152, thus traversing the entire Montseny massif. The road up from Sant Celoni, just off the *autovia* towards France, via Campins and Fogars de Montclus, arrives at the **Santa Fe hermitage**, a vantage point which seems little more than a stone's throw from Montseny's highest points at Turó de l'Home and Les Agudes.

Santa Fe, surrounded by oaks and poplars, becomes bright with colour as the leaves turn in autumn, an unusual sight in Catalonia where forests and deciduous trees are uncommon. **Viladrau**, to the north, and **Riells** are two more delicious villages, spiritual redoubts for thought and solitude.

The port at Blanes.

224

Montseny, no more than 40 minutes from Barcelona, is a botanical anthology, including some of the southernmost fir trees in Europe, other specimens from all over the continent, and evergreen oak which is found as far south as Andalucía. This rich natural treasure, a virtual symphony of greens, along with the sweep and force of the massif, make Montseny Barcelona's reservoir of thought and reflection, to be drawn upon in times of turmoil.

Country towns: An easy hour north by train or car, **Vic** is the meeting place of industry, commerce and agriculture, a mixture of rural and urban life with a strong ecclesiastical and cultural tradition. Especially known for its Romanesque bell tower, Josep Maria Sert's epic murals, and the wide, arcaded Plaça Major, Vic is an entity distinct from Barcelona. The Vic accent in Catalan is unmistakable and becomes, if anything, more acute in the Catalonian capital as natives of this small city emphasise their separate identity.

Rupit, a medieval town in the green and rocky Collsacabra region east of Vic, is a 40-minute drive for lunch. Built on a rock promontory over a stream, Rupit is known for its unique *patata*, a baked potato stuffed with duck, beef, lamb and secret ingredients.

Vic's **cathedral**, a neoclassical structure completed in 1803, is known for its graceful 11th-century bell tower. But the real story of Vic cathedral is that of the Herculean labours of the painter Josep Maria Sert who decorated the walls with murals in 1930, and again, after fire destroyed them at the beginning of the Civil War in 1936, working until he died in 1945.

Sert, a powerful, vital artist, left his personal vision in these voluptuous, neo-baroque figures performing colossal deeds, muscles bulging, building, straining. His triptych on the back of the cathedral's western door depicts the injustices in the life of Christ and, by association, in the history of Catalonia. With the cathedral in ruins as his back-

Evening *passeig* on the Costa Brava.

ground, Jesus expels the moneylenders from the Temple and is, in turn, condemned to be crucified while Pilate washes his hands and Barabbas, the thief, is cheered by the crowd. Certain faces (Pilate, Barrabas) are said to be those of Franco's lieutenants, but El Generalísimo himself, during a visit to Sert's work while it was in progress, did not seem to see the resemblance.

Philosopher Jaime Balmes (1810–48), a native of Vic, is buried in the 14th-century cloister, as is Sert. The **Museu Arqueologic Artistic Episcopal** contains a series of altarpieces and sculpted figures collected from local chapels and churches. One of the best of these is *El Davallament de la Creu* (The Descent from the Cross), an especially fine 12th-century sculptural work in carved, polychrome wood.

The Plaça Major, or central square, surrounded by low arcades, is a metaphor for the sense and feel of this agro-industrial town. Open, unrelieved by the equestrian statue some critics feel it should have, the square stands on its own, as the city itself does, flat and firm on the plain, the Plana de Vic.

Costa Brava: An hour north of Barcelona, between Blanes and Lloret de Mar, **Santa Cristina** is one of the first *calas* or inlets of Catalonia's famous Costa Brava. Whether by train to Blanes and bus to Santa Cristina, or by car along the coast, Santa Cristina's proximity to Barcelona has made this sandy enclave popular with Barcelonans. Other visitors might do well to stay in town at the weekend and save this trip for the week.

With its twin beaches bordered and divided by rocky promontories, Santa Cristina's lovely **hermitage** stands at the top of the steep paths down to the water. The chapel and house were left to the town of Lloret de Mar by a wealthy 18th-century landowner who moved to Cuba. At that time the shorefront was worth nothing; the valuable property in those days was inland, where there were arable fields. **Girona.**

The Costa Brava, which officially begins at **Blanes**, is distinguished by its bold, rocky shoreline punctuated by small sandy inlets. There are beaches all the way northwards from Barcelona, but the clear, bright water and rocky coastline make the coast unique.

During the summer months, passenger boats work in and out of the *calas*. You can board a boat at Blanes for Santa Cristina or be dropped at some remote *cala* which may be at the bottom of a sheer cliff and inaccessible from land.

At Santa Cristina there are several simple restaurants on the beach where paella can be prepared anytime during the afternoon. These places are relaxed, outdoor spots where dining in bathing suits is normal, and they might not mind adding a few crabs or mussels to the *paella* if you find any among the rocks. They also serve excellent seafood *tapas* or small specialities of squid, sardines, wild mushrooms, shrimp or prawns.

A day at Santa Cristina, especially if you can manage a drive up the N11 coast road in an open-top car, is a breather from a heavy diet of museums and Romanesque art. The only architecture available is the Santa Cristina chapel, a five-minute visit; the landscapes are provided by the Costa Brava and the Mediterranean.

Northern culture: The cities of Figueres and Girona can be combined for a memorable excursion. **Figueres**, 90 minutes north on the *autovia*, is the major city of the **Alt Empordà** (Upper Ampurdan), a fresh, busy country town which, in many ways, could be on either side of the border with France.

Like many provincial cities in Spain, Figueres seems to have some time on its hands, certainly in comparison to Barcelona where time is, somewhat ironically, a thing of the past. The Figueres Rambla is the scene of the legendary *passeig*, the constitutional, the midday or evening stroll, a chance to run into friends, share an aperitif with an old chum you haven't seen for years, an encounter tailor-made for a 20-minute

Left, Girona Cathedral. **Right**, the Arab baths.

chat. A morning visit to the spectacular **Salvador Dalí museum** and lunch in one of the excellent gourmet bistros scattered throughout the town would complete an excellent tour.

Girona, 30 minutes back towards Barcelona, is known for its *Ciutat Antiga* (Old Town) and especially for its 13th-century **Jewish quarter** which is considered, along with Toledo's, one of the two most important and best preserved in Spain. The Onyar river separates Girona's old section from the modern part of the city which lies west of the river. The footbridges over the Onyar provide some of Girona's most unforgettable views into the old city, including reflections of the buildings on the banks of the river as well as taller structures such as the Sant Feliu bell tower or the cathedral. The 12th-century **Sant Pere de Galligants** church is one of the city's oldest monuments, with a lovely Romanesque cloister built before 1154.

Girona's old city, built on a hill, is known for its lovely stairways, such as the baroque *escalinata* leading up to the cathedral or the stairs up to Sant Martí church. **Santa Maria Cathedral**, described by the ever-present Josep Pla as "literally sensational" in its force and magnitude, was built by architect Guillem Bofill who succeeded in covering the structure with Europe's largest Gothic vault.

The cathedral's **museum** is most notable for its *Tapis de la Creació*, an 11th-century tapestry depicting Christ surrounded by all the flora and fauna, fish and fowl of Creation, and for Beatus' *Llibre de l'Apocalipsi* (Book of the Apocalypse), dated 975. **Sant Feliu Church**, the **Arab baths**, and **Devesa Park**, with its lofty plane trees, are other important landmarks of this ancient city of sunless alleys, graceful stairways, and the Onyar flowing through as imperceptibly as the millennium itself.

Into the Pyrenees: Riding the cogwheel train up to **Núria** is an adventure not soon forgotten. Connections up to

228

Ripoll and Ribas de Fresser by train from Barcelona are simple enough. There are departures from Sants station (stopping at Plaça de Catalunya) every three hours or so. The morning train connects with the midday cogwheel. From Ribas, the cogwheel train, known as the *cremallera* or "zipper", clicks up to Núria, the first winter sports resort of the Catalan Pyrenees.

The shrine of *La Mare de Deu de Núria* (the Mother of God of Núria), *La Verge de la Vall de Núria* (The Virgin of the Valley of Núria), follows the Marian cult of Montserrat, the most important in Catalonia. Montserrat and Núria are Catalan women's names, perhaps the two most common. Núria, associated with the purity of the upper Pyrenees and all its natural connotations, has a spiritual image which is, if possible, even more pristine and unspoiled than the somewhat more suburban monastery of Montserrat.

Until 1916 Núria was open only in summer. The construction of the *cre-*

mallera railway in 1917 connected the town of Ribas with the sanctuary at Núria, and since that time the town has been accessible all year round.

According to legend, Sant Gil from Nîmes did penance in the valley of Núria during the 7th century, leaving behind his wooden image of the Virgin Mary, the bell he used to call the shepherds of the region to prayer, and his cooking pot. A Dalmatian pilgrim came to Núria several centuries later, around the year 1072, and discovered Sant Gil's cave with the wooden statue of Mary, the bell and the pot; these are still kept in the sanctuary.

The polychrome wood sculpture is a simple Romanesque carving which the poet Josep Maria de Sagarra described as "rigid and palpitating reality of wood and colour, dark rose of the Divine Shepherd". The bell and the pot came to have a special religious significance: the story is that, by placing their heads in the pot and pulling the bell cord, barren women desiring children, would

Rolling out the barrels at Puigcerdà.

have as many children as the number of times the bell pealed above them.

The **chapel of Sant Gil** lies at the foot of Puigmal, near the sanctuary. Next to the chapel is a spring, La Font de Sant Gil, famous for its freezing waters. The wooden image of Maria, La Verge de la Vall de Núria, sounds an essential chord in the Catalan spirit, remote, intimate, pristine, mysterious – a natural presence who, in the words of the poet Sagarra, "anoints in ecstasy the eyes of the sheep and the blue of the sky until the eagles tremble".

Last resort: Three hours away by train, two and a half by road, **Puigcerdà** has long been Barcelona's favourite mountain resort. Built on a small rise in the Cerdanya valley, *Puig* (hill) *Cerdà* (Cerdanya) the town is the county seat and key commercial centre of the Oriental Pyrenees.

The **Cerdanya Valley** stretches from Prades and Mont Louis in France all the way down to Martinet in the Catalonian province of Llèida, thus fragmenting this whole geographical entity into two countries subdivided by two provincial administrations and further complicated by the Spanish enclave at **Llivia**. The latter is a town surrounded by French territory yet remaining Spanish under the terms of a 17th-century treaty which declared all "villages" north of a certain point to be French. However Llivia, which was incorporated as a "town", remained part of Spain.

The Cerdanya, an east–west valley with an exceptional number of hours of sun each year, is rich pastureland bordered by two *cordilleras* of the Pyrenees to the north and south. Primarily dedicated to the breeding of cattle and horses, the Cerdanya is also known for pears and pigs and, increasingly, for tourism since the construction of the Cadí tunnel provided four million Barcelona residents with a safe, quick way to reach Puigcerdà.

The valley floor is dotted with lovely Pyrennean villages, some of which – for example, Aja or Guils – are within walking distance of Puigcerdà. **La Tour de Carol**, an hour's walk north of Puigcerdà in France, is another good hike via back roads, keeping the Carol stream on your left.

Llivia, 10 minutes away by car, has a lovely church, Europe's oldest pharmacy, and **Can Ventura**, a rustic village farmhouse which has been converted into a restaurant by the owners of the Hotel de Llivia, one of the finest in the Pyrenees. Surrounded by 15 ski resorts in France, Spain and Andorra, Puigcerdà has enough excursions and activities to last a lifetime: horseback outings, jeep safaris, trout fishing, cross-country skiing, wild mushroom hunting, or just sightseeing.

A night at the **Hotel Maria Cristina** in Puigcerdà should provide a spectacular evening and morning overlooking the Cerdanya, an opportunity to watch the sun drop off the far end of the valley at dusk and to catch its first rays hitting the top of the rock walls of the Serra del Cadí at dawn.

Left, the Spanish enclave at Llivia. **Right**, harvesting the hills.

TRAVEL TIPS

GETTING THERE

BY AIR

Barcelona's international airport, El Prat, is 7 miles (12 km) south of the city in the direction of Castelldefels. Most European capitals are served by Iberia and other international airlines. Charter flights are available from many European cities, particularly during the summer months, though the bargains are to be found off-season. Scheduled airlines offer reasonable price reductions with Superpex fares, which means committing to a flight date and time that cannot be changed once booked. Superpex availability is limited, so be sure to book well in advance especially for the peak summer season, Christmas and Easter.

A word of warning: departures from El Prat can be frantic, with endless queues at check-in and passport control, particularly on charter flights, so allow plenty of time. Charter flights are not usually announced and it is almost impossible to obtain information concerning their departure through the airport or Iberia, so try to get a contact number in Barcelona when you buy your ticket. All this may change with the airport extension, due to be completed by 1992.

It is now possible to fly direct from Barcelona to New York every day of the week. There are also flights to Tokyo and Rio de Janeiro, North Africa, Egypt and Israel. All other inter-continental flights have to be made from Madrid, but there are good connections, especially for flights to Central and South America.

The Iberia air-shuttle (*Puente Aereo* or air bridge) between Barcelona and Madrid runs hourly from 6.45 a.m. to 10.45 p.m. on weekdays. It is used by businessmen so the morning and evening flights tend to be very full. It is not possible to book the *Puente* and you may have to wait several hours to get on a flight in the rush hour. Try to travel at other times, or book on one of the regular flights to Madrid (essential if you do have to connect with an international flight); there are seven a day. In August and at weekends the shuttle service is reduced. Travelling by the *Puente* is no luxury, although it is charged at a luxury price: return fare (1990 prices) is 22,500 pesetas.

There are daily connections between Barcelona and other Spanish cities with Iberia or Aviaco, an affiliate of Iberia.

BY SEA

There is a regular passenger and car service from Barcelona to the Balearic Islands with the Trasmediterránea company (Via Laietana, 2, Tel: 319 8212 or through travel agents). There are daily crossings to Mallorca, to Menorca twice a week and to Ibiza four times a week (or more frequently via Mallorca).

The old service to Genoa has been replaced with weekly sailings to Livorno: contact Alimar, Tel: 412 3321.

The ferry terminal has been temporarily moved to the quay Sant Bertran (Moll de Sant Bertran), while Pei and Partners build the new World Trade Centre which will incorporate a new terminal. Make sure you arrive in good time in case there are more changes.

BY RAIL

International service, the Talgo, runs daily between Barcelona and Paris, Milan, Berne and Geneva. It is a high-speed, comfortable train. All other international connections involve a change at the French border, in Port Bou on entering Spain and Cerbère when leaving. These remain dismal frontier stations with few charms and less facilities, so travel prepared if you cannot get on the Talgo.

International trains terminate at Sants, Barcelona's central station, though most stop at Passeig de Gràcia station which is much more central, and very convenient if you are staying in the Eixample or the *barrí* Gotic. The former Estación de Francia, near the port, is being renovated and should reopen as an international terminus in 1991.

BY ROAD

Bus: the international bus companies Julià, Via Eurolines and Iberbus run a regular service all over Europe, linking up with the national bus companies in each country. Julià have a daily bus to and from the main European cities.

Car: Barcelona is 92 miles (149 km) from La Jonquera on the French border and easily reached by the A7 motorway (*autopista*) and then, nearer Barcelona, the A17. The tolls on this stretch total about 1,000 pesetas. If you can avoid travelling into Barcelona at peak times it is well worth it: the worst time throughout the year, but particularly from June to September, is Sunday afternoon/evening, or the end of a bank holiday, when the whole of Barcelona returns from the weekend at the sea or in the country. Tail-backs of 10–20 miles are quite common, even on stretches 35 miles (60 km) before the city. Similarly the Friday evening exodus is a nightmare. Normal weekday rush hour is from 8–10.30 a.m. and from 7–9 p.m.

Be very careful when you stop in a service stations or lay-bys on this motorway. Notorious professional gangs work this route, engaging travellers in conversation, or seeking help, while their companions skilfully rob you of your possessions. If you stop for a drink or a meal try not to leave the car unattended.

TRAVEL ESSENTIALS

VISAS & PASSPORTS

Valid passports are required for all nationalities entering Spain. In theory, nationals from member countries of the EC (European Community) should only need to carry a national identity card. However, there is still a lot of uncertainty, even among the authorities, about the current regulations and the relevant changes that will come in to force in 1992, so it is wiser to carry a passport. In fact, the National Police at Immigration points are quite perfunctory; avid collectors of passport stamps will be lucky if they add to their collection on entering Spain.

A passport is useful to have simply as a piece of identification, for spot checks on the street or for exchanging money. It is well worth carrying a photocopy for everyday use so that the original document can be left in a secure place (such as a hotel safe).

Visas are needed by non-EC nationals, unless their country has a reciprocal arrangement with Spain. In 1992, regulations for entry of non-EC nationals may get tougher as the Community drops its internal barriers. If in doubt consult the Spanish Embassy in your country before travelling, allowing plenty of time for the bureaucratic process.

If your passport is lost or stolen, report the fact immediately to the National Police, where you must make a statement (*declaración*). Once this is done, your consulate should be able to issue an emergency passport.

MONEY MATTERS

The Spanish national currency is the peseta. It is available in the following denominations: notes of 10,000, 5,000, 2,000, 1,000 and 500 pesetas; coins of 500, 200, 100, 50, 25, 10, 5, 2 and 1 pesetas.

Be sure to always carry small change as notes larger than 2,000 pesetas are always a cause of great consternation, especially amongst taxi drivers who are happy to wait outside a bank, meter ticking, while you queue for change. Alternatively, ask before getting into the taxi, or making a purchase, if they do have change: *"Tiene cambio de cinco mil (5,000) pesetas?"*

Coins of 5 pesetas are often referred to as *duros*, so 25 pesetas becomes 5 *duros* (*cinco duros*), 100 pesetas is 20 *duros* (*veinte duros*) and so on.

Banks and Saving Banks (Cajas/Caixas) abound in Barcelona, a reflection of the prosperity of Catalonia. Opening hours vary slightly according to the bank, but most open Monday–Friday, 8.30–2 p.m. and a few stay open until 4.45 p.m. On Saturdays they open 8.30–12.30 p.m., except June–September, when all are closed.

Two branches of the Caixa de Pensions offer a service for money exchange outside these hours: one in Sants railway station, open every day (including Sundays) 8 a.m.–10 p.m; the other at Las Ramblas, 30, open Monday–Friday, 8 a.m.–8 p.m; Saturday 8 a.m.–7 p.m.

Most banks now have automatic tills or cashpoints, operating 24 hours a day, where money can be withdrawn by credit card and personal identification number. Major international credit cards, Visa, Eurocard, MasterCard, Eurocheque, can be used. The larger hotels also exchange money, though usually at a less favourable rate.

Keep a record of the individual numbers of your travellers cheques. If they are lost or stolen they can be quickly replaced provided you have this information.

Some of the major foreign banks now open in Barcelona:

Banco Natwest March, Casp, 17.
Barclays Bank, Passeig de Gràcia, 45.
Banco de Londres/Lloyds, Rambla de Catalunya, 123.
Commerzbank, Consell de Cent, 357.
D.B. Aktiengesellschaft, Passeig de Gràcia, 111.
Dresdner Bank, Diagonal, 427.
Credit Lyonnais, Londres, 102–104.
Banque Nationale de Paris, Entença, 321.
Bank of America, Bori Fontestá, 23.
American Express has an office in Passeig de Gràcia, 101, offering the usual services to clients including poste restante. Tel: 217 0070.

HEALTH

Old tales of catching a "gyppy tummy" while on your holidays in Spain are really an anachronism today. Any such complaints are usually self-inflicted, from an excess of sun or cheap wine, though more often from the heady combination of both. Avoid too much of either, or at least break yourself in gently.

In most areas of Barcelona the tap water can be drunk without fear, but it is often dosed with purifying salts which make the taste unpleasant. Mineral water is a better option and easily available and Vichy Catalan is soothing for queasy stomachs.

Catalan cooking is healthy and nutritious, but a change of diet can affect some digestive systems. If you are wary go cautiously, particularly with shellfish, but not so cautiously that you miss many of the gastronomic delights available. Some northern stomachs are shocked by the generous use of olive oil, though it is medically proven to be much healthier than animal fats and polyunsaturate oils. An excess can be hard to take initially, however: avoid bars and restaurants where oil is obviously used to cook everything.

Another danger area can be in the ritual, adored by foreigners, of eating *tapas* (snacks), the tempting array of dishes spread out along most bars. In the hot weather they can be a source of infection, often prepared in the morning and left out all day. Most notorious is anything mayonnaise-based, such as *ensaladilla rusa*, a potential source of salmonella; in some parts of Spain homemade mayonnaise has been banned in favour of commercial substitutes, a real loss to Spanish cooking. With common sense it is easy to spot the "tired" *tapas* which should be avoided, being well past their eat-by date.

For these and other minor ailments any chemist's shop (*farmacia*) can offer advice and provide a wide range of remedies. Beware of antibiotics and other strong medicaments which are all too easily available across the counter in Spain. Normal opening hours are Monday to Friday, 9 a.m.–1.30 p.m. and 4.30–8 p.m., Saturday 9 a.m.–1.30 p.m. At lunch-times, weekends and night-time there is a rota of special opening hours (*farmacia de guardia*) in every area; a list should be hung in the window of every chemist's shop, with the nearest underlined.

For alternative treatment and an interesting local experience try one of the many herbalists that are in every district of the city. White-haired ladies offer herbs and potions and wise advice, a legacy of knowledge from their ancestors. Homoeopathic remedies are available at the chemist's on Rambla de Catalunya, 77.

WHAT TO WEAR

Winter or summer, Barcelona is basically smart. Catalan men and women dress elegantly, even to go to the market. Just take a look at the women selling fish in the market for an idea of standards – all coiffed and manicured, in dazzling white aprons as they rip out the guts of your squid. So if you prefer not to advertise yourself as a foreigner more than necessary, bring the smarter of your T-shirts and the better-cut jeans. If you don't mind being taken for a tourist, then try at least to respect local traditions: bathing costumes and bikinis are strictly for the beach, not for a stroll down the Ramblas; fashionable shorts are fine, especially for men, but avoid really short shorts.

The heat in the city can be extreme in July and August, due to the humidity, so cool cottons and loose-fitting garments are best for walking around. A light jacket is useful for the evenings, especially in the months of June and September. In fact, a jacket is an essential item at any time of the year. In the winter a warm jacket which can accommodate various layers, or be complemented with an umbrella, is more useful than an overcoat or a raincoat. The weather can be harsh in January and February, especially when the wind blows, but meals on pavements in the sun are equally common. The bright winter sun can be dazzling, so bring sunglasses at any time of the year.

Dress in Barcelona is stylish but not too formal, so unless you intend to dine or dance in the most expensive places you will not need formal wear: men rarely wear ties in the evening, and for dinner women tend to be casually smart, in elegant trousers rather than dresses.

Be sure to bring comfortable shoes – Barcelona is a very walkable city.

WHAT TO BRING

Since Spain became a member of the European Community, the availability of imported products has widened considerably, and most goods can be found in the shops. If you have a personal liking for a certain blend of tea or brand of muesli then bring it with you, though you ought to be able to find an adequate substitute here.

Bring your driving licence, in case you decide to hire a car; for EC members a national licence is valid, but non-EC members require an international licence.

ANIMAL QUARANTINE

There are no animal quarantine regulations in Spain, so think twice before you buy a parrot on the Ramblas – it might have something infectious. You will need health certificates before you bring your own animal into the country, but the regulations vary according to country of origin; from the UK a health certificate and proof of vaccination against rabies is sufficient. The airline with which you are travelling should be able to provide the information required. Remember that if you travel with pets you will be subject to your own national quarantine regulations on your return. In the UK quarantine is six months.

ON ARRIVAL

Whether you arrive in the airport, rail or bus station, or in your own car you probably will stand out as the vulnerable tourist, so be aware and keep your bags or car attended until you are established in a hotel or *pension*. Check that your return flight is confirmed.

Customs: The Customs officers are pretty lenient on European flights and rarely stop passengers. Entering Spain from the UK, the allowance for tobacco is 200 cigarettes or 50 cigars, or 250 grams of tobacco; one litre of alcohol over 38.8 degrees proof or two litres under 38.8 degrees proof. International airlines are the best sources of information on duty-free allowances both outbound and returning home.

Porter services: Both El Prat airport and Sants railway station have a porter service, with fixed rates according to the number and weight of bags.

Reservations: It is essential to book in advance for any form of travel and hotel accommodation at the end of July or beginning of August when Spain goes on holiday. Easter and the other major national and local holidays are the same.

Hotel reservation desks are available in the airport and at Sants railway station.

GETTING ACQUAINTED

GOVERNMENT & ECONOMY

Since the death of Franco in 1975, Spain has made a remarkable transition politically and economically from a country manacled by 36 years of dictatorship to a fully democratic society and a rapidly developing industrial nation. The General Elections of 1989 were won for the third successive time by PSOE, the Spanish Socialist Party, under the leadership of Felipe Gonzalez.

The king, Juan Carlos, originally nurtured by Franco to be his successor, has in fact played a decisive role in guiding the nation to democracy, backing political reform and a new constitution and effectively quelling an attempted military coup in 1981. He is probably one of the most popular and accessible monarchs in Europe.

Spain's entry into the European Community in 1986, which will become fully operational in 1992, represents an enormous challenge: the nation is rising to that challenge undertaking major industrial developments in preparation for the Single Europe of 1993.

Catalonia, and in particular Barcelona as its capital and industrial centre, is of outstanding economic importance to the Spanish state. Covering an area which is equivalent to only 6.3 percent of the whole of Spain,

it nevertheless has 15.5 percent of the population, 25 percent of the nation's industry, and supplies 19.3 percent of the Gross Domestic Product. In European terms, the economy of Catalonia has a greater turnover than Portugal or Ireland. Foreign investment has increased notably in recent years, a reflection of confidence in Catalonia as a dynamic, progressive region.

This economic viability combined with a strong cultural identity and sense of individuality distinguishes Catalonia from the rest of Spain and fuels the Catalan call for independence. Since 1979 Catalonia has been a semi-autonomous state. Emotionally this represents a step forward after the years of Franco's dictatorship when Catalan culture was suppressed and the language forbidden. However, the autonomy's political powers are limited, particularly compared with Catalonia's former strength as a nation.

The origins of Catalonia as a state date back to 988; by the 13th century it had one of the first parliaments in Europe, the Corts and the Generalitat, and by the 14th century it was an imperial force in the Mediterranean. It was not until 1716, following the Wars of Succession, that the Catalan political bodies were abolished, the language suppressed and Spanish introduced into the legal system, the administration and education.

Since then the history of Catalonia has included many conflicts with central government in Madrid over political independence and cultural recognition. Catalan dynamism and determination to progress led to rapid industrial development in the 18th and 19th centuries and gave Catalonia economic supremacy over the rest of Spain.

After various declarations of independence, the Generalitat was finally re-established as an autonomous regional authority in 1932, only to be abolished again under Franco in 1939. The current ruling party, first elected in 1980, is Convergència i Unió, whose leader, Jordi Pujol, is President of the Generalitat.

Barcelona has always been the energetic centre of Catalonia. As the second largest city in Spain and the largest city in the Mediterranean, it is representative of the independent and ambitious Catalan spirit. The driving force in recent progress is the City Council (Ajuntament), socialist since the first democratic municipal elections in

1979.

Led by the charismatic mayor, Pasqual Maragall, the Ajuntament was instrumental in winning the 1992 Olympic Games for Barcelona, which it sees as an opportunity for the city to regain lost time. In preparation for the Games, major works have been undertaken to modernise the city's infrastructure, improve communications, increase hotel accommodation and so on. The Ajuntament's vision is of a fully equipped Barcelona, for 1992 and beyond, that will function as a major European centre.

Meanwhile, political differences between the Ajuntament and the Generalitat handicap the progress of work on a regular basis, emitting waves of panic in the media about completion dates not being met. However, foreign interest in the city is on the increase and the city's self-confidence is soaring; Catalans see Barcelona as becoming the commercial and cultural capital of Southern Europe and the Mediterranean.

POPULATION

Barcelona's situation on the northeast coast of Spain on the Mediterranean Sea moulded its history as an imperial power in the 13th and 14th centuries. More recently it has solidified the city's role as a centre of trade and commerce with easy access to the rest of Europe, and as a centre for tourism. Jammed between the hills of Tibidabo and Montjuïc and the sea, it is the second most dense city in the world, after Calcutta, with 17,504 inhabitants per square kilometre.

Accordingly, the sea frontage is a relief, though traditionally the Barcelonans have turned their backs on the sea. However, current plans are encouraging the city and its inhabitants to look towards the water by developing leisure areas around the port.

Strictly speaking the population of the municipal area is 1.7 million, but the name Barcelona is usually taken as referring to the greater metropolitan area, whose population is 4.2 million. This represents 71 percent of the population of Catalonia, living in 10.2 percent of its land. With the industrial development of the 19th and 20th centuries, the population has increased sharply as waves of immigrants from more rural parts of Spain, especially the south, have come in search of work. Immigrants and their families make up 40 percent of the population of Catalonia.

CULTURE & CUSTOMS

Catalonia's millennial history, its geographic location, its former political strength and independence are all factors which have contributed to a culture that is deeply rooted in the past and is quite distinct from what is popularly considered "Spanish culture" of flamenco and bullfighting. It is a Mediterranean culture, influenced more by the Greek and Roman invasions (and its own empire building in the Mediterranean in medieval times) than by the Moorish influences in the rest of Spain. The Catalans' reputation as industrious, hard workers stems from the country's history as a trading nation.

People from other parts of Spain, especially Madrid, accuse the Catalans of being too serious and self-involved. They have been described as a "Nation of Shopkeepers", with connotations of a people looking after their own particular business in a small-minded way. Certainly, the immediate warmth and openness encountered further south is not always evident amongst Catalans, particularly in the city. People in shops and offices are often brusque, and even in service industries can be quite short with customers. By the same token, they are not obsequious and hardly ever expect tips, which is a refreshing reflection on Catalonia's democratic history and the absence of a dominant ruling class.

The *sardana*, the national dance, provides a telling analogy: the solemn, unbroken circle of linked hands represents the unity of the Catalan people, and their unified strength. However, that circle can be widened; outsiders can join in and are welcomed as long as they dance the same steps. Catalonia as a nation has always absorbed new ideas and outside influences, developing and progressing as a result, but from its own secure foundation. It is a successful formula, producing leaders in many fields, from the arts to science and politics.

On a personal basis, friendships with Catalans may take longer to develop; but once formed will be lasting and loyal. The way of life is Mediterranean and highly civilised: Catalans have a keen sense of perspective and know how to enjoy life to the full.

As a visitor it is important to be aware that you are in Catalonia rather than in Spain. Endeavour to experience what is genuinely Catalan, gastronomically, culturally and in its festivities. Of course, the influence of the rest of Spain is evident, but sangria, bull-fighting and flamenco are imported and not indigenous to Catalonia. To be fully appreciated they should be experienced in Andalusia.

Catalan is now an official language along with Castilian (Spanish) and is widely spoken. In the rural regions outside Barcelona you may come across Catalans who cannot speak Castilian, but usually people in the city will reply to your attempts at either language, especially when they see you are a foreigner.

Catalan is a Romance language; with a knowledge of French and Spanish you should find it possible to read a little. It is spoken in Catalonia, Valencia, the Balearic Islands, Andorra, the Catalan parts of Southern France and L'Alguer, a town in Sardinia. In the wake of its repression under Franco, when its use in public was forbidden, it is currently undergoing a resurgence with the aim of fully implementing it in every aspect of daily life. Most street names and maps are now in Catalan, but you may come across guides or listings in Castilian, so be prepared with both names.

TIME ZONES

In line with the majority of Europe, Barcelona is one hour ahead of Greenwich Mean Time (GMT) in the winter and two hours ahead in the summer:

Barcelona	12 noon
Bangkok	6 p.m.
Bonn	12 noon
Hong Kong	7 p.m.
London	11 a.m.
Lisbon	11 a.m.
New York	6 a.m.
Mexico City	5 a.m.
Moscow	2 p.m.
Paris	12 noon
Rome	12 noon
San Francisco	3 a.m.
Tokyo	8 p.m.

CLIMATE

Barcelona has a mild Mediterranean climate, with an average temperature of 54° F (12° C) in the winter and 75° F (24° C) in the summer. December and January have the lowest temperatures, though the cold is often accompanied by bright sunshine and blue skies. The rains tend to be in November and February/March. Spring and autumn are very pleasant with mild, sunny days. The heat of July and August is aggravated by Barcelona's humidity, which can be overbearing.

WEIGHTS & MEASURES

Barcelona, like the rest of Spain, follows the metric system. Occasionally, market produce is weighed in "libras" or pounds (equivalent to 400 grams).

ELECTRICITY

In general the power supply is 220/230 volts AC, though some old buildings still function on 125 volts. Plugs are two-pinned.

BUSINESS HOURS

Business hours vary according to the nature of the business, its location and the season: in general offices are open 9 a.m.–2 p.m. and 4–8 p.m. though some open earlier, close later and have shorter lunch breaks. Most official authorities are open 8 a.m.–3 p.m. and close to the public in the afternoon. Companies in the outer industrial zones tend to close at 6 p.m. From mid-June to mid-September many businesses practise *horas intensivas*, from 8 a.m.–3 p.m. in order to avoid the hottest part of the day and to get away early on a Friday.

HOLIDAYS

Religious and civil holidays are given due respect in Barcelona and enjoyed to the full. Many people leave the city during a fiesta, which makes it a good time to walk the streets. Unfortunately the best bars and restaurants tend to shut at this time and museums usually close in the afternoons. If a holiday falls on a Tuesday or a Thursday it is common to take a *puente* (bridge) to link the interim day with the weekend. August is the annual holiday month and many businesses, including restaurants, close for three or four weeks. Avoid travelling at the beginning and end of August, at Easter or one of the major holiday weekends: the roads become very congested and public transport can be fully booked.

Apart from Christmas, Easter and Whitsun the main public holidays in Barcelona are:

6 January - Reis Mags: Epiphany
19 March - Sant Josep
1 May - Festa del Treball: Labour Day
24 June - Sant Joan: Summer solstice
15 August - Assumpció: Assumption
11 September - Diada: Catalan national holiday
24 September - La Mercè: Barcelona's town fiesta
12 October - Hispanitat/Pilar: Spanish national day
1 November - Tots Sants: All Saints
6 December - Dia de la Constitució: Constitution Day
8 December - Immaculada Concepció: Immaculate Conception

FESTIVALS

Traditional celebrations of religious, civil and popular feast days take place throughout the year. If your visit coincides with one, don't miss the opportunity to join in. The Catalans may have a reputation for working hard but they also know how to play hard. Apart from the main fiestas described here, every district (*barri*) of Barcelona has its own, known as the Festa Major, centred on its own patron saint. These usually last several days and have certain key ingredients:

Sardanas: the national dance of Catalonia, a solemn affair in which young and old link hands in a circle and to the strains of the *cobla*, a special band, perform some very intricate footwork. The dance is full of symbolism about the unity of the Catalan people. Sardanas can be seen every Sunday and holiday in Plaça Sant Jaume at 7 p.m. (6.30 p.m. in winter).

Gegants and *Cap Grossos*: literally Giants and Big Heads. Giant kings and queens and comic characters with large heads who parade the streets and usually reunite in the evening at a Grand Ball in one of the public squares.

Castellers: awesome human towers (record height is nine human storeys) capped with the youngest and smallest.

CALENDAR OF FESTIVALS

Christmas: during December the Santa Llùcia Fair is held in the streets around the Cathedral, selling Christmas trees, mistletoe, baubles and all you need for a nativity scene, a traditional decoration in every Catalan household.

Sant Esteve, 26 December: an important holiday in Catalonia, when families meet for an even larger meal than on the 25th.

Reis Mags, Epiphany, 6 January: traditionally this is the time when children receive their presents from the Three Wise Kings, though modern commerce now indulges them in presents at Christmas as well. In Barcelona the Kings arrive from the Orient by boat, are greeted in the port and then process around the city showering excited children with sweets.

Carnival, Carnestoltes, before Easter: these wild celebrations which take place in the days prior to Ash Wednesday were banned from 1936 until 1980. The ceremonies close with the "Burial of the Sardine" on Ash Wednesday, symbolising the end of high living and the beginning of the restrictions of Lent. The best celebrations are at Sitges, on the coast, which becomes a mini Rio de Janeiro.

Sant Jordi, 23 April: Jordi is the patron saint of Catalonia. This is also the Day of the Book, in which men give a rose to their lady, and receive a book in return. Book stalls are set up all over town.

Fira de Sant Ponç, 11 May: marked by the sale of aromatic and medicinal herbs, crystalised fruit and honey in Carrer Hospital.

Sant Joan, 24 June: the day used to sleep off the excesses of the night before, the *verbena*: the revelry which takes place all through the previous night in celebration of the summer solstice. Beware the *petardos*, noisy fireworks or bangers, that are set off in the streets days before they are due. The Catalans are experts at beautiful firework displays, but unfortunately seem to have equal regard for the noisy *petardo* which has no aesthetic qualities and terrifies the young and old, but is a vital part of many fiestas. It is traditional to eat "coca", a Catalan cake made with pine nuts and crystalised fruit, on Sant Joan.

Diada de Catalunya, 11 September: the Catalan National Holiday, commemorating the fall of Barcelona to Felipe V in 1714. On that day Catalonia first lost sovereignty to the Spanish crown and its political institutions were abolished. A fiesta banned during the Franco regime, it now consists of political demonstrations.

The Feast of La Mercè, Barcelona's patron saint, 24 September: this is the city's main fiesta, with a whole week (*Setmana Gran*) of dancing, parades, concerts, theatre and merriment. Don't miss the Correfoc: fire-breathing dragons and devils chasing victims through the streets.

RELIGIOUS SERVICES

Mass is usually said between 7 a.m. and 2 p.m. on Sunday and Feast days. Evening mass between 7 p.m. and 9 p.m. on Saturday, Sunday and Feast days.

Mass in French: Paroisse Française, Carrer d'Anglí 15. Saturday 7 p.m., Sunday 11.30 a.m.

Mass in English: is said at the same church at 10.30 a.m. on the first and third Sundays of the month.

German services: are held in the German Parish Church, Carrer d'Avenir 14. Sunday 10 a.m., Tuesday 8 p.m. and on the second and fourth Sundays of the month at 11.30 a.m.

Anglican services: in English are held at Saint George's Church, Carrer Sant Joan de la Salle 41. Sunday 11 a.m., Wednesday 11.30 a.m.

Other venues:

The Synagogue, Carrer d'Avenir, 24. Tel: 200 6148.

The Greek Orthodox Church, Carrer d'Aragó, 181. Tel: 253 2508.

Al-Widadiyah Mosque, Carrer de Balmes, 13. Tel: 318 6709.

LANGUAGE

Spanish (Castilian) and Catalan are both official languages in Catalonia, but under the current resurgence of Catalan culture you will find that the Catalan language dominates in public signs, street names, leaflets and information on cultural events. However, if you can speak some Castilian, even the most ardent Catalinistas will respond in the same tongue, especially when they realise you are a foreigner. Also, many people you encounter in bars, restaurants and public transport will be from other parts of Spain, so Castilian is universally usable. If you want to win a Catalan's heart, however, here are a few expressions in Catalan:

Good morning: *Bon dia*
Good afternoon/evening: *Bona tarda*
Good night: *Bona nit*
How are you? *Com està vostè?*
Very well thank you, and you? *Molt bé, gràcies i vostè?*
Goodbye, see you again: *Adéu, a reveure*
See you later: *Fins després*
See you tomorrow: *Fins demà*
What's your name? *Com us dieu?*
My name is… *Em dic…*
Pleased to meet you: *Molt de gust*
Do you have any rooms? *Per favor tenen habitacions lliures?*
I'd like an external/internal/double room: *Voldria una habitaci exterior/interior/doble*
…for one/two persons: *…per a una persona/dues persones*
I want a room with a bath: *Vull una habitació amb bany*
I have a room reserved in the name of… *Tinc reservada una habitació a nom de…*
How much is it? *Quin és el preu?*
It's expensive: *Es car*
Could I see the room? *Podria veure l'habitació?*
At what time do you serve? *A quina hora es pot?*
Breakfast/lunch/dinner: *esmorzar/dinar/*

sopar

How do you say that in Catalan? *Com es diu això en català?*

Speak a little more slowly, please: *Parleu una mica més a poc poc, si us plau*

How do I get to…? *Per a anar a…?*

Is it very far/close? *Es lluny/a prop?*

Where's the nearest motor mechanic? *On és el pròxim taller de reparació?*

Can I change this traveller's cheque? *Pot canviar-me aquest xec de viatge?*

Where can I find a dentist? *On puc trobar un dentista?*

This tooth is hurting: *Em fa mal aquesta dent*

Don't take it out. If possible give me something for it until I get home: *No me l'extregui. Si és possible doni'm un remei fins que torni a casa*

Please call a doctor: *Cridi un metge, per favor*

Where does it hurt? *On li fa mal?*

I have a bad cold: *Estic molt refredat*

I want to make a phone call to… *Vull telefonar a…*

It's engaged: *La línea está ocupada*

I am… I'd like to speak to Mr… *Sóc… voldria parlar amb el senyor…*

What time will he be back? *A quina hora tornarà?*

Tell him to call me at this number: *Digui-li que truqui al número…*

I'll be in town until Saturday: *Seré a la ciutat fins dissabte*

COMMUNICATIONS

MEDIA

Newspapers: The national and regional newspapers maintain a reasonably high standard, leaving sensationalism and scandal for the plethora of glossy magazines. The main daily papers in Barcelona are:

El País: a national newspaper based in Madrid but with a Catalan edition published in Barcelona. It grew out of the new liberalism in the post-Franco era. Probably the most respected Spanish paper internationally, it has links with Britain's *Independent*, France's *Le Monde* and the *New York Times*. Issues a useful guide to events in Barcelona every Friday.

La Vanguardia: the traditional newspaper of Barcelona, it has recently been revamped by Milton Glaser (who created the much-imitated logo, *I Love NY*) which makes it much more readable. Good coverage of Barcelona news and activities.

El Periodico: the more popular Barcelona newspaper, but limited on international news.

Diari de Barcelona and *Avui*: the two papers published in Catalan in Barcelona. *Avui* was given authorisation to publish in 1976, several months after Franco's death, and has the widest circulation.

For sport enthusiasts there are two daily papers, *Sport* and *El Mundo Deportivo*.

European newspapers can be found on the newsstands on the Ramblas and Passeig de Gràcia, and some international bookshops, like Libreria Francesa (Passeig de Gràcia, 91) or Collector (Carrer de Pau Claris, 168). Some international editions such as *The Guardian*, *International Herald Tribune* and *Financial Times* are on sale first thing in the morning and many foreign dailies are available by the afternoon of the day of publication.

Magazines: A wealth of magazines are available in Spain, covering every interest and indulgence, from politics and business, fashion, sport and more. The main fashion magazines, such as *Vogue*, *Marie Claire* and *Elle* now publish a Spanish edition. Most notable of the national magazines are:

Cambio 16: a weekly news magazine, good on politics and controversial issues.

Hola: the most famous Spanish magazine, with fully illustrated scandal and gossip on the rich and royal. The magazine everyone loves to read but hates to be seen with. Strictly for the hairdresser's.

On Barcelona:

Guia del Ocio: an essential weekly guide to what's on in the arts, cinema, theatre, music, dance and any other activities or special events such as local fiestas. Useful listings of museums, art galleries, bars and restaurants.

Vivir en Barcelona: a monthly glossy, slightly self-indulgent for the "in" people in Barcelona, but with useful reviews of the month's events.

Barcelona Concept: even glossier and more indulgent, but with some useful information, especially if you want to know the latest places to see and be seen. Issued every six months.

Comics: Adult comics have a large following in Barcelona. The comic strip is an art form quite particular to the city. For a good selection of comics and books: Makoki, Plaça Sant Josep Oriol, 4.

Publications for foreign residents:

Lookout: a monthly for the English-speaking community, particularly those on the Costa del Sol. Well illustrated general articles on Spain.

TELEVISION

There is too much to discover in Barcelona to waste time on the television. However, with private channels coming on stream in 1990 and the proliferation of satellite stations, a new element of competition may improve present broadcasting standards. The principal channels are TVE1 and TVE2 (state-owned) and TV3, the autonomous Catalan channel. Private channels include Antena 3 (general programming), Tele 5 (directed towards housewives) and Canal Plus (more cultural, for subscribers).

Satellite programmes obtainable in Barcelona (in many of the larger hotels) are: in Spanish, Galavisión; in English, BBC, CNN, Discovery Channel, MTV Music, Super Channel, Eurosport, Screen Sport, Sky Channel and Sky Movies; in German, Sat 1; in French, TV5; in Italian, RAI UNO.

News bulletins in various languages are on TVE and TV3 from July to September. Check the daily press for timings.

POSTAL SERVICES

Stamps for letters, post cards and small packets can be bought very conveniently in the many *estancos* to be found in every district. These are state-owned establishments licensed to sell stamps, cigarettes and tobacco, and easily recognisable by their orange and brown logo, Tabacs S.A. Opening hours are loosely 9 a.m.–1.30 p.m. and 4.30–8 p.m. Post boxes are yellow, sometimes with two sections, one for Barcelona city, and the other for the rest of the province, Spain and abroad. Express letters can be posted in special red boxes, marked *Urgente*, but it is easier to find the post office than one of these, and possibly more direct.

The main post office, a monument to a bygone age, is at the bottom of Via Laietana near the port, in Plaça Antoni López. It has collections every hour and is open Monday–Friday 9 a.m.–9 p.m., Saturday 9 a.m–2 p.m. Other post offices close at 2 p.m. daily, apart from the one in Carrer d'Aragó, 282 (near Passeig de Gràcia) which is open until 7 p.m. but with limited services. Poste Restante letters can be sent to the main post office addressed as follows:

Name
Lista de Correos
08000 Barcelona

Be sure to take personal identification with you when claiming letters.

Telegrams: can be sent from the main post office from 8 a.m.–10 p.m. every day or from a small office in Ronda Universitat, 23, from 9 a.m.–7 p.m. Alternatively they can be sent by telephone. Tel: 322 2200.

Both telegram offices have a **telex** and **telefax service**, but will not receive a telefax unless the recipient is present. A more convenient and cheaper service for fax is offered by **Prismafax** (Carrer Jaume I, 18. Fax no: tel: 310 5865) who will accept in-coming faxes.

TELEPHONE

Telephone boxes and booths are well distributed throughout the city. They are easy to use and efficient, especially for international calls, once you have found one in working order. Most bars have either a pay-phone or a metered telephone, but be tactful and at least have a coffee while you are there. The coins accepted by public telephones are 5, 25 and 100 pesetas, and some will take credit cards. Minimum charge is 10 pesetas. International reverse charge calls cannot be made from a box.

You may prefer to use the central exchange, where you talk first and pay later: it is just off Plaça de Catalunya in Carrer de Fontanella, 4. A similar service is available in both branches of the department store El

Corte Inglés, one in Plaça de Catalunya and the other in Avinguda Diagonal, 617–619.

Some useful codes:

Barcelona (from outside the province) 93; (from abroad) 3.

International operator (Europe) 008; (Rest) 005.

Information 003

International direct dial 07 (await signal) + country code + town code + number

Country codes:

Australia	61
Austria	43
Belgium	32
Denmark	45
Eire	353
Finland	358
France	33
E. Germany	37
W. Germany	49
Great Britain	44
Greece	30
Holland	31
Italy	39
Japan	81
Luxembourg	352
Mexico	52
New Zealand	64
Norway	47
Portugal	351
Sweden	46
Switzerland	41
United States	1
Yugoslavia	38

EMERGENCIES

SECURITY & CRIME

Barcelona has the same security problems as any large city. No better, no worse. Because it is a tourist centre with quite a severe drug problem, it is inevitable that loosely swinging handbags and ostentatious cameras are snatched by the desperate who feel their need is great. Don't tempt them. Do not

be alarmed either: Barcelona is not a den of vice, and with due attention and common sense you can avoid dangerous situations.

The old town has a bad reputation, and it is also the area where tourists tend to congregate. So be aware when ambling down the Ramblas, meandering through the narrow streets or watching one of the many street performers. Wear your handbag across your chest, keep your camera hidden and do not flash your wallet around. Carry enough money for the day, leaving the rest in the safe deposit box of your hotel.

Other danger points can be the airport, railway and bus stations, where there is bustle and confusion and it is easy to be distracted. Keep your luggage together and don't leave it unattended.

Never leave anything valuable in a car, especially radios; follow the example of the locals who always have the car radio at their side in bars and restaurants. Even in a crowded street, car windows are quickly smashed and any objects dexterously removed.

Don't get caught by a few small gangs who perpetrate various tricks to waylay you, like commenting on the dirt on your back and while "helping" you to remove it, slip the purse from your pocket.

Another is a game known as *trila*, a variation of the three-card trick, played by crooks in the guise of innocent bystanders: it involves guessing which of three nutshells, or similar containers, hides a dried pea, for a wager of 5,000 pesetas. It looks easy but you can be sure you will never win. At first glimpse of a policeman they all miraculously disappear, as do your 5,000 pesetas. The authorities have run an advertising campaign warning against this game.

There is a marked increase in police presence on the streets, with constant patrols by motorbike and car. The confusion of which branch of police play which role remains an enigma, especially now that they all wear navy-blue uniforms. However, they can be roughly defined as follows:

Policia Municipal: the City Police, known as Guardia Urbana, responsible for traffic, civilian care and security; recognisable by the blue-and-white checked band around their caps and on their vehicles.

Policia Nacional: the State Police, who since Franco's death have changed from grey, to brown to navy-blue uniforms, a metamorphosis that seems to have made them less military and aggressive and more peaceful and civil. They are responsible for law and order and civilian security.

Mossos d'Esquadra: the autonomous police of Catalonia, in Toni Miró-designed navy-blue and red. Their powers are quite restricted within the city where they are mostly responsible for the Generalitat buildings. Basically they have replaced the Guardia Civil (those of the shiny black hats), who you will only catch a rare glimpse of now.

In the case of a theft, assault or loss, you should first contact the National Police to make a statement (*denuncia*). This is vital if you want to claim on an insurance or seek further help from the City Police or your consulate. The National Police operate a mobile office in a van, either at the top of the Ramblas (Plaça de Catalunya end), or halfway down where Carrer de Boqueria joins the Ramblas (opposite the Liceu); you can make your statement at one of these or at the police station in Carrer d'Ample. The main police station is in Via Laietana, 49.

For further help, contact the City Police who have pioneered a special 24-hour assistance scheme for tourists at their headquarters (Ramblas, 43. Tel: 301 9060) offering legal advice, medical assistance, provision of temporary documents in the event of loss or robbery and an international telephone line for the speedy cancellation of credit cards etc. They can cope in French, English, German, Italian or Russian.

LOST PROPERTY

There is a Lost Property Office in the City Hall (Ajuntament) in Plaça San Jaume, 1. Open: 9.30 a.m.–1.30 p.m., tel: 301 3923. At the main entrance ask for the Servei de Troballers. Lost or stolen bags and wallets are often found without their contents and handed in here. Official personal documents are passed on to the relevant consulate.

MEDICAL SERVICES

Permaments, residents of EC countries are entitled to receive state medical treatment in Spain if they present a form known as an "E111", which must be obtained in their own country. In the UK this can be done through the Post Office.

Similarly Austria, Finland and some Latin American countries have a bilateral agreement on medical services. Check it out and obtain the relevant papers before leaving. The alternative is to take out a private insurance which can be organised on arrival through any travel agency.

In an emergency: go to "*Urgencias*" at any of the main hospitals:

Hospital Sant Pau: Carrer de Sant Antoni Maria Claret, 167. Tel: 347 3133.

Hospital Clínic: Carrer de Casanova, 143. Tel: 323 1414.

Hospital Cruz Roja: Carrer de Dos de Maig, 301. Tel: 235 9300.

Or visit an *Ambulatorio*, (clinic/medical centre) which can be found in every district. With private medical insurance (or a large wallet) the scope widens to include the many private doctors. Consulates can advise on those who speak your language.

Dentists: not covered by any of the reciprocal agreements. The following clinics offer an emergency service:

Clínica Janos: Carrer de Muntaner 375, 6º 2ª. Tel: 200 2333. Open: 9 a.m.–1.30 p.m. and 4–8.30 p.m. daily (including weekends and holidays.)

Institut Dexeus: Passeig de Bonanova, 67. Tel: 418 0000. Famous for its gynaecological work and for producing the first test tube baby in Spain, this clinic also provides a dental service exclusively at weekends, on fiestas and in August when many dentists are away on holiday.

Amesa: Gran Vía, 680. Tel: 302 6682. Open: 9 a.m.–9 p.m.

Clínica Quirúrgica: Carrer d'Aragó, 293. Tel: 215 5700. For after 9 p.m. and fiestas.

LEFT LUGGAGE

Left luggage lockers (*consigna*) are available in Sants railway station from 7 a.m.–11 p.m. for approximately 200 pesetas. There is no equivalent service at the airport or other railway stations. At the sea terminal on Moll Barcelona there is a left luggage office which is open until the boat sails in the evening.

GETTING AROUND

Barcelona is a manageable city to get around, whether on foot or by public transport. The latter is efficient and good value. The only means of transport to avoid is your own: the parking problems, the threat of the police clamp or removal lorry, the wracked nerves as you struggle to adjust to local driving habits and the traffic system, the frustration at not being able to enjoy the sights you pass, all conspire to make travelling by car in this city a nightmare. Leave your car in a car park.

MAPS

The Tourist Board issue a good general map of the city (*plano de la ciudad*), indicating key places of interest and published in English, German, French, Italian, Catalan and Spanish. Combined with the public transport guide to buses and the Metro in the centre and metropolitan area, it makes a comprehensive package. Both are available free of charge from Tourist Offices (for details see under Useful Addresses), and the transport map is also available from the Metro stations in Sants and Universitat. Larger, more detailed maps in various languages can be bought at newsstands and most bookshops in the centre. For page by page detail of the city, there is the *Guia Urbana*, the taxi drivers' bible, but it is not practical for a short stay.

In addition the Tourist Board publish several leaflets on subjects such as Modernist architecture and places of interest.

FROM THE AIRPORT

Barcelona is only 7 miles (12 km) from El Prat airport and is easily reached by train or taxi. Trains to Sants, the central station, depart every 30 minutes from 6.30 a.m.–11 p.m. and take about 16 minutes. The same service from Sants to the airport operates

from 6 a.m.–11.30 p.m. Approximate cost is 125 pesetas. Although always advertised as the train to Sants, it actually continues to Plaça de Catalunya and Arc de Triomf which can be more convenient for central parts of the city.

There is a bus service (line EA) to and from Plaça d'Espanya but it is rather irregular, though the night service (EN) may be useful running every 80 minutes from 10.30 p.m.–2.30 a.m. It leaves from Plaça d'Espanya from 11.10 p.m.–3.10 a.m.

To reach most central parts of Barcelona by taxi will cost from about 1,300–1,700 pesetas, plus an airport supplement of 175 pesetas and 50 pesetas per suitcase. Tales are told of foreigners being taken on circuitous routes to reach their destinations. To avoid this try asking how much it will cost before getting in to the taxi. "*Cuánto vale el recorrido desde el aeropuerto hasta...* (e.g.) *Plaça de Catalunya?*". Get him to write down the answer if necessary and if it seems reasonable the deal is made. To be really thorough, you can check with the taxi authorities whose office is next to the Arrivals gate in the airport.

PUBLIC TRANSPORT

Metro: The Metro is Barcelona's underground network. It has four lines (lines I, III, IV and V: line II never got off the drawing board). Maps are outside every station. Trains are frequent and cheap, with a set price per journey, no matter how far you travel. Individual tickets cost 65 pesetas but it is practical and more economical to buy a card that allows you 10 journeys for 365 pesetas (*tarjeta multiviaje*) available at any station. Trains run from 5 a.m.–11 p.m. during the week and from 6 a.m.–1 a.m. at weekends.

The train service, Ferrocarrils de la Generalitat de Catalunya (FFCC), interconnects with the Metro, looks like the Metro and functions in the same way but extends beyond the inner city area to towns on the other side of Tibidabo, like San Cugat, Terrassa and Sabadell (all from Plaça de Catalunya) and to Manresa and Igualada (from Plaça d'Espanya). It is a useful service for reaching the upper parts of Barcelona and for parts of Tibidabo and the Parc de Collserola, the forested hills beyond.

The single Metro ticket is valid within the urban area, but to travel beyond is more expensive. The FFCC lines show in a darker blue on the Metro map. Within town the timetable is the same as the Metro, but beyond, it varies according to the line. Check in any of the stations or tel: 336 0000, a useful number for information on any form of public transport.

Buses: The bus service is good for reaching the areas the Metro doesn't, and for seeing more of Barcelona – at speed. Thanks to bus and taxi lanes journeys can be fast, so hold on tight. Single tickets (65 pesetas) can be bought from the driver or a multiple card (*tarjeta multiviaje* T-1: 410 pesetas) of 10 journeys can be punched inside the bus; this ticket is valid for bus, Metro, urban lines of FFCC and Tramvia Blau (the tram in Avinguda Tibidabo) and can be bought in the Metro or any Caixa (savings bank). Most buses run from between 5 and 6 a.m.–10 or 11 p.m. There are some night services, but lines vary so check on the map or at bus stops.

Taxis: All Barcelona taxis are black and yellow, and show a green light when they are available for hire. There are taxi ranks at the airport, Sants station, Plaça de Catalunya and other strategic points but taxis constantly move around town and can be hailed at any street corner. Rates are standard and calculated by meter: the meter starts at 225 pesetas and will clock up at a rate governed by the time of day, with night-times, weekends and fiestas being more expensive.

If you go beyond the urban limits, to the airport for example, the rate will increase slightly. The final charge is what shows on the meter, except when supplements are due for luggage, dogs or leaving from the airport or railway station. Drivers do not expect a tip though a small one is always appreciated.

If you can communicate with the driver it is a worthwhile experience and you will be enlightened on what's wrong with Spain, what's wrong with the traffic, what's wrong with politicians and what bizarre incidents occur in a taxi driver's typical day. Do not be alarmed if the driver leaps out at a red traffic light and opens in the car's boot (trunk) – many are fuelled by butane gas and he is just changing the bottle.

PRIVATE TRANSPORT

Cars are better left in a parking place while you travel around town. However, if you prefer to take the car be prepared for bad jams, horn-blowing if you hesitate and do not maintain local speed, and anarchic overtaking on both sides. Avoid parking anywhere that is not legal, particularly entrances and private garage doors: the police tow offenders away with remarkable alacrity and charge at least 11,000 pesetas for retrieval. Street parking, indicated by blue lines on the road and a nearby machine to buy a ticket for display in the car, is limited. Car parks charge approximately 150 pesetas an hour or 1,200 pesetas a day. Convenient ones are in Passeig de Gràcia, Plaça de Catalunya and many side streets, there are also several under construction.

Useful addresses: Royal Automobile Club of Catalonia: Carrer de Santaló, 8, Barcelona 08021. Tel: 200 3311/200 0755 (24 hours).

The German Automobile Club: Carrer de Muntaner 239–253, Barcelona 08021. Tel: 200 8800.

24-hour repairs: workshop/towing service: Detroit, Carrer de Biscaia, 326. Tel: 351 1203.

Towing service: Grúas García, Carrer Nou Pins, 24. Tel: 350 7535.

CAR HIRE

Both international and national firms are represented in Barcelona and several are at the airport. Some addresses:

Avis: Casanova, 209.
Tel: 209 9533; 379 4026 (Airport).
Europcar: Consell de Cent, 363.
Tel: 317 5876; 317 69 80 (Airport).
Godfrey Davis: Viladomat, 214.
Tel: 239 84 01.
Hertz: Tuset, 10.
Tel: 237 3737; 370 5752 (Airport).
Atesa: Balmes, 141.
Tel: 237 8140; 302 2832 (Airport).
Budget: Avinguda Roma, 15.
Tel: 322 9012.
Regente Car: Aragó, 382.
Tel: 245 2402.
Vanguard: Londres, 31.
Tel: 239 3880, 322 7951.
Motorcycle Hire: Vanguard: as above.

DOMESTIC TRAVEL

RAIL

As part of the preparation for the Olympics, railway lines have been moved and stations closed. The following stations currently function as described, but before planning any journey it is advisable to call RENFE (the national train network) for the latest information. Tel: 490 0202.

Sants station, Plaça Països Catalans s/n: long distance national trains. Some of these will also stop in Passeig de Gràcia station which is very convenient for central parts of town. However, do confirm with several different sources beforehand that your train really does stop there.

Regional trains leave Sants for the coast just south and north of Barcelona: these get very crowded in the summer months, so avoid travelling at weekends; it is common to stand all the way to Girona.

Plaça de Catalunya station, Plaça de Catalunya: apart from the Metro and Generalitat railways, RENFE has a station in Plaça de Catalunya. Trains to Manresa, Lleida, Vic, Puigcerdà and La Tour de Carol leave from here.

Plaça d'Espanya station, Plaça d'Espanya: trains to Montserrat, Igualada and Manresa.

Estación de Francia (or Estación Término), near Ciutadella park: currently undergoing renovation. Due to open as a national and international terminus.

It is advisable to purchase tickets in advance, especially at holiday times. The easiest way is through a travel agency which is a recognised RENFE agent. In Sants queues can be long and ticket clerks impatient and not very helpful. RENFE offers all kinds of discounts.

ROAD

There are regular long-distance coach lines running all over Spain, operated by different companies. Most buses leave from the Bus Station Norte in Avinguda Vilanova. For general information on services, tel: 336 0000.

For services in Catalonia:
For the Costa Brava, contact Sarfa. Tel:

318 9434.

For the Costa Maresme, contact Trapsa. Tel: 232 0459.

For Montserrat, contact Julià. Tel: 318 3895.

Vall d'Aran/Lleida:

For the Pyrenees, contact Alsina Graells. Tel: 302 6545.

For the Delta del Ebro, contact Hife. Tel: 322 7814.

WHERE TO STAY

HOTELS

There are over 300 hotels in Barcelona offering a wide range of accommodation from the humble *pension* to 5-star luxury. The choice is still quite limited at the upper end of the scale, though the prospect of the 1992 Olympics spurred plans for new hotels. Travellers with a small budget have the consolation that there is much more on offer at the cheaper end of the scale, but demand of course is much greater, particularly in the summer months. Take care when choosing a *pension*: it could have all the charms and comforts of staying with a local family or it could equally well be the local brothel.

New regulations for the classifications of establishments in Catalonia are being introduced: *hostales*, *hostal-residencias*, *casas de huespedes* (CH – Guest Houses) and *fondas* will all be re-categorised either as hotels or as *pensions*. If they cannot adapt to the necessary standards (i.e. size of bedroom, or minimum percentage of bathrooms) they will be phased out. The aim is to produce a higher standard of tourist accommodation in Barcelona. It will probably take some time to enforce the new categories so be prepared to find the old names above the door – and in this listing.

The new categorisation is:

Hotels (one star to five star) – a bathroom in every room is obligatory.

Pensions: One star – 15 percent of rooms with bath. Two star – 25 percent of rooms with bath.

The following selection is categorised according to price based on the cost of a double room with bath. Luxury rooms cost from 15,000 pesetas to more than 24,000; moderate, from 6,000 pesetas to 15,000; low is below 6,000 pesetas. All those mentioned are hotels unless specified otherwise. Remember that a flight and hotel package always works out cheaper. If you are planning to stay a while, find out what packages are on offer from your home country.

LUXURY

Ritz: Gran Vía, 668. Tel: 318 5200. Telex: 52739.

Luxury maybe, but really exorbitant even for business accounts. Splendid entrance hall and lobby where tea can be taken.

Avenida Palace: Gran Vía, 605–607. Tel: 301 9600. Telex: 54734.

Classic old-world gilt and chandeliers at new world prices. Comfortable, good service. Request one of the rooms that still has original fittings, on fourth floor upwards for good city views.

Duques de Bergara: Carrer de Bergara, 11. Tel: 301 5151. Telex: 81257.

Very attractive new hotel in a typical Eixample building from the turn of the century, with some original features well preserved. Intimate atmosphere. A rare alternative to impersonal chain hotels.

Ramada Renaissance: Rambla, 111. Tel: 318 6200. Telex: 54634.

A large hotel recently well renovated in keeping with the refurbishing of Barcelona for 1992. It has already become a favourite with touring rock stars.

Rivoli: Rambla, 128. Tel: 302 6071.

A renovated bank. Behind its striking facade is a modern hotel with features designed by some of Barcelona's leading talent.

Condes de Barcelona: Passeig de Gràcia, 75. Tel: 215 0616. Telex: 51531. Contemporary elegance in a Modernist building.

Colón: Avinguda Catedral, 7. Tel: 301 1404. Telex: 52654.

A Barcelona classic, overlooking the cathedral in the centre of the *barri* Gótic. Bedrooms can be disappointing after the comfort of the ground floor.

Regente: Rambla de Catalunya, 76. Tel: 215 2570. Telex: 51939.

Pleasant hotel in excellent position. Some attractive original features have survived amidst the standard hotel furnishings. Rooftop swimming pool. Moderately priced for this upper bracket.

MODERATE

Suizo: Plaça d'Angel, 12. Tel: 315 4111.

Pleasant, homely, comfortable in a good position in the *barri* Gótic. Request room on Baixada Llibreteria for an attractive outlook and more peace.

Rialto: Carrer de Ferran, 42. Tel: 318 5212.

Modernised and pleasant in this bustling street just off Plaça Sant Jaume.

Regina: Carrer de Bergara, 4. Tel: 301 3232. Telex: 59380.

Reasonable-standard hotel in good position near Plaça de Catalunya.

Aparthotel Bonanova: Carrer de Bisbe Sevilla, 7. Tel: 418 1661.

In a quiet residential area in the upper part of Barcelona. For those who prefer independence. Rooms equipped with kitchen/dining areas. Reasonably priced. Ask for a room with terrace.

Granvia: Gran Vía, 642. Tel: 302 5046.

Faded baroque splendour which has its charms. Well situated near Passeig de Gràcia. Interior rooms are preferable to avoid Gran Vía traffic.

Hostal Residencia Urbis: Passeig de Gràcia, 23. Tel: 317 2766.

Dark and dull but clean and in a good position on Passeig de Gràcia. Ask for exterior room.

San Agustín: Plaça Sant Agustí, 3. Tel: 317 2882.

Comfortable and clean, overlooking quiet square. Well worth paying 2,000 pesetas more for one of their "de luxe" rooms on the fourth floor, with rooftop views.

Oriente: Rambla, 45. Tel: 302 2558. Telex: 54134.

One of Barcelona's best known hotels. Not what it was despite the price increases but still has its charm.

LOW

España: Carrer de Sant Pau, 9. Tel: 318 1758. Telex: 50574.

Magnificent Modernist decor on the ground floor by Domènech i Montaner is refreshingly mixed with kitsch and a Fifties bar. Rooms modernised. Popular amongst American intellectuals. Visit it at least: the set lunch is good value and the surroundings worth every peseta.

Peninsular: Carrer de Sant Pau, 34. Tel: 302 3138.

Fairly basic but comfortable, with some attractive Art Nouveau touches recently restored with taste.

Hostal Residencia Windsor: Rambla de Catalunya, 84. Tel: 215 1198.

A gem: impeccably clean, light and airy in contrast to the usual drab, sad *hostales*. Essential to book in advance and request a room looking on to Rambla de Catalunya. Excellent position near Diagonal.

Nouvel: Carrer Santa Anna, 20. Tel: 301 8274.

Attractive old hotel in pedestrian street off the Ramblas.

Jardí: Plaça Sant Josep Oriol 1/Plaça del Pi. Tel: 301 5900.

Fairly basic but clean and very well situated overlooking two of the most attractive squares in the *barri* Gòtic. Extremely popular so book in advance if possible.

Hostal Palacios: Gran Vía, 629 bis. Tel: 301 3792.

Convenient, pleasant *hostal*.

Hostal El Casal: Carrer de Tapineria, 10. Tel: 319 7800.

Clean and pleasant, in the shadow of the cathedral.

The *barri* Gòtic is full of *hostales* and *pensiones* but choose them with care: the streets between Carrer de Ferran and Plaça de Catalunya are better than those nearer the port. Several reasonable places are in Carrer de Carme, Portaferrissa and Santa Anna. For those who prefer to visit the *barri* Gòtic by day and sleep in another part of town here are two recommendations:

Hostal Ciudad Condal: Carrer de Mallorca, 255. Tel: 215 1040.

Hostal Felipe II: Carrer de Mallorca, 329. Tel: 258 7758.

There are 300 camp sites in Catalonia, 70 percent of the total number in Spain. Twelve of these are within easy reach of Barcelona. Most are south of the city, near the stretch of beach which begins at the end of the airport tarmac and runs through Viladecans, Gavá and Castelldefels. The road into Barcelona is notoriously busy and dangerous, the beaches and sea are crowded and of dubious cleanliness, but the air provides a refreshing change from the city. Sites in this area:

El Toro Bravo: (2,100 sites). Ctra. (Carretera.) C-246, Km 11, Viladecans. Tel: 658 1250.

At Km 12 and Km 12.5 on the same road are:

Filipinas: (1,050 sites). Tel: 658 2895.

La Ballena Alegre: (1,825 sites). Tel: 658 0504.

Also on the same road, but in Gavá, at Km 13.5, Km 14.5 and Km 15 are:

Tres Estrellas: (450 sites). Tel: 662 1176.

La Tortuga Ligera: (700 sites). Tel: 662 1229.

Albatros: (1,400 sites). Tel: 662 2031.

Just along the road in Castelldefels, the most popular of these resorts, is the Estrella de Mar (550 sites). Tel: 665 3267.

North of Barcelona:

Masnou: (135 sites). Tel: 555 1503.

Hispano: (120 sites). Tel: 555 0875.

Both are on the N-11 in Masnou, at Km 639.8 and Km 641 respectively.

FOOD DIGEST

Eating is an important part of Catalan culture, something to be taken seriously and enjoyed to the full. The traditional gathering together of the family for Sunday and feast day lunches is an ancient ritual, providing an opportunity to eat well and converse long into dinner time. On Sunday mornings the *pastelerias* are full of freshly cologned fathers and sons buying indulgent pastries for dessert, then between 2 p.m. and 5 p.m. a sacred quiet descends over the city. Even on working days most shops and offices close during this time while lunch is seriously observed. The Catalans have just cause to preserve the tradition: real Catalan cooking is delicious and nutritious and considered, along with the Basque, the best in Spain. It is certainly part of the experience of visiting this country which should not be missed.

Catalan food is said to embody the key elements of Catalonia, having evolved from using the freshly available produce of the Mediterranean sea, the fertile plains and the mountains. It is the pride of Catalans that their country can offer miles of rugged coastline and sheltered beaches, as well as awesome mountain ranges and rich valleys, all within easy access of each other. Similarly the cooking combines *mar i montanya* (sea and mountains) which makes for strange sounding marriages on the menu, though delicious in the tasting, such as meat balls with cuttlefish, or chicken with shellfish.

If anything Catalan gastronomy can err on the side of richness: it has all the goodness of Mediterranean cooking which is increasingly being considered as one of the healthiest, based on olive oil and fresh vegetables. Its strong flavour is due to abundant use of garlic and sauces made with almonds and cognac.

A rich meal can be well balanced by the omnipresent fresh salad and simple, but often the most delicious, grilled fish or meat; the best is *a la parrillada*, food grilled over charcoal. Eaten with *allioli* (a Catalan garlic sauce, not to be missed) and *pa amb tomàquet* (bread or toast dressed with tomato and olive oil) this is one of the most typical Catalan meals.

It is worth adapting to local meal times during your stay, so as to eat when food is at its freshest.

Breakfast: Coffee or milk with a sweet cake or croissant first thing in the morning, followed by a mid-morning break of a hearty sandwich often with beer or wine.

The *Aperitivo*: an aperitif before lunch, around 1 p.m., of a *vermut* (usually red vermouth, often with soda) and olives, or some other *tapa* (snack).

Lunch: peak time is 2 p.m. lingering on to 4 p.m. or later at weekends. After 3.30 p.m. there is a danger of not being served. Lunch is the main meal of the day and the best time to find fresh food and the most economical meals. Every restaurant has a *menú del día* (set menu), offering a choice of starters (soup, salad, vegetables), a main course of meat or fish, a dessert (flan, yogurt, tinned peaches or fresh fruit) and wine, beer or a soft drink. Standard and price vary according to the establishment, but it is always good value. For around 600 pesetas you can have an excellent meal. If the *menú del día* is not in immediate evidence, ask for one: "*hay menú?*". Some restaurants may try and withhold it from rich-looking tourists.

Merienda: a kind of afternoon tea, from 5–7 p.m., consisting of milky coffee or hot chocolate and sticky cakes and often a large plate of cream eaten just on its own. For a classic *merienda* try the cafés around the Plaça del Pi, especially in Carrer Petritxol.

Dinner: at home this is usually a light meal, often *tortilla* a Spanish omelette, around 10 p.m. Restaurants do not have a set menu at night, so eating out can be more expensive than at lunch time.

Tapas: if you have had a good lunch, the evening is the ideal time to "do *tapas*" i.e. to visit several bars having a glass of wine and a snack in each. Only foreigners eat *tapas* at lunch time, and it can prove to be a much more expensive way of eating.

WHAT TO EAT

The French saying *On connais les gens à table* is as valid here as anywhere in the world: the *barcelonéses* are what they eat. On the white tablecloths of the city are laid the very best produce from the sea, the mountains, the valleys and the plains. From the mountainous regions during the autumn months come the succulent *setas* (wild mushrooms), cooked in elaborate sauces or braised with a little garlic and parsley. Cured and smoked meats are another speciality of the Catalan cuisine: *butifarra* (black sausage), *fuet*, Vic sausages and so on.

The *escudella i carn d'olla* is a typical Catalan standby whose principal ingredients are meatballs made from minced pork, breadcrumbs, parsley and eggs. A dish such as *pan tomàquet*, slices of country bread rubbed with tomatoes and flavoured with a dash of home-grown olive oil, is a typical speciality that bridges all social classes. And, of course, no self-respecting *barcelonés* would dream of finishing a meal without a flan dessert topped with burnt sugar called *crema catalana*.

In Barcelona the number of pastry shops per square metre must rank among the world's highest. For each feast day and festival there is a corresponding traditional sweetmeat: *Bunyols* during Lent, *Las Monas* for Easter, *Panellets* (marzipans) for All Saints. Throughout the long summer months the *barcelonéses* celebrate their numerous local festivals with an abundance of fireworks, champagne and *cocas* (pastries covered in sugar and pine nuts).

The best menus vary according to what is in season. These will be singled out under "*Platos del Día*" or "*Recomendaciones*", or the head waiter will advise. Here are some typical Catalan dishes:
•**Starters**
Escalivada: salad made of cooked peppers and aubergines.
Esqueixada: salad of raw salted cod, onions and peppers.
Ensalada Catalana: a mixed salad with cold meat/sausage added. Can be dull.
Xató: salad of *frisée* lettuce with tuna, anchovies and a romesco sauce. Speciality of Sitges.
Bolets: generic name for the various wild mushrooms in season in the Autumn. *Rov-*

elló is one of the best, especially just grilled with garlic and parsley. Often used in meat dishes at this time of the year.

Espinacs a la Catalana: spinach cooked with raisins and pine nuts.

Faves a la Catalana: small broad beans stewed with herbs and pork and sausage meats. Best in spring.

Escudella: the most traditional Catalan soup, usually followed by the *carn d' olla*, i.e. the meat and vegetables which have been cooked in the soup. A Christmas dish though formerly staple diet of every Catalan household.

Canelons: another Catalan tradition despite their Italian associations.

Calçots: spring onions cooked on a charcoal grill and served with a sauce. Only in season.

Arros negre: one of the many traditional rice dishes. Black rice with squid, cooked in the squid's ink.

Fideus: an excellent and lesser known variation on paella, in which noodles replace the rice making a moister dish. A good paella is increasingly difficult to find.

•Main courses

Botifarra amb mongetes: the local, very tasty, sausage served with haricot beans.

Estofat: stews, made from beef or older veal, usually have a rich, succulent sauce.

Oca amb naps: goose with turnip.

Conill: rabbit, grilled and served with allioli, or stewed.

Xai: lamb. Cutlets (*costelletes*) are especially good in Catalonia.

Fricandó: classic stew with *moixernons*, a small, delicate wild mushroom.

Bacallà: salted cod can be served in many ways: *a la llauna* - with garlic, parsley and tomato; *amb xamfaina* - with a sauce of tomato, pepper and aubergine. This sauce often served with meat.

Suquet: a seafood stew.

Fish and shellfish should not be missed in Barcelona. Often served in rich sauces, the simplest and perhaps best way is grilled or done in the oven, *al forn*.

•Desserts

Crema catalana: an essential during your stay, a cinnamon flavoured custard with a burnt caramel top.

Mel i mató: a curd cheese with honey.

Postre de músic: roasted nuts and dried fruits usually served with a cold glass of moscatel.

Apart from these classic *postres*, the usual run of commercial ice-creams, sorbets and *macedonia* (fruit salad) are always available, as well as fresh fruit.

•Tapas

The best way to choose *tapas* is to look and point, so you can be sure to only select the freshest. Ham, spicy cold meats and cheese eaten with *pa amb tomaquet* are often the best bet. *Tapas* tend to be more Spanish than Catalan in origin, so are given here in Castilian rather than Catalan.

Jamon serrano: cured ham. *Jabugo* is the best.

Queso: cheese. Try *manchego seco* for a strong flavour, *cabrales*, a potent blue cheese from Asturias in or *cabra*, goat cheese.

Salchichón, *chorizo*: spicy sausages.

Anchoas: anchovies.

Boquerones: small, pickled fish.

Berberechos: cockles; normally out of a tin but delicious with an aperitivo.

Tortilla: Spanish style omelettes. *Española* (potatoes and onions); *espinacas* (spinach); *payés* (mixed vegetables); *ajos tiernos* (young, tender garlic). *Francesa* is the classic French omelette made without a filling.

Patatas bravas: fried potatoes with a hot spicy sauce, or garlic mayonnaise.

Ensaladilla: "Russian" salad, with potatoes, vegetables and mayonnaise.

Pescaditos: small fried fish.

Pulpo: octopus, a speciality from Galicia.

WHERE TO EAT

In a short holiday there are not enough meal times to visit all the restaurants that should be visited in Barcelona. The following have been selected for their good food combined with atmosphere or pleasant location. Nearly all serve Catalan food and other regional dishes. At lunch time try any corner bar with a reasonable looking *menu del día*.

The following selection is divided into "prime", "moderate" and "economic" categories on a financial basis. Prime will cost a minimum of 3,000–4,000 pesetas a head, moderate a minimum of 2,000 pesetas and economic 500–1,000 pesetas. Many establishments close on a Sunday/Monday or in August.

•Prime

Jaume de Provença: Carrer de Provença, 88. Tel: 230 0029.

Eldorado Petit: Carrer de Dolors Monserdà, 51. Tel: 204 5153. Attractive situation complete with garden in the top part of town. Excellent Catalan *nouvelle cuisine*.

Botafumeiro: Carrer de Gran de Gràcia, 81. Tel: 218 4230. This is a Galician restaurant but it is also one of the best places to eat sea food in Barcelona. Oysters at the bar.

Café de Colombia: Carrer d'Iradier, 12. Tel: 418 7504. Striking decor in an elegant building, shades of colonialism. One of *the* restaurants in Barcelona, though more for its clientele and appearance than its food.

Les Noies: Major de Sarrià, 109. Tel: 205 0959. Charming old surroundings in the middle of the Sarrià district. Unusual Catalan dishes from times past, combining sweet and savoury.

Passadís de'n Pep: Pla de Palau, 2. Tel: 310 1021. For people "in the know", the kind of place you will walk past if you are not. Excellent seafood.

La Venta: Plaça Doctor Andreu. Tel: 212 6455. Attractively decorated building and leafy terrace at the foot of the funicular to Tibidabo. Perfect for spring-time lunches or summer nights.

La Vaqueria: Carrer Deu i Mata, 139–141. Tel: 419 0735. Another of the latest places to be seen, especially for a certain bejewelled section of Barcelona society who will later be dancing in the trendy night club Up and Down. Two interior decorators from the same set have given a beautiful, dream-like quality to this old cowshed.

Can Majó: Carrer d'Almirante Aixada, 23. Tel: 310 1455. One of the best and most established of the Barceloneta fish restaurants, and one of the few places you can be sure of a good paella.

•Medium

Senyor Parellada: Carrer d'Argentería, 37. Tel: 315 4010. Unusual and classic Catalan dishes in a sophisticated, very pleasant environment.

Casa Leopoldo: Carrer de Sant Rafael, 24. Tel: 241 3014. Worth hunting down in the narrow streets of the *barri* Xines, a family-run Barcelona classic. Favourite of artists and intellectuals. Reasonable priced menu at lunch time.

Siete Puertas: Passeig Isabel II, 14. Tel: 319 3033. Over 150 years old and recently sympathetically restored, recapturing the original atmosphere. Another classic, popular for family Sunday lunches. Specialises in rice dishes, one for each day of the week. Also has the advantage of remaining open through the afternoon and evening until 1 a.m.

Café de l'Academia: Carrer de Lladó, 1. Tel: 315 0026. Delicate Catalan cooking, well presented. Stylish, modernised medieval building in an attractive square in the *barri* Gótic.

Carballeira: Carrer de Reina Cristina, 3. Tel: 310 1006. Excellent Galician fish. At lunch time on Sundays try a simple *tapa* at the bar of *arroz a banda*, delicious rice cooked in fish stock. Accompany it with a glass of Ribeira, Galician white wine; try the cloudy one, *turbio*.

The following six venues fall into a "classic" category, as white table-clothed bustling Catalan restaurants with dignified service. They never change and are always fun and good value:

El Caballito Blanco: Carrer de Mallorca, 196. Tel: 253 1033.

Restaurant Ponsa: Carrer d'Enric Granados, 89. Tel: 253 1037.

Madrid–Barcelona: Carrer d'Aragon, 282. Tel: 215 7026.

Bilbao: Carrer de Perill, 33. Tel: 258 9624.

Can Massana: Plaça del Camp, 6. Tel: 417 0674.

Agut: Carrer de Gignás, 16. Tel: 218 4230.

•Economic

The following are especially good (and economic) at lunch time.

Egipte: Carrer de Jerusalén, 12. Tel: 317 7480. Just behind the Boqueria market, a popular, lively place that grew from being a small market restaurant into several well decorated floors and two annexes.

La Morera: Plaça Sant Agustí, 1. Tel: 318 7555. Bustling town restaurant with above average menu.

La Ribera: Plaça Olles, (behind Passeig del Born). Friendly, charming owner creates the atmosphere. Excellent food presented with more style than many restaurants, for half the price.

La Cassola: Carrer de Sant Sever, 3. Tel: 318 1580. Family run. Good home-made Catalan food.

Rodrigo: Carrer d'Argenteria. Another endearing family-run busy restaurant, popular with foreign language teachers. Delicious food.

Casa Joana: Major de Sarriá, 59. Also **Goliard**: Major de Sarriá. Both are very good value for this up-market part of town.

Can Tripas: Carrer de Sagués, 16. Cheap, cheerful and crowded: a paradox amid the elegant shops of the Diagonal/Plaça Francesc Macià area.

Casa Julio: Carrer de Regomir. No nonsense, wholesome dishes, served on shared formica tables. One of the cheapest menus in town.

Also very good value are the Regional Centres, which are clubs for people from different regions of Spain, open to the public at midday. Try **Hogar Extremeño** (Extremadura) at the bottom of Avinguda Portal de l'Angel, or **Centro Murciano** (Murcia) in Carrer de Portaferrissa.

MISCELLANEOUS CUISINE

•Vegetarian
Biocenter: Carrer de Pintor Fortuny, 24. Delicious salads with a difference – difficult to find in Barcelona.

Botiga Restaurant Les Corts Catalanes: Gran Vía, 603. Soothing surroundings reminiscent of the Avenida Palace Hotel next door. A relief from the usual vegetarian pine.

•Morrocan
La Rosa del Desierto: Plaça Narcís Oller 7, Tel: 237 45 90

Syrian
Xix Kebab: Carrer de Córcega 193, Tel:321 82 10

•Japanese
Koyuki: Carrer de Córcega, 242. Tel: 237 8490. As the Japanese population of Barcelona increases so does the number of restaurants. This is one of the simplest but best, less expensive than most and frequented by comic-reading Japanese.

•Chinese
Dragon Inn: Carrer de Buenos Aires, 12–14. Tel: 419 1929. High-style Chinese, with none of the usual flock wallpaper.

•Pizzas
Chicago Pizza Pie Factory: Carrer de Provença, 300. Tel: 215 9415. Deep pan pizzas, the all-American way.

•*Tapas*
Available nearly everywhere but to be chosen with care. Some of the best are:

Mundial Bar: Plaça Sant Agustí Vell 1. Especially good for shellfish.

Bar Roure: Carrer de Lluis Antúnez, 7. Tel: 218 7387. Also well-known for paella on Thursday lunch, but you must book.

La Gran Bodega: Carrer de Valencia, 193. A glimpse of the rest of Spain in the middle of Barcelona.

El Gran Colmado: Carrer de Consell de Cent, 318. This is high-tech Barcelona, a grocer's shop with a difference.

Montesquieu: Carrer de Mandri, 56. Good sea food.

Cristal: Carrer de Balmes, 294. Bar/bookshop with good *tapas* and delicate sandwiches. Comfortable alternative but with good atmosphere.

José Luis: Avinguda Diagonal, 520. For those who want *tapas* without roughing it. Sophisticated snacks at elevated prices – beware the bill.

Xampanyet, Carrer de Montcada, near Passeig del Born. Ceramic-tiled pretty bar that serves a fizzy white wine of the same name. Perfect for an aperitif.

El Raval: Carrer de Doctor Dou. A bar that serves pâtés, cheese and salads. Ideal for after concerts or theatre. Frequented by artists and actors.

Carrer de Mercè is a street behind Passeig de Colom which is full of good *tapas* bars, but hold on to your handbag.

DRINKING NOTES

Despite the proliferation of bars and drink available at reasonable prices, there is little evidence of drunkenness in public places. Such excess is popularly associated with tourists from Northern Europe overcome by the accessibility of alcohol in Spain, though hopefully that image is becoming a cliché of the Costas of the past. First-time visitors to Spain should be aware that measures of spirits are larger than in most other countries. Also, it is important to specify the brand when asking for a drink in a bar, to avoid rough imitations. Beware the bottles that look remarkably similar to your own favourite brand.

Beer is served in bottles of a fifth (*un quinto*), a half litre (*una mediana*) or draught from the tap; for the latter ask for "*una caña*". When ordering water, soft drinks or wine you will often be asked if you want it "*fresco o natural?*", chilled or room temperature. Red wine is usually served "*fresco*" in the summer unless you specify "*natural*".

Sangria can be dangerously refreshing; often made from cheap wine, cheap brandy and an excess of sugar and drunk under a hot sun it can take its toll. Best avoided.

Wine is regarded as a drink to accompany meals. Table wine is often drunk with "*gaseosa*", a light lemonade, at lunch time. There are a lot more wines to Spain than the Riojas which have put the country on the food and wine map. Catalonia is the second largest producer of wines in Spain, so make the most of the range of local wines on offer. The official mark of quality is D.O. (Denominacion de Origen). The main regions are:

Penedés: The most important and internationally famed area, just to the west of Barcelona and easily visited. Known for its *cava* (champagne-style sparkling wine) and white wines, but also produces some good reds and rosés. Try any of the following producers: Torres (Gran Coronas or Gran Viña Sol and Viña Esmeralda), Masia Bach, Marqués de Monistrol (especially whites), René Barbier, Cavas Hill.

Alella: A few miles north of Barcelona, this region is best for its whites, Alella Marfil and Marqués de Alella.

Empordà–Costa Brava: A region near the French border in the northeast. Perelada wines are good. Blanc Pescador is a refreshing, reasonably priced white that slips down easily at lunch time.

Costers del Segre: In the province of Lleida. The company Raimat produces excellent wines that are often overlooked. Try their Clos Abadía and Cabernet Sauvignon, Clos Casal and Chardonnay.

Priorat: Quite heavy reds. Main producers are Scala Dei, De Muller and Priorat Unió.

•CAVA

Another pride of Catalonia, *cava* is the sparkling wine made by the *méthode champenoise*. Produced in the Penedès region for over 100 years it has now gained international recognition, especially in the United States where certain brands have gained popularity over French champagnes. In Catalan homes it is drunk at festive occasions and with Sunday lunch, usually to accompany sticky cakes at dessert.

Codorniú and Freixenet are the most established labels but other well regarded producers are Conde Caralt, Juve i Camps, Segura Viudas and Marqués de Monistrol. Try "*brut*" and "*brut nature*" for the best quality. A visit to the cellars of various producers in Sant Sadurní d'Anoia, a small town near Vilafranca del Penedés, which is the centre of *cava* country is a pleasant excursion. Codorniú have impressive modernist buildings designed by Puig i Cadafalch and along with Freixenet offer organised tours. Call to arrange visits: Codorniú tel: 891 0125. Freixenet tel: 891 0700.

Keen *cava* drinkers who cannot make it to Sant Sadurní could visit Xampany, Carrer de València 200, in Barcelona; this specialist shop sells over 100 different *cavas* and offers tastings.

THINGS TO DO

Barcelona is densely built between the hill of Tibidabo and the sea and bordered by Montjuïc to the south. It is worth making a trip up either hill or over the port in the cable-car for a good view and instant orientation of the city's layout. Avoid misty or heavily polluted days.

•Tibidabo

The highest peak in the Collserola range of hills which lie behind Barcelona, Tibidabo's name comes from the biblical story of the devil tempting Christ from the summit of a hill: "all this will I give to you…" or "*tibi dabo*" in Latin.

The most enjoyable way up is in the Tramvia Blau (Blue Tram), which runs from the foot of Avinguda Tibidabo (Metro/FFCC station Av. Tibidabo) to the Funicular Railway which continues to the summit. The services interconnect, running frequently every day 7 a.m.–9.35 p.m. and later at weekends and in the summer, according to the opening hours of the amusement park.

While waiting for the tram note "La Rotonda", a former hotel turned hospital. There are also some magnificent modernist *torres* (villas) on the route, where the rich Barcelonans used to summer, now mostly converted into flats or offices.

The amusement park on the summit comprises fairground attractions, a museum of automata (some from the early 19th century), a lookout tower and restaurants. A good spot for a drink with a view on a balmy summer evening. An unexceptional church at the entrance, the Sagrada Corazon Temple, is popular for weddings.

Opening times: Winter: 11 a.m.–8 p.m., weekends, school holidays, fiestas. April–September: every day, but June–August, 5 p.m.–1.30 or 2.30 a.m. to avoid the heat of the day, except Sundays 12 –11 p.m.. These timings could easily change; to be safe confirm on tel: 211 7942.

Entrance fee: "*de paseo*" costs 450 pesetas, and covers the entrance charge and six attractions, including the famous "*Avion Tibiair*" and the museum; "*pasa libre*" costs 1400 pesetas, and gives access to all the attractions.

Reductions are available for half-days, groups, very young and old. An alternative excursion, if you can't face the fairground at the top, is to take the tram to the funicular station but then walk up through the gardens as far as Carretera de les Aigües, a rough road that skirts the mountains for several miles: the view is excellent and the pine-scented air is the perfect antidote to Barcelona. (This road can also be reached from Metro/FFCC Peu del Funicular). Returning to the tram pause for a drink in the Merbeye or Mirablau bars, or treat yourself to a meal on the terrace of La Venta, good food in very charming surroundings.

•Montjuïc

Having played an important strategic role in the defence of the city, Montjuïc hill was developed and landscaped for the 1929 International Exposition. History is now repeating itself as the buildings and sports facilities are dusted down and redeveloped for the 1992 Olympics. There is something for everyone on Montjuïc: good views from the castle, museums, fairground attraction, Poble Espanyol (the "Spanish village"), the Olympic complex, walks or bicycle rides through the gardens.

You can get to Montjuïc by cable car from the port, by the Metro to Plaça d'Espanya or Paral.lel, by bus to Plaça d'Espanya (Nos. 9, 27, 50) or Palau dels Esports (No. 55). A bus from Plaça d'Espanya (No. 61) to Avinguda Miramar covers key areas of the hill. A final alternative is to take the funicular from Paral.lel to the amusement park, from where there is a cable car to the castle and military museum.

Poble Espanyol: the Spanish village was built for the 1929 exhibition to show the different regional styles of architecture. Recently refurbished and injected with new life it can be fun, but remains a tourist showcase and seems to lack a genuine heart. There is plenty on offer: daily entertainments in the main square and streets (from 11.30 a.m.), an audio-visual on Barcelona and shops selling crafts. There are bars and restaurants of every type: for cocktails, *tapas*, fruit juices or even sherry and olives in an Andalusian *patio* (though beware of being talked into the most expensive item on the menu here; not much sign of the warm Andalusian spirit in this *patio*). The village has bars with live music, jazz, and floor shows. There are restaurants which offer regional dishes, Mediterranean food, pizzas or tea and cakes. Naps, a vegetarian restaurant, has refreshingly different salads. The Tablao de Carmen offers a set dinner and flamenco show: both are good, but try and go in a crowd or on a busy night for greater atmosphere.

Village opening times: daily 9 a.m.–2 a.m., and later at weekends. Entrance fee: 400 pesetas; family ticket: 800 pesetas. For more information tel: 325 7866.

Olympic complex: The most important of the four Olympic locations, Montjuïc has the stadium (built within the 1929 stadium) and the Palau d'Esports Sant Jordi. Both can be visited 9 a.m.–7 p.m. on week days. Enquire at the stadium entrance.

A recommended way of seeing Montjuïc is by bicycle, which can be hired at Bicisport, tel: 214 4046, just by the Palau Nacional (Museu d'Art de Catalunya). Open: weekends and fiestas 10.30 a.m. till dusk.

•The Port
Barcelona has had a reputation of "turning its back to the sea", but the present municipal authorities are endeavouring to open the town up by developing the port for popular recreation. Thanks to the recent developments, particularly the Moll de la Fusta, there is much more contact with the activities of the port, and no mistaking that this is a Mediterranean city. For a different angle, walk round to Barceloneta and along the sea wall, or to the beaches along the Passeig Marítim, or try *tapas* in one of the many bars that line the Passeig Nacional (Bar Hispano is recommended). These pavement cafés can be a suntrap in the winter months. Barceloneta is the next bit of waterfront scheduled to be developed and may lose some of its seedy charms, but it will always be a part of Barcelona not to be missed.

Cable car: Another relic of the 1929 exhibition and still going strong. For a spectacular view catch it at any of the three stations – Barceloneta, Moll de Barcelona or Miramar on Montjuïc. It runs daily, from 11.30 a.m. till dusk.

Columbus monument: This monument to Christopher Columbus at the foot of the Ramblas is one of the landmarks of Barcelona. For a fine aerial view of the city take the lift which runs inside the column. From 10 a.m.–2 p.m. and 3.30–6.30 p.m. in the winter; closed: Monday. From 9 a.m.–9 p.m. daily in the summer (mid-June to mid-September).

Golondrinas: For a trip round the harbour take one of these pretty boats moored near the Columbus monument. Every 30 minutes from 11 a.m. till dusk. Tel: 412 5944.

Bicycle hire: To get around the port and beaches the healthy way, hire bicycles, tricycles or tandems opposite the Estacion de Francia on Avingudia Marquès de l'Argentera. (See *Sport* for details). On Sundays a cycle route is closed from traffic in the central Eixample; follow the signs.

•Parc de Ciutadella
A real family park with a happy atmosphere. On Sunday morning the park is still full with families parading before going off to large lunches. Apart from the Museum of Modern Art and the Zoological Museum housed in old buildings, look out for the Catalan Parliament building in the former Governor's Palace, the Umbracle with its tropical vegetation and the Hivernacle, where concerts and exhibitions are often held. The concerts are particularly enjoyable on a summer night. Boats can be hired on the lake, from 10 a.m.–6 p.m. November–February and until 7 p.m. the rest of the year.

The zoo is in Ciutadella park. Its main claim to fame is "Snowflake", the white gorilla (the only albino gorilla in captivity). Open: 10 a.m.–5 p.m. and in the summer 10 a.m.–7.30 p.m.

COUNTRY

•Parc de Collserola
Collserola is a natural park area formed by the forested hills which lie between Barcelona and Sant Cugat (the hill of Tibidabo and

beyond). An excellent leaflet available at tourist offices shows the walks, tracks, picnic spots etc., and gives names and addresses of riding centres, restaurants and other places of interest. The whole area is easily reached from Barcelona (FFCC from Plaça de Catalunya) but feels like "real" country, not just over the hill.

•Montserrat

The sacred centre of Catalonia, the mountain and monastery of Montserrat is where the Black Virgin, the patron saint of Catalonia, is worshipped. Montserrat is within easy reach of Barcelona by car, or by organised excursions. Daily visits leave Barcelona at 9.30 a.m., or from April–August in the afternoons. The Montserrat choir sings only in the mornings.

For excursions contact:

Julià Tours: Ronda Universitat, 5. Tel: 317 6454/318 3895.

Pullmantur: Gran Via, 635. Tel: 317 1297/ 318 0241.

Wine Country: Vilafranca del Penedès and Sant Sadurní d'Anoia are in the heart of the most important wine region of Catalonia and make a pleasant trip from Barcelona. In Vilafranca the Wine Museum is open every day except Monday, and in Sant Sadurní the cellars of *cava* producers Freixenet and Codorníu can be visited. (See *Food Digest* for details).

Spas: There are many different spas in Catalonia, offering diverse treatments. Some are quite near Barcelona. For details contact: Associació Catalana de la Propietat Balneària, Passeig de Gràcia, 34. Tel: 317 9312.

Tour Guides: For professional tourist guides/interpreters to accompany groups contact the Professional Association of Barcelona Tour Guides. Tel: 345 4221.

CULTURE PLUS

The combination of Catalonia's rich cultural heritage and the dynamism of contemporary movements makes Barcelona one of Europe's cultural capitals. Apart from its architecture and nearly 40 museums, there is a busy calendar of music and arts festivals, visiting exhibitions and constant activity in design, theatre and the arts in general, to say nothing of daily performances from street artists in the Ramblas and small squares of the *barri* Gòtic. Furthermore, as part of the 1992 Olympic Games, a programme known as the Olimpíada Cultural, the Cultural Olympics, is taking place, re-evaluating the cultural wealth of Barcelona past, present and future, and drawing international talent to the city.

Whatever time of year you visit, there will be some cultural activity. Posters, banners, the daily and weekly press all herald what's on. The City Council have a Cultural Information Centre in the Palau de la Virreina, Rambla, 99, which is very helpful and has leaflets and information on nearly all cultural activities. It also sells tickets. For information tel: 010 or 301 7775. For tickets tel: 318 8599.

MUSEUMS

Apart from the permanent collections, check what itinerant exhibitions are in town, particularly in the Museu Picasso, Fundació Joan Miró and Museu d'Art Modern, as well as the cultural and exhibition centres listed below.

In preparation for 1992 and beyond, Barcelona is undergoing major changes, not least in the renovation of museums and the re-housing of works. Confirm locations and opening hours before visiting anywhere. Except where specified below most museums are closed on Mondays, lunch-times, and Sunday and holiday afternoons.

Museu Arqueològic: Passeig Santa Madrona, Montjuïc. Tel: 423 2149. Open: Tuesday–Saturday 9.30 a.m.–1 p.m. and 4–7 p.m, Sunday 9.30 a.m.–2 p.m. Archaeological discoveries from the first inhabitants of Catalonia and the rest of the Iberian Peninsula.

Museu Etnològic: Passeig Santa Madrona, Montjuïc. Tel: 424 6402. Open: Tuesday–Saturday 9 a.m. –8.30 p.m., Sunday 9 a.m.–2 p.m., Monday 3 –8.30 p.m. Ethnographical items from all over the world, especially the Philippines and New Guinea.

Museu d'Art de Catalunya: Palau Nacional, Montjuïc. Tel: 423 1824. Open: Tuesday–Sunday 9 a.m.–2 p.m. Undergoing major renovation work for re-opening by 1992, this rather forbidding building that overlooks the fountains of Montjuïc houses an impressive collection of Catalan Romanesque art. Many of the frescos were painstakingly salvaged from remote churches in the Pyrenees and brought down the mountain-side by donkey at the beginning of the century. It also houses a collection of Gothic art and some baroque and Renaissance pieces.

Institut i Jardí Botànic: Avinguda Montanyans, Montjuïc. Tel: 325 8050. Open: Sunday–Thursday 9 a.m.–2 p.m.

Fundació Joan Miró: Plaça de Neptú, Montjuïc. Tel: 329 1908. Open: Tuesday–Saturday 11 a.m.–7 p.m., Thursday 11 a.m.–9.30 p.m., Sunday 10.30 a.m.–2.30 p.m. Cafeteria, restaurant and bookshop. One of the largest collections of Miró's work in the world, including paintings, drawings, sculptures, tapestries and the complete graphic work, well exhibited in this modern building designed by Sert. Regular exhibitions of contemporary art.

Museu Militar: Montjuïc Castle. Tel: 241 6829. Most impressive for its view over the port.

Museu Marítim: Portal de la Pau, 1. Tel: 318 3245. Open: Tuesday–Saturday 10 a.m.–2 p.m. and 4–7 p.m., Sunday 10 a.m.–2 p.m. Housed in well-preserved 14th-century royal shipyards, this maritime museum has an interesting collection of models, navigational instruments, figureheads, drawings and replicas, including an outstanding one, to scale, of the galleon used by Don Juan de Austria in the Battle of Lepanto. A haven for boat enthusiasts of all ages.

Museu de Cera: Passatge de la Banca, 7. Tel: 317 2649. Open: Monday–Friday 10 a.m.–1.30 p.m. and 4–7.30 p.m., Saturday and Sunday 10 a.m.–8 p.m. The Wax Museum near the end of the Ramblas. Not exactly a Madame Tussauds, but an option for entertaining the children.

Museu d'Història de la Ciutat: Plaça del Rei. Tel: 315 1111. Open: Tuesday–Saturday 9 a.m.–8.30 p.m., Sunday 9 a.m.–1.30 p.m. The museum of the city's history, including archaeological remains in the cellars and adjoining streets.

Museu Frederic Marès: Plaça Sant Iu. Tel: 310 5800. Open: Tuesday–Saturday 9 a.m.–2 p.m. and 4–7 p.m., Sunday 9 a.m.–2 p.m. Sculpture, from Roman to baroque, and interesting portrayal of daily life from the 15th to the 20th centuries.

Museu de la Catedral: Cathedral Cloister. Tel: 315 3555. Open: daily 11 a.m.–1 p.m. Cathedral treasures.

Museu Picasso: Carrer de Montcada, 15–19. Tel: 319 6310. Open: Tuesday–Sunday 10 a.m.–7.30pm. Essential on any itinerary of Barcelona's museums. The museum has a particularly absorbing collection of Picasso's early work, his sketches in school books, a masterly portrait of his mother accomplished when he was 16, his early days in Barcelona and Paris, but it is limited on the later periods apart from the series *Las Meninas*. Housed in the magnificent gothic palaces of Berenguer Aguilar and Barón de Castellet, this museum is the answer to the clichéd "My three-year-old could do that!". Unfortunately, it offers poor support in foreign languages; for details buy the catalogue in the bookshop, though the arrows and dates provide a chronological guide. Go at lunchtime to avoid queues. Attractive cafeteria.

Museu Tèxtil i de la Indumentària: Carrer de Montcada 12–14. Tel: 310 4516. Open: Tuesday–Saturday 9 a.m.–2 p.m. and 4.30–7 p.m., Sunday 9 a.m.–2 p.m. The Textile and Clothing Museum is housed in yet another elegant palace. It is worth visiting if you are interested in period costume, but limited on textiles and documentation. Occasional visiting exhibitions.

Museu d'Art Modern: Parc de la Ciutadella, Plaça d'Armes. Tel: 319 5728. Open: Tuesday–Saturday 9 a.m.–7.30 p.m., Sunday 9 a.m.–2 p.m., Monday 3–7.30pm.

Under threat of being moved to another location, this large collection of mostly Catalan 19th and 20th-century paintings, drawings, sculpture and decorative art is currently in the former Ciutadella Palace in the middle of the park, a perfect setting that makes a soothing excursion. Little really contemporary art, but a good collection of Fortuny, Nonell, Casas, Rusiñol and Sert from around the turn of the century. Well worth visiting.

Museu de Geologia: Parc de la Ciutadella. Tel: 319 6895. Open: Tuesday–Sunday 9 a.m.–2 p.m.

Museu de Zoologia: Parc de la Ciutadella. Tel: 319 6912. Open: Tuesday–Sunday 9 a.m.–2 p.m. Zoological collection well presented in an extrovert building designed by Domènech i Montaner which was built as the restaurant in the 1888 universal exhibition.

Museu de la Ciència: Carrer de Teodor Roviralta, 55. Tel: 212 6050. Open: Tuesday–Sunday 10 a.m.–8 p.m. The Science Museum at the "top end" of Barcelona near Av. Tibidabo station, providing an opportunity to see another part of Barcelona. It is well thought-out and funded by the benevolent and wealthy bank, the Caixa de Pensions. Good for children.

Museu-Monestir de Pedralbes: Baixada Monestir, 9. Tel: 203 9282. Open: Tuesday–Sunday 9.30 a.m.–2 p.m. This is the perfect antidote to several days of intense living in the centre of Barcelona. The 14th-century three-tiered cloisters of the Monastery of Pedralbes still occupied by Clarista nuns, are pure serenity. They contain some remarkable paintings by the Catalan Ferrer Bassa, a leading Italo-Gothic artist in the 14th century. The museum, a glimpse into monastic life, make the visit even more worthwhile. The upper cloisters, undergoing restoration work, may be used to house part of the Von Thyssen collection that is being given to Spain.

Museu de la Música: Diagonal, 373. Tel: 217 1157. Open: Tuesday–Sunday 9 a.m.–2 p.m. This collection of musical instruments from the 16th to the 20th centuries is housed in the modernist building "Casa Quadras" designed by Puig i Cadafalch.

Casa-Museu Gaudí: Parc Güell, Carrer Olot. Tel: 214 6446. Open: March–November 10 a.m.–2 p.m. and 4–7 p.m. daily. Closed: December–February. House within the park where Gaudí lived from 1905 to 1926, displaying furniture he designed, drawings and projects.

Museu Verdaguer: Vil.la Joana, Vallvidrera. Tel: 204 7805. Open: Tuesday–Sunday 9 a.m.–2 p.m. The Catalan poet Jacint Verdaguer lived and died here. The museum is a collection of his personal belongings. It also offers an opportunity to visit this small, pleasant suburb of Barcelona at the top of the hill, reached by FFCC train to Baixador de Vallvidrera.

Palau Reial de Pedralbes: Diagonal, 686. Tel: 203 7500. Open: Tuesday–Friday 10 a.m.–1 p.m. and 4–6 p.m., Saturday and Sunday 10 a.m.–1.30 p.m. Often closed for offical receptions, so check before visiting. Standing in elegant, spacious gardens, the palace was built in the 1920s for King Alfonso XIII. It contains some personal belongings of the Royal Family and furniture, paintings, sculptures.

EXHIBITION CENTRES

The following centres regularly hold good temporary exhibitions of visual arts. Consult local press for details:

Palau de la Virreina: Rambla, 99. Tel: 301 7775.

Palau Robert: Passeig de Gràcia, 107.

Centre Cultural de la Caixa de Pensions: Passeig Sant Joan, 108. Tel: 258 8907.

Sala d'Exposicions de la Fundació Caixa de Pensions: Via Laietana, 56. Tel: 404 6130.

Sala Sant Jaume de Caixa de Barcelona: Jaume I, 2. Tel: 318 4744.

Centre d'Art Santa Monica: Rambla Sta. Monica, 7. Tel: 412 2279.

Centre de Cultura Contemporania Casa de la Caritat: Carrer Montealegre, 5. Tel: 412 0782. This venue holds seminars as well as exhibitions of contemporary art. Due to be developed into a large centre for contemporary culture, possibly including the modern art museum.

ART GALLERIES

The galleries are congregated into specific areas of the city: the first is the Passeig de Gràcia/Rambla de Catalunya and interconnecting streets (notably Consell de

Cent); the second is the old town, classical around Plaça San Josep Oriol and contemporary near the Born; and thirdly the streets behind Plaça Francesc Macià. Opening hours are usually 10.30 a.m.–1.30 p.m. and 4.30–8.30 p.m. Tuesday–Saturday.

A selection of the most interesting by area:
Ambit: Consell de Cent, 282.
Carles Tache: Consell de Cent, 290.
D Barcelona: Diagonal, 367.
Dau al Set: Consell de Cent, 333.
Eude: Consell de Cent, 278.
Joan Prats: Rambla de Catalunya, 54.
Kreisler-Barcelona: Valencia, 262.
Subex: Mallorca, 253.

Key galleries in the Old town:
Benet Costa: Comerç, 29.
Berini: Plaça Comercial, 3.
Duna: Amargós, 6.
Jordi Boronat: Passeig del Born, 17.
Lino Silverstein: Antic de Sant Joan, 3.
Maeght: Montcada, 25.
Sala Pares: Petritxol, 5–8. The oldest gallery in Barcelona.
Sala Artur Ramon: Palla, 23.

Key galleries by Plaça Francesc Macià:
ASB Gallery: Diagonal, 606.
Fernando Alcolea: Plaça Sant Gregori.
Tache Editor: Juan Sebastián Bach, 22.
Trade Art: Riera de Sant Miquel, 30.

CONCERTS

•Classical Music
A busy season of concerts by the Barcelona City Orchestra (Orquestra Ciutat de Barcelona) and visiting orchestras and soloists runs all the way from September to early July, complemented by various international music festivals outside Barcelona in July and August. Barcelona's different Arts Festivals also include classical music. The main locations are:
Palau de la Música Catalana: Carrer d'Amadeu Vives, 1. Tel: 301 1104. If you have an opportunity to go to a concert in this extravagant modernist palace by Domènech i Montaner's, go – whatever the programme.
Centre Cultural de la Fundació Caixa de Pensions: Passeig de Sant Joan, 108. Tel: 258 8907.
Saló de Cent: Ayuntamiento de Barcelona, Plaça de Sant Jaume, 1. Tel: 317 1096.

•Contemporary Music
Fundació Miró: Montjuïc. Tel: 329 1908. The gallery hosts a season of 20th-century music, with particular emphasis on Catalan composers.
Nick Havanna: Rosselló, 208. Tel: 201 4095. More known for late night drinking, this trendy bar also holds a season of 20th-century music.

•Jazz
The Terrassa Jazz Festival in the spring and the Barcelona International Jazz Festival in the autumn gather together some leading names. In addition there are regular jazz sessions in:
La Cova del Drac: Carrer de Tuset, 30.
Harlem: Carrer de Comtessa de Sobradiel, 8.
L'Eixample Jazz Club: Carrer de Diputació, 341.
Sam's: Poble Espanyol, Montjuïc.

•Rock/Pop
Barcelona is now on the itinerary of most major international tours. Booking for these is usually through banks and record shops, notably Discos Castelló in Carrer de Tallers, just off the Ramblas. On a smaller scale, some interesting off-beat musicians and eternal old timers often pass through, and are usually to be found in:
Zeleste: Carrer d'Almogàvers, 122.
Studio 54: Avinguda Paral.lel, 65.

OPERA & BALLET

A season of opera, including some classical ballet, runs through from September to early July in the Gran Teatre del Liceu, the opera house on the Ramblas. This is the best place to see Barcelona's very own opera star Montserrat Caballé.
Gran Teatre del Liceu: Rambla, 61. Booking office open: Monday–Friday 8 a.m.–3 p.m., Saturday 9 a.m.–1 p.m. and on the day 11.30 a.m.–1.30 p.m. and 4 p.m. to performance.
There are guided tours of the building Monday–Friday at 11.30 a.m. and 12.15 p.m. depending on rehearsal schedules.

•Contemporary Dance
The Barcelona Contemporary Ballet have a short season, supplemented throughout the

year by visiting groups. Dance is an important part of the Mercat de les Flors programme. Teatre de l'Institut, Carrer de Sant Pere Més Baix 7, has a programme of contemporary dance. For information tel: 322 1037.

THEATRES

Catalonia boasts a long tradition of theatrical talent from Margarita Xirgu, actress and Lorca's collaborator, to Nuria Espert, internationally renowned for her performances and directing. Outstanding amongst contemporary talent is Josep Maria Flotats and company who usually perform classical works. The notorious La Fura dels Baus is an *avant-garde* company who can make theatre-going an uncomfortable but worthwhile experience. On a lighter level, and sometimes to be found in the streets of Barcelona are La Cubana – satirical and fun. Naturally productions are in Catalan, but for true enthusiasts the theatrical experience should compensate for language problems. Occasionally some Spanish theatre is performed. The main theatres are:

Poliorama: Rambla, 115. Tel: 317 7599. Flotats usually performs here.

Goya: Carrer de Joaquim Costa, 68. Tel: 318 1984.

Romea: Carrer de Hospital, 51. Tel: 317 7189.

Mercat de les Flors: Carrer de Lleida, 59. Tel: 426 1875. This is the former flower market converted into two theatrical areas. Its dome was painted by Miquel Barceló. It has a very active programme with many visiting groups and unusual productions.

Teatre Lliure: Carrer de Montseny, 47. Tel: 218 9251. Good contemporary productions from the theatre's own company. The venue also has a season of chamber concerts, poetry recitals and a very pleasant restaurant.

Malic: Carrer de Fussina, 3. Tel: 310 7035. Predominantly a puppet theatre.

In addition, the Catalonia National Theatre and the Barcelona Auditorium are being built near the Plaça de les Glòries.

CINEMAS

Unfortunately the dubbing industry is well established in Spain, so most international films are no longer shown with their original soundtrack. However, of the 52 cinemas in Barcelona, a handful specialise in *"version original"* (VO in the daily listings). The main ones are listed below. Most sessions begin around 4 p.m. and the last and most popular one is around 10.30 p.m., with some late-night shows at weekends. Seats are still reasonably priced and some cinemas offer discounts on certain days of the week. You should tip the usher about 25 pesetas – one of the very few places tipping is still expected.

Alexis: Rambla de Catalunya, 90.
Arcadia: Carrer de Tuset, 14.
Arkadin: Travessera de Gràcia, 103.
Capsa: Carrer de Pau Claris, 193.
Casablanca: Passeig de Gràcia, 115.
Maldà: Carrer del Pi, 5.
Moderno: Carrer de Gerona, 175.
Rex: Gran Vía, 463.
Verdi: Carrer de Verdi, 32.
Vergara: Carrer de Vergara, 14.

The Filmoteca de la Generalitat de Catalunya in Travessera de Gràcia, 63, is a film theatre showing less commercial films and retrospectives.

FESTIVALS

The Barcelona International Film Festival takes place in June/July, centred on Rambla de Catalunya, which becomes duly festive and glossy with visiting directors and exhibitions. It can be a struggle to obtain programmes and information but these should be available through tel: 215 2424. The Sitges International Festival of Fantasy Film is a well established annual event every October. Tel: 317 3585.

The Grec Festival: held from late June until early August, the Grec is Barcelona's summer festival, bringing together a high standard of national and international talent in theatre, music and dance. Performances take place all over the city, but one of the most impressive and appealing venues on a summer night is the Grec Theatre itself on Montjuïc: an outdoor amphitheatre. For information and booking: Palau de la Virreina, Rambla, 99. Tel: 318 2525 or the city council information service, tel: 010.

The Tardor Festival: An autumn festival of mostly theatre and dance which is part of the Olimpiada Cultural. For information on this or any aspect of the Olimpiada Cultural tel: 317 0024.

NIGHTLIFE

The first thing to understand about nightlife in Barcelona is that night means night, and nothing really gets going until after 1 a.m. For an authentic Barcelona night out, start to think about cocktails around 9 p.m. and dinner, at a leisurely pace, from 10-ish. This way you will be all set to begin the *juerga* (fun/wild time) by 1 a.m. with enough energy to keep going until at least 4 in the morning. This demanding schedule is usually practised from Thursday to Saturday – though the hardy are out playing any day of the week and still miraculously make it to their offices at 9 a.m.

BARS

Of the trendy bars which are regularly featured in international design magazines, the "in" place changes every few months when yet another one opens and becomes the bar where anybody who is anybody goes. Some are just for drinking and socialising (and being seen) and some are for drinking and dancing (and being seen). This selection is loosely divided into pre-dinner and post-dinner bars, the former including some classics which never go out of fashion and those which are pleasant at any time of day; the latter includes discos and bars which only open from 8 p.m. at the earliest.

•Pre-dinner bars
Boadas: Carrer de Tallers, 1. A classic Barcelona cocktail bar. The cartooned figure of the original owner watches from highly polished walls while his elegant daughter mixes the snappiest martinis and her waiters attend your every need. Their *mojito* –Hemingway's Cuban favourite – is highly recommended.

Dry Martini: Carrer d'Aribau, 162. A sophisticated cocktail bar that serves excellent Martinis to a middle-class clientele.

Ideal Cocktail's Bar: Carrer d'Aribau, 89. Professional service in British club style complete with hunting scenes.

Gimlet: Carrer de Santaló, 46. Slick, modern design. Good for post-dinner too.

Snooker Club: Carrer de Roger de Lluria, 42. Elegant, modern snooker club for a cool cocktail or an after-dinner drink.

Velódrom: Carrer de Muntaner, 213. An old bar in the middle of the Eixample with high, nicotine-stained ceilings, peeling paint and fluorescent lighting, but which never loses its charm or popularity.

Bar Pastis: Carrer de Santa Mònica, 4. Over 40 years old this small corner of Marseilles at the bottom of the Ramblas offering *pastis* to the strains of Brel and Piaf, is a welcome alternative to the high design and high tech of bars elsewhere.

Merbeyé: Plaça Doctor Andreu. At the foot of the Tibidabo funicular. Attractive shady terrace for lunch times and summer evenings.

Mirablau: Opposite the Merbeyé, with a spectacular view over Barcelona day and night.

Berimbau: Passeig del Born, 17. Brazilian bar with stunning *caipirinhas* – the Brazilian cocktail you'll never forget.

Café del Sol: Plaça del Sol. Terrace on the square. A good start to an evening in the Gràcia district, with its many alternative bars and restaurants.

In addition, there are several bars on the Moll de la Fusta, the new development along the waterfront.

•Post-dinner
Nick Havanna: Carrer de Rosselló, 208. Famed for its design and in-crowd. Several years on and still a leader.

Universal: Carrer de Mariano Cubí, 184. Striking decor on three floors. An essential stop on the nocturnal tour.

Satanassa: Carrer d'Aribau, 27. The latest of the latest. And the wildest.

Si Si Si: Avinguda Diagonal, 442. In a beautiful modernist building.

La Fira: Carrer de Provença, 171. Fun bar with the atmosphere and bustle of the fairground; fascinating old automatons on display.

292: Carrer de Diputació, 292.
Velvet: Carrer de Balmes, 161.

DISCOS & BARS

Otto Zutz: Carrer de Lincoln, 15. Bouncers vet your trendiness at the door. Best after 2 a.m.

KGB: Carrer d'Alegre de Dalt, 55.

Ars Estudio: Carrer d'Atenes, 27.

Distrito Distinto: Avinguda Meridiana, 140.

Centro Ciudad: Carrer de Consell de Cent, 294.

Artículo 26: Carrer Gran de Gràcia. Live music including salsa.

Up & Down: Carrer de Numancia, 179. One of the most famous nightspots of Barcelona, its members are somewhere between the jet set and Dallas. With the required amount of style, lip-gloss or jewellery you'll pass.

TABLAOS

A "Tablao" is a bar/restaurant that has a flamenco show. Strictly not Catalan, though recently this import from Andalusia has become popular among Catalans to the point of being trendy. It is advisable before hand to confirm the times of the shows and whether dinner is obligatory or not.

El Tablao de Carmen: Poble Espanyol. Tel: 325 6895. A good authentic show and reasonable dinner.

El Patio Andaluz: Carrer d'Aribau, 242. Tel: 209 3378.

Los Tarantos: Plaça Reial, 17. Tel: 317 8098. Quite touristy but plenty of atmosphere.

Romeria: Carrer de Casanova, 54. Somewhere you can learn to dance *Sevillanas* during the evening.

MUSIC HALLS/CABARETS

Barcelona has a long and colourful tradition of show business, centred on the area known as the Parallelo, the harbour end of Avinguda del Paral.lel. The shows, the surrounding bars, the characters involved all provide a sharp contrast to the high design and yuppiedom of the Eixample and upper parts of town. For a global view of Barcelona today you should have a night out at one of these places. Anything you lose in the language will be more than made up for in colour and atmosphere.

El Molino: Carrer de Vila i Vilà, 99. Tel: 241 6383. Tuesday–Sunday shows at 6 p.m. and 11 p.m., Saturday at 10.15 p.m. and 1 a.m. Ticket includes a free drink.

Arnau: Avinguda del Paral.lel, 60. Tel: 242 2804. Two shows nightly, apart from Wednesday.

Barcelona de Noche: Carrer de Tàpies, 5. Tel: 241 1167. Shows at 11.45 p.m. and 1.30 a.m.

Bodega Bohemia: Carrer de Lancaster, 2. Tel: 302 5081.

DANCEHALLS

La Paloma: Carrer de Tigre, 27. Tel: 301 6897. Orchestra Thursday–Sunday. Sessions 6 p.m.–9.30 p.m. and 11.30 p.m.–3.30 a.m.

Apolo: Carrer Nou de la Rambla, 113. Tel: 242 5183. Open: Saturday 6 p.m.–9 p.m. and 11 p.m.–3 a.m., Sunday 5.30 p.m.–9.30 p.m.

CASINOS

Gran Casino de Barcelona: Sant Pere de Ribes. Tel: 893 3666. About 30 miles (40 km) out of Barcelona in the hills behind Sitges.

Casino Castillo de Perelada: Perelada. Tel: (972)50 3162. In the province of Girona, only 13 miles (20 km) from the French border.

SHOPPING

If you can't face trudging home with virgin olive oil, or fear your holiday budget will disappear if you venture into leather at Loewe, it is still worth seeing the spectacle of the food markets and doing some serious window shopping while in Barcelona.

WHAT TO BUY

As Europe rapidly becomes one and most goods are available in most countries, the bargain which cannot be found back home is a rarity. However, in certain products the choice is much wider and anything bought abroad always has good sentimental value once the holiday is over.

Leather: it is questionable whether leather garments are still worth buying in Spain, except perhaps at the top end of the market, where design and quality are outstanding. But shoes, handbags and suitcases are worth considering. The best in clothes, bags and accessories is Loewe; their shop in the Casa Lleó Morera (Passeig de Gràcia, 35) is an experience in itself. There are many cheaper shops specialising in leather, particularly in and around the Ramblas and Portal de l'Angel, where you can also find shops in strange first-floor surroundings selling at factory prices; here there are bargains if you are not too worried about style.

Shoes are good value. Look out for Catalan and Spanish designers such as Yanko, Farrutx (sophisticated elegance), Lotusse (contemporary classical and very well made), Camper, Make-Up (off-beat). The best areas for shoes and bags are Portal de l'Angel, Rambla de Catalunya, Passeig de Gràcia, Diagonal and the shopping malls (Bulevard Rosa, Halley, Via Wagner).

Fashion: if you can afford the investment, a snappy little outfit from one of the latest Catalan or Spanish designers will set you aside from the crowd. Choose from Toni Miró (his shops called "Groc" are in Rambla de Catalunya and Carrer de Muntaner), Adolfo Dominguez (Passeig de Gràcia), Roser Mercé, Purificación Garcia, Jordi Cuesta, Sybilla, Joan Tomas.

Lesser known designers at more approachable prices can be found in boutiques in the galleries, and around Passeig de Gràcia, Rambla de Catalunya, etc. For cheap and cheerful clothes and accessories try Carrer de Portaferrisa and adjoining streets, including the galleries. Gralle Hall in Portaferrisa has boutiques with more off-beat, individual designs. Galon Glacé (Passeig de Gràcia, 76) has a classic collection of 1950s and 1960s clothes and accessories at 1990s prices, as well as their own unique garments.

Design: much of Barcelona's current image rests upon its fame in design. For a souvenir of Mariscal (designer of Cobi, the Olympic mascot, and much more besides) or just to have an idea of how trendy Barcelonans decorate their homes, don't miss Vinçon (Passeig de Gràcia, 96), especially its first floor. Or Pilma, just around the corner in Aving003uda Diagonal. On a smaller scale, Dos i Una (Carrer de Rosselló, 275) has David Valls socks, Mariscal ear-rings and gimmicks to help solve gift problems.

•**Traditional crafts**
Ceramics: from earthenware cooking pots to elegant dishes or hand-painted tiles, the ceramics of Catalonia and other regions of Spain can be found all over the city, particularly in the *barri* Gòtic, at Molsa in Plaça Sant Josep Oriol (who also have some antique pots) and La Roda in Carrer de Call. Traditional ironmongers usually have a good collection of the classic brown earthenware pots at non-tourist prices, as well as wonderful cooking utensils.

Lladrò porcelain remains popular and collectable. Several shops specialise in it and will dispatch abroad. García (La Rambla, 4) boasts of a large collection at near factory prices. Department stores also stock Lladrò.

Wickerwork: a rustic chair may not be very manageable on a charter flight, but baskets, mats etc. are easy to carry and are appreciated as presents. There is a wide choice on the corner of Carrer de Banys Nous and Carrer Ave Maria.

Candles: from religious to decorative,

candles are quite a speciality of Barcelona. Visit the shops near the cathedral, especially Cereria Subirá (Baixada Llibreteria, 7) founded in 1761.

Alpargatas: these are the classic rope-soled canvas shoes (*espadrilles*). For an infinite variety of design, colour, size, and to see them being made, go to La Manual Alpargatera, just off Carrer de Ferran (Carrer d'Avinyó, 7).

For really original footwear, sturdy leather boots, Mallorcan sandals or rustic shoes from different regions in Spain, visit Calzados E. Solé (Carrer d'Ample, 7).

Many traditional crafts still exist in Barcelona, as do the small shops specialising in them. Whether you are looking for lace, embroidery, feathers, fans, gloves, hats, musical instruments, glass, religious artefacts, or whether you want to commission a guitar, walking stick, glass eye or lightning conductor, you can be sure that somewhere in Barcelona there is someone who specialises in it, particularly in the *barri* Gòtic, around the Born or on the streets Hospital and Carme. Most of these establishments are over 100 years old.

Antiques and books: there are many elegant and expensive antique shops in the Eixample and the *barri* Gòtic, notably the streets Banys Nous and Palla. Prints and antique books are also a feature of Barcelona, particularly in the labyrinth of pretty streets around the Cathedral: visit Librería Violán just off the Plaça del Rei for its unusual books, prints and striking Deco Posters.

Food and drink: a taste of Spain back home always extends the holiday. Olives marinated in garlic direct from the market, sausages (*chorizo*, *sobrasada*), ham (*jamon serrano* is the best), cheese (Manchego, Mahon, Idiazabal) nuts, dried fruit, handmade chocolates are all easy to carry. Virgin olive oil, wine, *cava*, and moscatel are less portable, but probably worth the effort. Buy from the markets or *colmados* (grocer's shops, on street corners in every district of the city).

Specialists in *turrón* (sticky nougat-type delicacy eaten mostly at Christmas) are Planelles Donat in Portal de l'Angel and Cucurulla. For chocolates try Fargas, a decorative old shop (corner of Carrer del Pi and Cucurulla) or the famous chocolate "sculptor" Antoni Escribà who has a beautiful modernist shop on La Rambla, 83. The only Spanish outlet of French chocolate maker Richart is at Carrer de Muntaner, 463, where you can buy the finest chocolates exquisitely presented.

Serious purchasers of *cava* should visit Xampany (Carrer de Valencia, 200), an attractive shop brimming over with more than 100 different types of *cava*, essential accessories and memorabilia.

SHOPPING AREAS

Apart from the specific areas mentioned, the entire length of Passeig de Gràcia and Rambla de Catalunya and the interconnecting streets provide enjoyable shopping, as does the Avinguda Diagonal, from the top of Rambla de Catalunya up to the roundabout which forms Plaça Francesc Macià (still often referred to as Calvo Sotelo). The streets behind the Plaça, Pau Casals, Mestre Nicolau and Bori i Fontesta with its Galerias Wagner are good but expensive for fashion.

The upper parts of town have their own local district atmosphere and make a refreshing change from the Eixample and *barri* Gòtic. Try Carrer de Muntaner, around its Metro station and upwards: interesting shops and bars, one of the best shoe shops in town in Las Maravillas (No. 356), and good wines by the glass to accompany delicate snacks in the Tivoli (No. 361).

The largest department store in Barcelona is El Corte Inglés, with one branch in Plaça de Catalunya and the other in Avinguda Diagonal, 617–619. The latter is rather isolated amongst office blocks, apart from a new Bulevard Rosa shopping arcade next door. (Metro Maria Cristina). Open: 10 a.m.–9 p.m. Monday–Saturday. Galerias Preciados has branches in Portal de l'Angel and Diagonal, 471–473. Open: Monday–Friday 10 a.m.–8 p.m., Saturday 10 a.m.–9 p.m.

Main shopping malls:

Bulevard Rosa (3 locations): Passeig de Gràcia, 55; Diagonal, 474; Diagonal, 609–615.

Galerías Halley: Passeig de Gràcia, 62.

La Avenida: Rambla de Catalunya, 68.

Galeries Maldà: Carrer de Portaferrissa, 22.

Diagonal Center: Diagonal, 584.

Via Wagner: Carrer de Bori i Fontesta, 17.

Useful for their opening hours, including Sundays, are the **Drugstores:**

Drugstore: Passeig de Gràcia, 71. Open: 24 hours daily. Restaurant, supermarket, tobacconist, bookshop, gifts, perfumes.

Drugstore David: Carrer de Tuset, 19–21. Open: daily from 9 a.m.–5 a.m..

VIP'S: Rambla de Catalunya,7. Open 8 a.m.–1.30am and until 3 a.m. on Friday and Saturday.

MARKETS

There are covered markets in every district of the city selling fruit, vegetables, meat and fish. A trip to Barcelona would be incomplete without visiting at least one of them. Markets open every day except Sunday from early in the morning until around 3 p.m. Avoid Mondays; the selection is poor because the central wholesale market does not open on a Monday.

The largest and most colourful market is the Boqueria on the Ramblas, which stays open until 8 p.m. Monday–Saturday. The most exotic and expensive fare is in the entrance; the bargains are to be found exploring the maze of stalls behind.

The Mercat de Concepció: (on Carrer de Valencia, between Carrer de Bruc and Carrer de Girona) is worth a visit for the flower market outside, which remains open day and night except on Christmas Day.

Els Encants: Plaça de les Glòries. A genuine flea market. Some expensive antiques, some old clothes, and a lot of trash, but in amongst it all bargains can still be found. Very hot in the summer; early morning is better for bargains and comfort. Open: Monday, Wednesday, Friday and Saturday 8 a.m.–7 p.m. (winter) and until 8 p.m. (summer).

Mercat Gòtic d'Antiguitats: Plaça del Pi. Antique market every Thursday (except in August) in Plaça del Pi and adjoining Plaça Sant Josep Oriol. Some interesting collections.

Coin and stamp market: Plaça Reial. Sunday 10 a.m.–2 p.m.

Coin and book market: Mercat Sant Antoni. Sunday 10 a.m.–2 p.m. Attractive market building on the junction of Carrer de Tamarit/Comte d'Urgell.

Craft fair: in Turó Parc, Carrer de Pau Casals. First Sunday of every month 10 a.m.–3 p.m.

Book and **Antique Fairs** are held with great regularity in Barcelona: look out for posters or announcements in the press.

SHOPPING HOURS

Most shops open between 9 and 10 a.m. and close religiously for lunch between 1 and 2 p.m., opening again between 4 and 5 p.m. until 8 p.m. Many clothes and food shops close at 8.30 or 9 p.m.. The large department stores and some of the shopping galleries remain open through lunchtime. In the summer many shops will close on Saturday afternoons.

EXPORT

Under current laws anyone resident outside Spain, including Spanish citizens of Ceuta, Melilla and the Canary Islands is exempt from IVA (Value Added Tax) on individual purchases worth more than 52 000 pesetas. The IVA rate is 6, 12 or 33 percent, according to the goods. The relevant forms to fill in for Customs on leaving and on entering one's own country will be provided by the store. Ask for details at the time of purchase. Bear in mind that the goods may be subjected to an even higher tax on return home. Large stores such as El Corte Inglés have a packing/despatch service.

SPORTS

Proud host of the 1992 Olympic Games, Barcelona has a fistful of new and redeveloped sports centres. Various international events and championships have already been held here.

Venues for paricipant sports are:
Can Caralleu: Carrer Esports, s/n. Tel:

203 7874. (Bus 94 from Tres Torres/Via Augusta). A sports centre in a pretty location on the hill of Tibidabo which offers tennis courts, fronton, volley ball and two swimming pools. Indoor facilities: open to public Monday–Friday 8–10 a.m. and 2–3.30 p.m. Sunday 10 a.m.–1 p.m. Outdoor facilities open: mid-June to mid-September 10 a.m.–5 p.m. Tennis courts available from 8 a.m.–11 p.m.

•Swimming Pools

Piscina Marítim: Passeig Marítim, s/n, Barceloneta, Tel: 309 3412. Two indoor pools. Open: Monday–Friday 7 a.m.–9 p.m.

Parc de la Creueta del Coll: Castellterçol, s/n. Tel: 237 7303. Large outdoor pool/lake, in one of Barcelona's new urban parks complete with Eduardo Chillida sculpture. Boats can be hired in the winter. Swimming: June to mid-September Monday–Friday, 10 a.m.–4 p.m. Sunday and holidays 10 a.m.–7 p.m.

Piscina Municipal Sant Pau: Ronda Sant Pau, 46. Tel: 329 9806. Indoor pool open: Monday–Friday 8 a.m.–9 p.m. Closed: for classes from 7–8 p.m. Less crowded in the morning.

Club Natació de Catalunya: Carrer Ramiro de Maeztu, s/n. Tel: 213 4344. Two indoor and one outdoor pool. Open to public: 7 a.m.–2 p.m. daily.

•Tennis

Vall Parc: Carretera a Sant Cugat, 79. Tel: 212 6789. Courts open: 8 a.m.–midnight. Quite expensive.

•Cycling

Bicitrans: Avinguda Marqués de l'Argentera, 15. Tel: 792 2841. Bicycles, tandems, and child seats, near Parc de la Ciutadella. Open: weekends and holidays 10 a.m.–dusk. Easy access to park, port, beach at Barceloneta. Occasionally a circuit is opened in the Eixample with traffic restrictions. Bicycle hire also on Montjuïc: see *Things to Do.*

•Bowling

AMFF: Carrer de Sabino de Arana, 6. Tel: 330 5048. Open: 11 a.m.–1.30 a.m.

Pedralbes Bowling Alley: Avinguda Doctor Marañón, 11. Tel: 333 0352. Open: 10 a.m.–1.30 a.m.

•Horse Riding

El Ecuestre: Carrer de Ciutat de Balaguer, 68. Tel: 417 3039. Saturday and Sunday: individual classes, and two hour excursions on Tibidabo.

Hípica Sant Cugat: Finca La Pelleria, Carretera de Cerdanyola. Tel: 674 8385. Bus from Sant Cugat to Cerdanyola will drop you off. Excursions from one hour to whole day in Collserola hills.

Hípica Severino: Carrer Príncep/Passeig Calada, Sant Cugat. Tel: 674 1140. Off La Rabassada, the road which winds over Tibidabo between Barcelona and Sant Cugat. Take the train to Sant Cugat and bus V42, or taxi.

•Golf

Many new courses are being built all over Catalonia. To play it is essential to prove membership of a recognised club. For the moment three courses within easy reach of Barcelona are:

Sant Cugat: Sant Cugat del Vallès. Tel: 674 3958. Bar, restaurant, swimming pool. Hire of clubs and trollies. Closed: Monday. Open: Tuesday–Friday 5,000 pesetas., Saturday and Sunday 10,000 pesetas.

Vallromanes: Montornès del Vallès. Tel: 568 0362. Bar, restaurant, sauna, swimming pool, tennis. Hire of clubs and trollies. Closed: Tuesday. Open: weekdays 4,500 pesetas, Saturday and Sunday 9,000 pesetas.

El Prat: El Prat de Llobregat. Tel: 379 0278. A premier course, often host to international competitions. Hire of clubs and trollies. Open: Monday–Friday 7,500 pesetas., Saturday and Sunday 15,000 pesetas.

•Skiing

During the season many cheap weekend excursions are available in the Pyreneean resorts, with transport from Barcelona. Most travel agencies have information.

SPECTATOR SPORTS

Check the weekly entertainment guides or the daily sports magazines, *Sport* and *El Mundo Deportivo,* for a full calendar. The daily papers also have good sports coverage.

Most local fiestas have various sporting activities as part of their programme, notably the Barcelona fiesta of La Mercé at the end of September.

•Football

When the favourite local team "Barça" is playing you will know all about it: firstly from the traffic jams to get to the match or to the television, secondly because the town goes silent, and thirdly thanks to the explosion of fireworks, car horns and bugles. Celebrations of important matches are centred at the top of the Ramblas.

Fútbol Club Barcelona: Carrer Arístides Maillol. Tel: 330 9411. The stadium, Nou Camp, can be visited from 10 a.m.–1 p.m. and 4–6 p.m. Closed: Sunday and match days. Winter hours: closed Monday. It is the second largest stadium in the world.

•Basketball

Basketball is gaining as ardent a following as football. The "Barça" basketball team is part of the Fútbol Club and matches are played in the Palau Blaugrana, next to Nou Camp. Tel: 330 9411.

•Tennis

The Conde de Godó trophy is an annual event at the Real Club de Tenis Barcelona, Carrer de Bosch i Gimpera, 5. Tel: 203 7758.

FURTHER READING

There are very few translations of Catalan works of literature into other European languages; those that do exist are difficult to find in Barcelona and are probably more available abroad.

Tirant lo Blanc, Joanot Martorell. A 15th-century novel of adventures.

Gatherings from Catalonia, John Langdon-Davies.

Handbook for Travellers in Spain, Richard Ford.

On Barcelona:

La Ciudad de los Prodigios, Eduardo Mendoza.

Barcelona Modernista, Cristina y Eduardo Mendoza.

Barcelonas, Manuel Vázquez Montalban.

La Soledad del Manager and *Los mares del Sur*, two of the Carvalho series by Manuel Vázquez Montalban, detective stories that vividly depict the atmosphere of Barcelona and its restaurants.

Nuéva Guía Secreta de Barcelona, José María Carandell.

Guía de Arquitectura de Barcelona, published by the Ajuntament de Barcelona.

USEFUL ADDRESSES

TOURIST OFFICES

Run by Generalitat:

Gran Via: 658. Tel: 301 7443 or 317 2246. Open: Monday–Friday 9 a.m.–7 p.m., Saturday 9 a.m.–2 p.m.

El Prat Airport: Tel: 325 5829. Open: Monday–Saturday 9.30am–8 p.m., Sunday 9.30am–3 p.m.

Run by Barcelona Tourist Board:

Sants Station: Tel: 490 9171. Open daily: 8 a.m.–8 p.m.

In the summer tourist information is available at:

City Hall: Plaça Sant Jaume. Open: 8 a.m.–8 p.m.

Palau de la Virreina: Rambla, 99. Open: 10 a.m.–9 p.m.

SPANISH TOURIST OFFICES ABROAD

•United Kingdom

The Spanish Tourist Office: 57–58 St James' Street, London SW1A 1LD. Tel: 071-499 1169.

•Germany

Spanisches Fremdenverkehrsamt: Graf Adolfstrasse, 81. Düsseldorf 1. Tel: 37 04 67.

•France

Office Espagnole du Tourisme: 43 ter. Avenue Pierre 1er de Serbie, 75381 Paris. Tel: 720 90 54.

•United States of America

Tourist Office of Spain: 665 Fifth Avenue, New York, NY 10022. Tel: 759 88 22.

CONSULATES IN BARCELONA

United Kingdom: Avinguda Diagonal, 477. Tel: 322 2151.

Ireland: Gran Via Carles III, 94. Tel: 330 9652.

Germany: Passeig de Gràcia, 111. Tel: 217 6162.

France: Passeig de Gràcia, 11. Tel: 317 8150.

Netherlands: Passeig de Gràcia, 111. Tel: 217 3700.

Switzerland: Gran Via Carles III, 94. Tel: 330 9211.

Italy: Carrer de Mallorca, 270. Tel: 215 1654.

Belgium: Carrer de Diputació, 303. Tel: 318 9899.

Portugal: Ronda de Sant Pere, 7. Tel: 318 8150.

Japan: Avinguda Diagonal, 662. Tel: 204 7224.

USA: Via Laietana, 33. Tel: 319 9550.

Sweden: Carrer de Còrsega, 289. Tel: 218 1566.

USEFUL TELEPHONE NUMBERS

General information: Tel: 010. This is the Barcelona City Council's service that will provide a wealth of information, or at least tell you where to telephone. Can handle English and French.

Police assistance for tourists: Tel: 317 7020.

Police station with interpreter service available: Via Laietana, 49. Tel: 302 6325.

National Police: Tel: 091.

Municipal Police: Tel: 092.

Fire Brigade: Tel: 080.

Directory enquiries: Tel: 003.

Ambulance services: Tel: 329 7766 or 300 2020.

Road accidents: Tel: 352 4142.

Lost property: Tel: 301 3923.

Public Transport: Tel: 336 0000.

Iberia information: Tel: 302 7656.

Airport: Tel: 379 2762.

RENFE (National and international rail services): Tel: 490 02 02.

Radio Taxi: Tel: 300 3811 or 300 3905.

Credit cards:

American Express: Tel: 279 6200.

Diner's: Tel: 302 1428.

Visa España: Tel: 315 25 12.

MasterCard: Tel: (91) 435 4905.

CREDITS

INDEX